BECOME FIRST

FRANCESCO VITALI

First edition: 2026

Published by VITSIA ENTERTAINMENT GROUP, INC.

To you—
for trying to become First.

TABLE OF CONTENTS

MY STORY

I didn't write this book because I figured it all out. I wrote it because I didn't. This isn't a victory lap; it's a confession. *Become First* didn't start as a concept. It started as a cry—my own. After a lifetime of showing up for everyone else—friends, partners, clients, strangers—I finally admitted something I had never said aloud: I have never truly come first. Not in relationships. Not in life. Not even with myself.

I've been fortunate in my career. I've built companies, produced major projects, consulted leaders, artists, and entrepreneurs. I've lived across industries—journalism, entertainment, marketing, branding, global festival production. But none of that made me prioritize myself. In fact, I used my success as a distraction from the truth: that I was constantly placing other people's needs above my own. Always the fixer. Always the problem-solver. Always the one emotionally, financially, spiritually carrying what others couldn't carry themselves. It became my identity. I saw people's potential and made it my mission to pull it out of them—while quietly abandoning my own.

And I still struggle. The weight issues, the smoking, the anxiety—the old patterns live inside me. The belief that choosing my own happiness is selfish, or worse, unsafe. There's a part of me still scared to be happy because happiness never felt safe. But I'm working on it. That's why I'm writing this. This book isn't a message from the mountaintop; it's from someone who finally stopped carrying everyone else on the way up.

I've been the strong one, the reliable one, the "you'll figure it out" guy. I never asked for that title—I became it out of survival. Someone had to keep things together. Someone had to absorb the chaos. And when I finally stopped, when I stepped back and chose myself, the backlash came. I wasn't applauded—I was punished. I wasn't seen—I was accused. Suddenly I was selfish, cold, distant, simply because—for once—I didn't abandon myself to save someone else.

I don't regret choosing me. I've spent years being the support system for people who never once asked if I was tired. People who loved the way I made *them* feel, not who I was. The moment I stopped carrying them, the truth surfaced: some people don't love you. They love their access to you. And when you stop giving them that access, they call you the problem.

I've told the truth to powerful people—the ones others tiptoe around—not to challenge them, but because I don't know how to perform. The truth is the only language I speak. And here's mine: I wrote this book because *I* needed to Become First. I needed to stop bleeding for other people's comfort. To stop being last on my own list. To stop apologizing for wanting more—for myself.

If you're reading this and thinking, "That sounds like me," good. It means you're ready. Not to impress anyone. Not to perfect anything. But to be honest. Clear. Real. This book is about returning to yourself before the world taught you to come last. No more waiting. No more justifying. No more hiding behind the identity of "the strong one." Become First. Even if it's messy. Even if it scares people. Even if you're still figuring it out. Just start.

HOW TO USE THIS BOOK

Read this book like your life is trying to get your attention. It wasn't written to inspire you—it was written to interrupt you. To challenge the roles you've accepted. To confront the lies you've made comfortable. To unhook you from the belief that putting yourself last is noble. This isn't a feel-good guide. It's a mirror. And once you see what it reflects, you won't be able to unsee it.

There's no timeline here. No right way to move through the chapters. You'll stop where it hurts. You'll highlight what scares you. And wherever you feel resistance—that's where your real work begins. Read this like a conversation between the version of you that's been surviving and the one who's ready to lead.

Don't read to agree. Don't read to feel good. Read to wake up. Because *Become First* isn't a strategy; it's a decision. You won't leave this book with answers. You'll leave with clarity. And from clarity, everything changes.

"You've spent long enough watching others rise. It's your turn now. No guilt. No apology. Become First."

—Francesco Vitali

INTRODUCTION

We've all said it: "I wish they'd just understand me." "If only he would try harder." "She needs to change—not me." And maybe you're right. Maybe they should be more patient, show up better, love you the way you deserve. But here's the truth most people don't admit: waiting for someone else to change is a losing game.

We've been conditioned to look outward—to blame, to complain, to wait. To expect someone else to give us what we refuse to give ourselves. We say we want peace, love, respect—but we expect them to go first. And in that space of waiting, we abandon the one person who could actually change everything: ourselves.

I know that space too well. I gave, I compromised, I tried. But underneath it all, I was keeping score—waiting for someone else to become who I needed, so I wouldn't have to. Until one day something cracked open inside me. Quietly. And a voice—my own—rose up with clarity: *Become First.*

Not because it's fair. Not because it's easy. But because no one else is coming to save you. *Become First* isn't about fixing others. It's not about waiting for closure or justice or validation. It's not about people-pleasing, being liked, or playing small. It's about truth. It's about leadership. It's about choosing to rise—even when no one else is ready. It's about breaking the pattern of self-abandonment that's been quietly running your life.

You want real love? Become First.

You want respect? Become First.

You want peace, clarity, intimacy, success, alignment? You already know—Become First.

This book is a mirror. It's not here to flatter you. It's here to reflect what you've been avoiding. Some pages will hurt. Some will hit too close. Some will free you. But all of them point to the same truth: it starts with you.

Read this with your whole heart—not to feel good, but to get clear. The life you want isn't coming from someone else. It's coming from who you're willing to become. You've waited long enough. Now it's your turn. Become First.

CHAPTER 1

THE MIRROR NEVER LIES

The Mirror Never Lies

People love the idea of accountability—until it becomes personal. We praise honesty only when it is directed outward, because it costs us nothing to be truthful about someone else's shortcomings. We celebrate calling others out, but calling ourselves in is where the ego starts negotiating, editing, justifying, and rewriting reality. Most people spend years trying to adjust the people around them, hoping they will show up better, love them cleaner, validate them louder, and finally stop triggering the parts they refuse to face. They call it standards. They call it boundaries. They call it discernment. Sometimes it is. But often, if we are honest, it is something else: a way to stay busy pointing, so we never have to look.

Because there is one question most people avoid their entire lives, not because they do not know the answer, but because the answer would dismantle the identity they built to survive: Who are you when no one is watching? Not the curated version you manage in public. Not the role you mastered to avoid rejection. Not the persona you perfected because it kept you safe, respected, or untouchable. I mean the raw, unedited you—the one that appears when the room goes quiet and there is no one left to impress. The person you are in silence, when you cannot use charm, logic, productivity, or performance to distract yourself from what you feel. That version is the one that drives your life, no matter how sophisticated your explanations sound.

At some point, you stop pointing at the world and turn toward the only place where the truth refuses to hide: the mirror. Not because you are looking for flaws, and not because you are assigning blame, but because you are finally ready to see the one thing that keeps repeating in every chapter of your life. Your relationships. Your disappointments. Your familiar cycles that masquerade as bad luck. The names and details may change, but the emotional wound stays eerily similar, like the same scene shot with a different cast. And while that does not mean you are always wrong, it does reveal something most people never want to admit: you are the common denominator. Not in a way that shames you—in a way that frees you, because freedom begins the moment you recognize where your leverage actually is.

Your life cannot evolve beyond your willingness to look at yourself with honesty. Not self-punishment, not overthinking, not the kind of "self-awareness" that is really self-criticism dressed up as maturity. Honest examination—the type that makes you uncomfortable because it removes your favorite excuses. It is easy to say "people do not respect me," but much harder to ask if you respect yourself in the ways that matter, not in words, but in choices. It is easy to say "they do not listen," but far more revealing to explore whether you communicate cleanly or emotionally negotiate, whether you speak from truth or from the need to manage the other person's reaction. It is easy to say "I always give," but more honest to ask whether you give as a gift or as a strategy—whether you give to love, or to control the outcome, or to earn what should be freely offered. These are not accusations; they are invitations, because the only type of accountability that transforms you is the kind that returns your power.

One night, after a fallout I had rehearsed emotionally a hundred times, I stood in front of a mirror and asked myself a question I had avoided my entire life: "If I met me, would I trust me?" The question did not feel poetic; it felt surgical. It sliced through every justification, every narrative I had used as armor, every image I had built to feel safe. Because for all the loyalty, fire, and presence I believed I brought into my relationships, I also saw what I had buried under intention. I saw control disguised as concern, the type that pretends it is love while it quietly demands compliance. I saw insecurity dressed as independence, a posture that looked like strength but functioned like distance. I saw bitterness camouflaged as boundaries, where "protecting myself" had slowly turned into punishing people for not reading my mind. I saw fear so subtle I had convinced myself it was not there, because fear does not always scream; sometimes it whispers through tone, through certainty, through the need to be right.

The mirror did not show me who I meant to be—it showed me who I had been. And that is what most people cannot face, not because they are weak, but because acknowledging the truth requires letting go of the version of themselves they have tightly defended. We defend our identity because it once protected us, because it gave us a role we could survive inside, because it kept us from feeling too much, wanting too much, hoping too much. A survival identity always comes with conditions: stay impressive, stay composed, stay in control, stay above the mess of being human. The problem is that what kept you safe at one stage of life can keep you small in the next, and the mirror is the moment you realize you have been paying for safety with intimacy.

Most people repeat the same heartbreak with different names because they refuse to confront their role in the pattern. They recycle the same argument with different partners, live the same disappointment in different stories, feel the same emotional hunger in every connection. They call it coincidence. They call it fate. They call it "I keep attracting the same type." Patterns do not lie. Energy does not lie. The mirror does not lie. And that does not mean you are "bad"—it means you are predictable, and predictability is not a moral failure; it is a map of what your nervous system recognizes as normal.

When you finally stop lying to yourself, something shifts. Not dramatically, not with fireworks, not with a social-media announcement about your "healing journey." Quietly. A clarity forms beneath the discomfort, and for the first time, you can feel the structure behind your reactions. You recognize how your past shaped your reflexes, how your family dynamics taught you what love looks like, what safety costs, what truth gets you punished for. You understand why you protect yourself the way you do, why you default to certain roles under stress. Self-awareness is not pain; it is release, because it removes the confusion that keeps you repeating the same loop with different details. It frees you from narratives that have held you hostage—stories you built to justify what hurt you and explain what you could not control. But clarity always comes with a cost: the loss of the identity you constructed for survival, because once you see the mechanism, you cannot unsee it.

The truth is this: your reflection will always reveal what your patterns have been trying to teach you. Every emotional loop carries a message. Every repeated wound is an unopened letter. Every conflict you keep reliving is a mirror—inviting you to understand where you have abandoned yourself, where you have overstayed, where you have performed, and where you have hidden. And once you see it, life does not collapse; life reorganizes. The people who once matched your unhealed parts no longer feel familiar. The habits that once soothed you now feel heavy, because you can finally feel their real function. The excuses you relied on lose their power, because you can no longer pretend you do not know. Self-awareness redraws the architecture of your emotional world, not because you become someone else, but because you finally meet the version of yourself who was buried underneath survival.

Most people think growth requires inspiration. But transformation rarely begins with hope; it begins with interruption—the disruption of the story you have been telling yourself about who you are and why you are the way you are. For me, that interruption came in a conversation where I thought I was being composed, grounded—even mature. I was not yelling. I was not reacting. I thought I was doing everything right. And then I heard words that hit me harder than any argument ever had: "You are always right. You are never wrong. You think you know everything—but you do not know how I feel. You think you do. Your tone is judgmental." I stood still because I recognized the truth: they were not describing my intention; they were describing my impact. And intention never outweighs impact.

In that moment, I was not present. I was not curious. I was not connected. I was performing composure to maintain control, and I had mistaken emotional distance for maturity. I had confused calm with wisdom, because calm looks impressive, especially when you grew up around chaos. I had used silence as armor and called it restraint, when it was really a way to stay untouchable. The mirror—whether literal or emotional—showed me the version of myself I had refused to confront: the strategist who avoids vulnerability by staying "above" the conversation, the one who wins the room while losing the person.

That is the thing about truth: it does not break you; it breaks what has been breaking you. And once it does, something inside you rearranges, not loudly, not dramatically, but quietly, deeply, permanently. You begin to see the gap between who you think you are and who you have been acting as. You recognize the outdated version of yourself you have been dragging into adult life. You see the survival traits that once kept you safe but now keep you distant. You notice the emotional habits you inherited without questioning, the reflexes you call personality because you have carried them for so long. And slowly, the illusion unravels, because the mirror does not let you hide behind vocabulary; it shows you behavior.

The mirror is not your enemy; it is your doorway. The entrance to the life you were meant to live once you stop replaying the one you outgrew. And when you walk through it—fully, honestly, without excuses—you do not become perfect. You become real. Real enough to stop performing, real enough to stop blaming, real enough to stop negotiating with the parts of yourself you have outgrown. Real enough to lead your life instead of surviving it. Becoming First is not about becoming better than others; it is about becoming the version of yourself you abandoned to make others comfortable. It is about reclaiming the authority you gave away each time you chose peace over truth, approval over boundaries, performance over presence. It is not easy, but it becomes inevitable the moment you decide to stop running from the one place where nothing can be denied: your own reflection.

The Pattern You Keep Calling Fate

After the mirror hits, the mind tries to soften the blow. It tries to turn truth into something inspirational so you can admire it from a distance instead of applying it in real time. It tries to make self-awareness a concept rather than a confrontation, because concepts are safe and confrontation demands change. But the mirror does not care whether you "understand" it; it cares whether you repeat. The most dangerous lie is not the one you tell others; it is the one you tell yourself while staying convinced you are honest. It is the lie that says, "This is just who I am," when "who I am" is really a set of strategies you learned under pressure. It is the lie that says, "I cannot help it," when what you mean is, "I do not want to feel the discomfort of doing something different." It is the lie that says, "It is always them," because that lie protects your identity as the good one, the rational one, the loyal one, the one who keeps getting hurt by the world.

One of the most seductive lies is the one that makes you sound innocent: "I keep attracting the wrong people." It gives you a clean story. It makes life the problem and you the victim of a mysterious universe. But attraction is rarely a mystery; it is a memory. You do not attract what you want; you attract what your nervous system recognizes. You attract what matches your unspoken contract, what fits the emotional climate you are trained to tolerate. You attract what mirrors the parts of you that are still negotiating worth, still asking for love in ways that require you to earn it.

People get offended by that because they confuse recognition with blame, but recognition is not blame; it is leverage. You are not being accused of choosing pain as a preference; you are being invited to notice that you choose familiar sensations because familiarity feels safer than the unknown. That is why you can meet someone calm, consistent, emotionally mature—and feel nothing. No spark, no obsession, no adrenaline. You call it boring, but your body is not bored; it is suspicious, because calm is unfamiliar to a system trained by unpredictability. Then you meet someone inconsistent, unavailable, emotionally avoidant, and your whole system lights up. Your mind calls it chemistry. Your body calls it home. And you build relationships on nervous system activation, then wonder why love always feels like hunger.

The mirror shows you that what you call passion can be panic with perfume on it. It shows you how you confuse intensity with intimacy and how you mistake being needed for being loved. It shows you how you confuse anxiety with desire because your early experience taught you that love comes with a threat: the threat of leaving, the threat of punishment, the threat of coldness, the threat of not being chosen. So you become someone who tries to manage love instead of receive it. You monitor tone. You monitor timing. You monitor reactions. You control the narrative. You stay one step ahead so you never feel powerless. You call it maturity, but often it is fear dressed in good posture.

That is why people repeat patterns across years while insisting the details are different. They change partners, friends, careers, cities, aesthetics, and they are convinced they have "moved on." But the emotional theme returns like a soundtrack they cannot mute. The same wound in a different scene, the same conversation with a different accent, the same disappointment wearing a different face. The mirror does not debate you; it holds up the evidence. Not one relationship, but the repetition. Not one breakup, but the same dynamic rebuilt, again and again. And the mirror asks a question that removes fantasy: What do you keep recreating because it allows you to remain loyal to your old identity?

Because the old identity has perks. It gets to be the strong one who never needs anyone. It gets to be the one who "sees through people," the one who stays above the mess of vulnerability. It gets to be the one who is always right, because being right feels like safety when you have learned that being wrong gets you hurt. It gets to keep distance and call it standards. Distance can feel like superiority when you are afraid of intimacy, and if you are not careful, you will build a life where you are never truly harmed because you are never truly open. You will be respected, admired, and alone. You will call it success while you quietly starve.

The mirror is not here to shame you for that; it is here to expose the cost. Every defense protects you from something and blocks you from something. It protects you from rejection and blocks you from being known. It protects you from disappointment and blocks you from receiving. It protects you from humiliation and blocks you from intimacy. It protects you from grief and blocks you from love. So, the question becomes less poetic and more honest: What has your protection cost you? If you are brave enough to answer, the mirror stops being cruel and starts being useful, because usefulness is what turns awareness into change.

Leverage, Not Guilt

People hear "common denominator" and they flinch because they think it is a verdict. They hear it as a courtroom sentence. They assume it means everything was their fault, and shame rushes in to protect them from the deeper truth: that they have power. But the common denominator is not guilt; it is leverage. It is the moment you stop living as if your future depends on other people suddenly becoming emotionally mature, suddenly becoming honest, suddenly becoming capable. Being the common denominator does not mean you caused someone else's cruelty, addiction, immaturity, or avoidance. It means you have a pattern of participation, and participation can be loud or quiet, direct or subtle.

Sometimes participation is staying too long. Sometimes it is explaining yourself to someone committed to misunderstanding you, because you are addicted to the fantasy that if you find the right words, they will become the right person. Sometimes it is tolerating inconsistency because the chase makes you feel alive. Sometimes it is abandoning your needs because you want to be "easy" and never risk being labeled difficult. Sometimes it is choosing people who cannot meet you because unavailable love feels familiar, and familiarity feels safe. Sometimes participation is not an action; it is an absence—the absence of boundaries, the absence of leaving when you should, the absence of asking directly for what you want, the absence of enforcing what you claim matters to you.

The mirror reveals how you have been negotiating worth. That is why the common denominator is leverage: once you see where you negotiate yourself, you can stop. And when you stop negotiating yourself, your life changes faster than your mind can rationalize. Most people do not lack awareness; they lack self-loyalty. They know what is wrong early. They feel it in the tone, in the inconsistency, in the subtle disrespect, in the way they keep shrinking. But they stay because leaving would mean admitting they tolerated something beneath their worth, and that admission feels like humiliation. They stay because leaving would mean grieving the fantasy, and grief is honest. They stay because leaving would mean starting over, and starting over forces you to face the emptiness you have been distracting yourself from.

So they compromise, but it is not compromise if you are the only one sacrificing. They call it patience, but it is fear of being alone. They call it understanding, but it is self-abandonment with a polite name. They call it loyalty, but it is attachment to a story that is already dead. The mirror does not call you stupid for doing this; it calls you trained. And then it asks you to choose differently, not because you deserve punishment, but because you deserve your life.

Here is the brutal clarity of leverage: you cannot change what you refuse to own. Owning is not blaming; owning is telling the truth about your participation. Owning is admitting the ways you stay in loops because they protect your identity. Owning is admitting the ways you prefer familiar pain you can manage over unfamiliar peace you cannot control. Owning is admitting the ways you want love without the vulnerability of being fully seen. When you own your participation, you stop begging for permission to be happy. You stop waiting for people to understand you. You stop hoping someone will finally treat you right. You start acting like your life is yours.

There is grief in that, because you lose the comfort of the victim story. You lose the dopamine of righteous anger. You lose the identity of being misunderstood and, therefore, morally superior. But you also lose something else: the excuses that kept you small. And in that loss, you gain responsibility. Responsibility is not oppression; it is access. It is the key to the door you keep standing in front of, praying it opens, while refusing to touch the handle.

Your Nervous System Writes the Script

If you want to understand your patterns, do not start with your thoughts. Start with your body. Your body is always first. Your body knows when something is off before your mind can defend it, rationalize it, or romanticize it. Your body knows when a person is not safe before your ego can label them "different" or "challenging" or "exciting." Your body knows when you are performing before you can admit it. Your body knows when you are shrinking before you can call it "being polite." Most people live as if their patterns are intellectual. They are not. They are neurological.

Your nervous system is not interested in your intentions; it is interested in survival. It will choose familiarity over health, if familiarity once kept you alive. It will choose what you recognize over what you deserve, if what you recognize once meant home. That is why you can feel attracted to what hurts you and bored by what is good for you. That is why you can feel anxiety and call it love and feel calm and call it suspicious. Your nervous system has been writing your love story long before you had language, and it writes in sensations: tight chest, stomach drop, jaw clench, restlessness, numbness, hyper-vigilance, the impulse to fix, the impulse to prove, the impulse to run. These are not random; they are old instructions.

So, when you stand in front of the mirror, you are not just confronting personality traits. You are confronting the script—the inherited script, the learned script, the script you have been calling "who I am," because it has been with you so long you cannot imagine life without it. The mirror shows you the moment you become someone else to keep love. It shows you when you become smaller to keep peace. It shows you when you become sharper to feel powerful. It shows you when you become calm to avoid conflict. It shows you when you become "fine" to avoid rejection. It shows you when you become the rescuer, because being needed feels safer than being wanted and when you become the judge, because judgment keeps you above vulnerability.

Intelligence can make this harder, because intelligence can justify anything. Intelligence can build beautiful explanations for ugly behaviors. Intelligence can turn avoidance into philosophy, control into "standards," fear into "discernment," emotional distance into "maturity." The mirror does not argue with your intellect; it exposes your body, and your body does not lie. It remembers the relationships where you had to perform to be loved. It remembers the environments where you had to anticipate mood swings to survive. It remembers the times you were punished for speaking, ignored until you became impressive, praised only when you were useful. So now you unconsciously recreate what you know, not because you want pain, but because you want predictability. Predictability feels safe even when it is miserable.

That is why people return to the same type of partner, the same type of friendship, the same type of workplace, the same type of emotional dynamic.

Different face, same energy. Different story, same wound. The mirror is the moment you stop calling it coincidence. Because once you see that your nervous system is driving, you can stop pretending chemistry is destiny. You can start asking better questions: not "Do I like them?" but "Do I feel safe with them?" Not "Do we have passion?" but "Do we have honesty without punishment?" Not "Do they say the right things?" but "Do they do the right things consistently?" The nervous system is not impressed by words; it is regulated by consistency, and consistency is the thing people claim to want until it demands they become consistent too.

A regulated relationship requires you to stop using chaos as stimulation. It requires you to stop mistaking intensity for intimacy. It requires you to stop chasing what is unavailable so you can feel in control of distance. It requires you to receive love without testing it, and that is where most people collapse, because receiving requires vulnerability, and vulnerability requires trust, and trust requires risk. So, people build relationships where they can stay armored and call it love. The mirror exposes that and it is humiliating, not because you are broken, but because you realize how much of your life has been organized around not feeling.

Impact is the Receipt Your Intention Cannot Burn

There is a specific immaturity that hides inside "good intention": the belief that meaning well makes you safe. That because you did not intend to hurt someone, they should not feel hurt. That your self-image should outweigh their experience. People use intention as a shield, because it allows them to avoid accountability while still feeling like good people. "That is not what I meant" becomes a magic eraser. "You are too sensitive" becomes a way to blame someone for feeling. "You misunderstood me" becomes a way to protect pride. But relationships do not live in your intention; they live in your impact. Impact is the receipt your intention cannot burn.

That is why the sentence "You do not know how I feel" is devastating. It exposes the place where your intelligence becomes distance, where your certainty becomes a wall, where your composure becomes control. You can be calm and still be cruel. You can be composed and still be controlling. You can be silent and still be punishing. You can be honest and still be emotionally reckless. Calm is not automatically maturity, and silence is not automatically wisdom. Sometimes calm is a strategy to stay above vulnerability. Sometimes silence is a weapon used to starve connection. Sometimes "honesty" is a permission slip to say what you want without considering the cost.

The mirror shows you the moments you choose being right over being connected. It shows you the moments you correct someone's feelings instead of meeting them. It shows you the moments you turn vulnerability into debate. It shows you the moments you withdraw presence and call it "space." That is why intention never outweighs impact, because impact is what the other person lives with after you leave the room. You cannot argue someone out of their experience without making yourself unsafe. And you cannot call that maturity without lying to yourself.

When I recognized that in myself, I saw the deeper truth: the need to be right is rarely about truth. It is often about power, not domination, but protection. If I am right, I am safe. If I am right, I cannot be blamed. If I am right, I do not have to risk being wrong, and risk is what vulnerability feels like. The mirror does not shame you for that; it shows you the mechanism. And the moment you see the mechanism, you have a choice: keep defending your identity or start protecting your connection.

The Doorway is Honesty

The mirror is not here to make you hate yourself; it is here to make you stop abandoning yourself. And abandoning yourself does not always look like weakness. Sometimes it looks like strength. Sometimes it looks like independence. Sometimes it looks like being the reliable one, the composed one, the one who can "handle anything." But if you are always handling everything, you are often not feeling anything. If you are always composed, you are often not present. If you are always the strong one, you are often not known. And being unknown is a quiet kind of loneliness that people learn to call normal.

Here is the truth most people do not want: you cannot enter a new life with an old identity. You can carry wisdom forward, but you cannot carry the survival version of you that was built purely to avoid pain. That version does not create intimacy; it creates function. It creates strategy. It creates performance. Performance might get you praise, but it will never get you peace. The mirror is the doorway because it forces you to stop performing. It forces you to meet yourself where excuses do not work, where self-image cannot save you, where your patterns speak louder than your words.

Looking at yourself clearly is not a one-time moment. It is a decision you renew in real time. It is pausing mid-conversation before you correct. It is asking a question instead of making a statement. It is listening for meaning instead of waiting for your turn to speak. It is admitting, "I did not realize that landed that way, but I hear you," without turning the moment into self-defense. It is allowing impact to teach you, because if impact cannot teach you, nothing can. It is choosing closeness over winning, because winning the argument while losing the person is not intelligence; it is fear with good grammar.

This is where Becoming First begins. Not with inspiration, but with interruption. Not with a new identity you announce, but with an old identity you stop feeding. The mirror is your beginning, because it returns you to the only place transformation can actually happen: your own behavior, your own participation, your own choices. It does not ask you to become perfect; it asks you to become real. And real is dangerous to the old version of you, because real removes the last excuse: "That is just who I am." No. That is who you were while surviving. Now you get to decide who you are when you stop running.

The Moment You Stop Negotiating with Yourself

Most people think the turning point is dramatic. They expect a breakdown, a betrayal, a public humiliation, a loss so loud it forces them to wake up. And yes, sometimes life does it that way because some people only respond to impact. But more often, the real turning point is quiet. It is not the moment you finally scream. It is the moment you finally stop bargaining with your own knowing. It is the moment you stop arguing with the part of you that has been whispering the truth for years. It is the moment you stop turning your intuition into a debate.

Because you have always known more than you admitted. You knew the tone was off. You knew the "joke" was not a joke. You knew the inconsistency was not "busy," it was avoidance. You knew the apology was performance. You knew the affection was conditional. You knew you were shrinking. You knew you were over-explaining. You knew you were walking on eggshells and calling it love. You knew you were over-functioning and calling it loyalty. You knew you were forcing clarity out of people who survive on fog. You knew. The mirror just removes the last excuse: pretending you did not know.

This is where the hardest truth lives, and it is not poetic, it is practical: you cannot build a clean life with a dirty agreement. And most people are living under agreements they never consciously chose. Agreements like: "If I am useful, I will be loved." "If I stay calm, I will be safe." "If I never need anyone, I cannot be disappointed." "If I am impressive, I cannot be rejected." "If I can control the room, I cannot be hurt." Those agreements are not morals. They are survival math. They are the equations you learned as a child, the ones you keep solving as an adult, even when the numbers have changed.

And because you do not name the agreement, you think the problem is always the person in front of you. You think the problem is their mood, their immaturity, their distance, their selfishness, their "issues." Sometimes it is. But even when it is, there is still a mirror question waiting behind it: why did that agreement feel acceptable to you? Why did you stay inside an emotional contract that required you to betray yourself? Why did you keep paying for love with performance? Why did you keep calling anxiety "chemistry" and absence "mystery" and disrespect "miscommunication"? Why did you keep negotiating your worth with people who were never going to pay full price?

The mirror does not ask these questions to punish you. It asks them because answering them ends the loop. People want closure from others, but closure is an internal act. Closure is when you stop handing your self-respect to someone else's behavior. Closure is when you stop waiting for the apology you will never receive and start giving yourself the honesty you have been postponing. Closure is when you stop needing the other person to admit what they did, because you finally admit what you tolerated. That admission is not shame. It is the first clean breath you have taken in a long time.

Most people think boundaries are sentences you say out loud. But boundaries are not words. Boundaries are decisions you uphold when you are lonely. Boundaries are what you do when you miss them. Boundaries are what you do when the old version of you wants to go back for one more hit of familiarity. Because that is what these patterns are: a dopamine economy. A nervous system addiction. A cycle that gives you intensity, uncertainty, and the illusion of control. You keep returning because it is familiar, not because it is good. You keep negotiating because negotiation makes you feel involved, and involvement feels like love when you grew up starving.

So, the mirror asks: what if the reason you are tired is not because you loved too much, but because you negotiated too long? What if the exhaustion is not from giving, but from performing? What if you are not "too sensitive," you are simply too self-betraying? What if the reason your relationships keep collapsing is not because you are unlucky, but because you keep bringing the same survival identity into spaces that require a different version of you?

That is when the work becomes real. Because at some point, self-awareness stops being an insight and starts being a responsibility. You do not get to "know better" and keep doing the same thing without paying a price. The price is always the same: your nervous system. Your peace. Your dignity. Your time. Your capacity to feel love without fear. You pay in sleep. You pay in weight. You pay in inflammation. You pay in reactivity. You pay in distrust. You pay in the way your mind never stops scanning for danger. You pay in the way you cannot relax even when nothing is happening, because your body is still living in the old climate.

And this is where people misunderstand Becoming First. They think it is an ego statement, like "I come first." They hear it as selfish. They hear it as arrogance. But Becoming First is the exact opposite of ego. It is the decision to stop abandoning your inner authority. It is the decision to stop outsourcing your worth to outcomes. It is the decision to become internally consistent. Not perfect—consistent. The kind of consistency that makes your life quieter, not because the world becomes easier, but because your internal arguments stop.

You stop negotiating with yourself. You stop making exceptions for what disrespects you. You stop explaining your boundaries to people who use explanations as loopholes. You stop trying to be understood by people who benefit from misunderstanding you. You stop collecting evidence that you are lovable. You stop auditioning for basic decency. You stop trying to earn what should have been freely offered.

That is when something shifts in your identity. The mirror stops being a threat and becomes a tool. You stop fearing what you will see because you are no longer trying to protect the old image. The old image needed everyone to approve of you. The old image needed you to be the "good one," the "rational one," the "mature one." The old image needed you to be right. The old image needed you to be impressive. The old image needed you to be untouchable.

The new version of you does not need that. The new version of you needs alignment.

Alignment is a word people throw around like perfume. But alignment is not a vibe. Alignment is what happens when your words, your actions, and your self-respect stop contradicting each other. Alignment is when you do not have to hype yourself up to do what you know you should do. Alignment is when you do not have to "forgive" people for the same thing every month. Alignment is when your boundaries are not threats; they are reality. Alignment is when you can be kind without being available for disrespect. Alignment is when you can love without losing yourself.

This is why the mirror is a doorway. Because it is the place where you stop pretending your patterns are accidents. It is where you stop calling your coping mechanisms personality. It is where you stop turning your history into your identity. It is where you finally see the difference between who you are and what you learned to do.

And that difference is everything.

The Identity You Built to Survive Will Fight You

Do not romanticize this process. The mirror moment is not only painful because of what you see. It is painful because of what it threatens. It threatens your familiar identity, and your familiar identity will fight you like it is your job to stay the same. Because it once was. Your identity was not just "you." It was a set of protective moves that kept you intact in a certain emotional environment. So when you try to change, it can feel like betrayal, not of others, but of yourself. Your body can interpret growth as danger because growth means stepping out of the old strategy.

This is why people relapse into old patterns even after they "understand." They do not relapse because they are stupid. They relapse because their nervous system is loyal to the old solution. The old solution may have been toxic, but it was predictable. Predictability feels like safety. And safety is what your nervous system will choose, even if it is miserable, because miserable and familiar is still familiar.

So, you will feel resistance the moment you begin to act differently. You will feel it when you do not text back. You will feel it when you do not explain yourself. You will feel it when you do not chase clarity from a fog machine. You will feel it when you say no without a paragraph. You will feel it when you leave without begging them to understand. You will feel it when you stop proving your innocence. You will feel it when you let someone be disappointed in you. You will feel it when you stop trying to be liked by people who cannot love cleanly.

That resistance will try to shame you. It will call you cold. It will call you dramatic. It will call you selfish. It will call you "changed." It will call you arrogant. It will call you heartless. It will call you too much, or not enough, depending on what keeps you small. And if you are not careful, you will return to your old identity just to stop hearing those voices.

But the mirror teaches you something harsh and liberating: not every voice inside you deserves a vote. Some voices inside you are old programming. Some voices inside you are the echo of people who benefited from your lack of boundaries. Some voices inside you are fear pretending to be wisdom. Some voices inside you are guilt pretending to be morality.

Guilt is one of the biggest chains in human behavior, because guilt can masquerade as goodness. People think if they feel guilty, they are moral. But guilt does not mean you did something wrong. Sometimes guilt simply means you stopped doing what you were trained to do. You stopped pleasing. You stopped over-functioning. You stopped absorbing other people's discomfort. You stopped sacrificing yourself to keep peace. You stopped being the convenient version of you. Of course you feel guilty. Your system has been trained to believe that your job is to make others comfortable.

Becoming First breaks that training.

And that is why it feels like you are doing something wrong when you are finally doing something right.

The mirror shows you that you have confused kindness with self-erasure. You have confused love with tolerance. You have confused patience with delay. You have confused loyalty with self-abandonment. You have confused "understanding" with accepting behavior that is not acceptable. You have confused peace with silence. You have confused maturity with emotional distance.

So yes, the identity you built to survive will fight you, because it thinks you are removing its purpose. But you are not removing its purpose; you are updating it. You are telling it, "Thank you for keeping me alive then. But you are not needed like this now." That conversation is not soft. It is firm. It is leadership. It is you becoming the authority inside your own life.

This is where most people fail. They want transformation without authority. They want peace without boundaries. They want a new life without becoming the type of person who can hold it. They want self-respect without the discomfort of disappointing people. They want deep love without the risk of being truly known. They want to be chosen without choosing themselves first.

But becoming First is exactly that: choosing yourself first in the moments that matter. Not in the cute self-care way, not in the "treat yourself" way, but in the real way: the way where you do not betray your own truth for connection. The way where you do not shrink your needs to keep someone. The way where you do not stay in a dynamic that requires you to bleed quietly. The way where you do not keep returning to what breaks you and calling it love.

And when you practice that, your life begins to reorganize again, but this time it is not only external. It is internal. Your self-respect becomes louder than your fear. Your boundaries become cleaner than your guilt. Your standards stop being speeches and start being behavior. Your nervous system slowly learns a new baseline: calm without suspicion, closeness without panic, love without war.

That is the real miracle. Not a new partner. Not a new job. Not a new city. A new internal climate.

And it starts here, at the mirror, because the mirror is where the war ends. Not because you defeat the world, but because you stop fighting yourself.

The Mirror is Where Your Authority Returns

Authority is a word most people associate with dominance, with power over others, with ego. But the kind of authority I am talking about is quieter. It is internal. It is the ability to stay loyal to what you know when your emotions try to negotiate. It is the ability to hold your standard when your loneliness begs for an exception. It is the ability to keep your boundary when someone offers you the exact thing that used to hook you: attention with a side of disrespect, affection with a hidden cost, intimacy that turns into punishment the moment you speak.

When you have internal authority, you stop needing external permission to do what is right for you. You stop needing someone to validate your feelings before you take them seriously. You stop needing a courtroom-level case before you leave something that is draining you. You stop needing the other person to admit it. You stop needing the "perfect reason." You stop needing to be angry enough. You stop needing to be betrayed dramatically.

You just know.

And that "just knowing" is what terrifies people, because knowing demands action.

Most people do not lack knowing. They lack the courage to act on it without drama as fuel. They wait until the situation becomes unbearable so they can leave without guilt. They wait until the other person crosses a line so obvious they can finally stop defending them. They wait until their health collapses, their nervous system crashes, their dignity is exhausted. Then they call it a wake-up call.

The mirror asks you to wake up earlier, before you lose years.

That is what makes it premium. That is what makes it serious. It is not "feel better." It is "stop bleeding."

Because bleeding is expensive. Bleeding costs time. It costs presence. It costs your capacity for joy. It costs your ability to trust someone who actually deserves it, because you are too busy repairing the damage from the last person. Bleeding costs your body. Your sleep. Your metabolism. Your hormones. Your immune system. It costs your confidence. And the worst part is that bleeding becomes normal if you do it long enough. You start to think that love is supposed to hurt, that success is supposed to exhaust you, that relationships are supposed to confuse you, that peace is unrealistic, that calm is boring, that safety is for other people.

No. Safety is for the version of you who stops negotiating.

The mirror returns your authority because it returns your honesty. And honesty is not only "telling the truth." Honesty is living it. Honesty is when you stop saying, "I deserve better" while continuing to accept less. Honesty is when you stop calling someone "amazing" while constantly feeling anxious around them. Honesty is when you stop telling yourself you are "overreacting" every time your body signals danger. Honesty is when you stop narrating your life in a way that makes you look noble while you remain stuck.

That is why the mirror never lies. It does not flatter you, but it does not attack you either. It just reflects. It reflects the way you show up. It reflects what you tolerate. It reflects what you chase. It reflects what you avoid. It reflects your relationship with yourself, because that relationship is the blueprint for every other relationship you build.

And once you understand that, you stop asking "Why do I keep meeting the same people?" and you start asking "Why do I keep being the same version of me inside different rooms?" Because that is the real question. The room changes. The cast changes. The storyline shifts. But the version of you remains the same until you decide it will not.

This is the part where people want motivation. They want a boost. They want an inspiring quote. They want hope. But hope is not the beginning. Hope is the result. The beginning is interruption. The beginning is the moment the mirror disrupts your identity and you do not run away. The beginning is when you stop defending your old story and start tolerating the discomfort of being honest.

Because honesty feels like loss at first. It feels like you are losing your excuses, losing your identity, losing the fantasy. It feels like you are losing people. And you are, in a way. You are losing the people who could only access you through your unhealed parts. You are losing the dynamics that required you to be smaller. You are losing the relationships that survived because you kept abandoning yourself.

And that loss is not tragedy. It is correction.

Life reorganizes, not to punish you, but to match you.

When you change your internal climate, your external reality follows. Not instantly, not magically, but inevitably. Your choices become cleaner. Your tolerance becomes lower. Your standards become lived. Your boundaries become behavior. Your voice becomes simpler, because you are no longer trying to convince anyone. You no longer need to persuade people to treat you well. You simply stop participating in environments that require you to beg.

This is what Becoming First actually is. It is not competing. It is not proving. It is not being better than others. It is becoming the version of you that does not abandon yourself to keep anything.

And that is why the mirror is not a threat. It is a doorway. Because the moment you step through it, you stop surviving your life and start leading it.

The Vow After the Mirror

There is a moment after the mirror that nobody warns you about. Not the breakdown. Not the guilt. Not the grief. The quiet after. The strange stillness where you realize the truth did not destroy you—it simply removed your ability to pretend. You do not feel instantly healed. You feel exposed. And that exposure is the beginning of integrity, because integrity is not a moral identity; it is alignment between what you know and what you choose next.

This is where people usually go back. Not because they did not "get it." Because the mirror is not the hard part. The hard part is what comes after: living like you saw what you saw. Not in a dramatic way. In a daily way. In the subtle moments where your nervous system begs for the old deal—one more explanation, one more chance, one more conversation, one more compromise that you already know will cost you. The mirror does not ask for perfection. It asks for consistency. And consistency is the only proof your self-respect has.

So here is the redemption most people miss: you do not need to punish yourself for your patterns. You need to stop protecting them. You do not need to hate the version of you that survived. You need to retire it. You do not need to rewrite your past. You need to stop letting it write your present. That is the shift from awareness to authority. That is the moment you stop being a witness to your life and become the one who decides what continues.

Because once you see your participation, you also see your power. You realize you do not have to win arguments to be safe. You do not have to be understood to be free. You do not have to convince anyone to value you. You do not have to chase clarity from someone committed to confusion. You do not have to make your boundaries poetic. You just have to make them real.

The mirror gives you one clean question to carry forward: "What would the healed version of me do next?" Not what it would feel. Not what it would say. What it would do. Would it stay to avoid loneliness? Would it text to manage anxiety? Would it explain to earn decency? Would it soften a boundary to keep approval? Would it accept a half-love and call it progress? Or would it choose the unfamiliar discomfort of a clean exit, a clean no, a clean standard, a clean life?

This is not where life becomes easier. This is where life becomes honest. And honesty does something brutal and beautiful: it reduces your options. Not because you have less freedom, but because you stop entertaining choices that violate you. Your world gets smaller for a moment, and that can feel like loss— until you realize it is space. Space to breathe. Space to stop scanning. Space to stop negotiating. Space to meet yourself without the noise.

So if you are standing here—at the end of this chapter—do not rush to feel inspired. Do not rush to forgive. Do not rush to "move on." Just make one vow: no more deals that require you to disappear. No more intimacy that costs you dignity. No more peace purchased with silence. No more love that feels like hunger. No more identity built around being right, being strong, being untouchable, while you quietly starve.

The mirror was not the ending. It was the first honest beginning. Because now you are not asking, "Why does this keep happening to me?" Now you are ready to ask the only question that changes everything: "What am I choosing—moment by moment—that keeps my old life alive?"

And that is exactly what the next chapter is about.

CHAPTER 2

ACCOUNTABILITY IS FREEDOM

You cannot lead your life if you are still blaming someone else for how it is going. That sentence is not motivational. It is structural. It is physics. You cannot steer a car from the passenger seat and then complain about the route. You cannot keep handing the wheel to other people and then acting shocked when you end up in the same ditch, on the same road, in the same weather, with a different soundtrack and the same damage.

There is a moment—right after the mirror hits—when you get to make a choice. It is not dramatic. It is not cinematic. It does not arrive with a choir behind it. It arrives like a pause in your nervous system, the kind of pause where your body knows something your pride is still trying to debate. You can ignore it. You can tell yourself it is not that deep. You can blame the other person. You can distract yourself with the next goal, the next text, the next story. Or you can stop running. You can own it. You can do the thing most people never do: take full responsibility for who you have been—without apology, without excuse, and without the need for someone else to go first.

That is accountability. And contrary to what we have been taught, accountability is not punishment—it is power.

Most people hear "responsibility" and feel accused. They feel cornered. They feel the old childhood sensation of being blamed for something they did not fully understand. That is why they fight it. That is why they intellectualize it.

That is why they turn accountability into a performance—saying the right words, posting the right realizations, using therapy language like perfume— while changing nothing about the behaviors that keep producing the same results.

But real accountability is not the ability to admit you were wrong. Real accountability is the ability to **stop being loyal to the version of you that keeps paying for comfort with dignity**. That is why accountability is freedom. Freedom is not "feeling better." Freedom is **access**. Access to the one lever that actually changes your life: your choices.

Here is the truth, and it is sharp on purpose: if someone mistreats you and you keep showing up, that is on you. If every relationship feels the same and ends the same, that is on you. If you are constantly waiting for people to change, so you can finally feel peace, that is on you. Not because you deserve mistreatment. Not because you are weak. Because you are participating. Because you are still available. Because you are still negotiating with what is already obvious.

That line is where people start panicking. "So it is my fault?" No. It is not your fault that someone lied, betrayed, disappeared, manipulated, or withheld. But it becomes your responsibility the moment you recognize the pattern and keep returning anyway. Responsibility is not a verdict. Responsibility is a key. And if you refuse the key, you stay locked in a room you keep calling "bad luck."

Scientifically, this is where people confuse morality with control. In psychology, there is a concept called **locus of control**—the degree to which you experience your life as primarily determined by external forces or internal agency. When you live in external control, you can talk for hours about who did what to you, why the world is unfair, why people are disappointing, why you "keep attracting" the same type. You can build a perfect case. You can be correct. You can be wounded and righteous and technically accurate. But your life will still not move, because you placed your power in the hands of someone else's behavior.

Accountability is the moment you pull the locus back inside. Not in a self-blaming way. In a **self-leading** way. You stop saying "I need them to do X so I can be okay," and you start saying "I will do what is required to be okay, regardless of whether they do X." That is the pivot. That is where you stop being a character and become the author.

This is not self-blame—it is self-liberation. Because the moment you stop outsourcing your peace, your healing, and your power, you start building the life you were meant to lead. You stop performing worthiness and start practicing it. You stop waiting for permission. You stop negotiating with people's limitations like they are laws of nature.

And yes, there is grief in that. Because blame gives you a story where you are trapped by the world. Accountability gives you a story where you are trapped by your own choices until you change them. That is harder. That is why most people avoid it. Blame is comforting. Blame is warm. Blame lets you keep your identity intact.

Accountability changes your identity.

There was a time when I carried resentment like a second skin. Someone had betrayed my trust, lied to me, disappointed me. And for a while, I let it own me. I replayed the conversations, rehearsed the comebacks, fantasized about justice. I told myself I was processing. I told myself I was "healing." What I was really doing was **ruminating**—running the same emotional file through my mind because it gave me the illusion of control.

That is another scientifically observed trap: the brain thinks repetition is problem-solving. It is not. Rumination is not resolution. Rumination is your nervous system staying activated because activation feels like doing something. It keeps you busy, and being busy feels safer than being honest.

Being honest would require you to admit something that hurts more than the betrayal: that you stayed attached to the injury because the injury gave you identity. The wronged one. The noble one. The loyal one. The one who "did not deserve it."

And then one morning, I asked myself: "What am I protecting by refusing to let this go?" The answer was brutal: a version of myself that still needed to feel right instead of becoming whole. A part of me that thought holding pain would prevent it from happening again. But that is not protection. That is self-abandonment. That is you choosing a familiar cage over unfamiliar peace.

So I made a decision—not to forgive them, but to Become First. To become the one who ends the pattern. To become the one who chooses peace, even without closure. To become the one who takes their power back by refusing to stay stuck in a story they did not write but kept repeating.

This is where people misunderstand me. They think "Become First" means "I come first." They hear ego. They hear selfishness. No. Becoming First is the choice to **stop coming last in your own life**. It is the choice to stop being the last person you protect. The last person you listen to. The last person you take seriously. It is the choice to stop living as if your self-respect is optional.

You want to feel peace? Become First. You want to stop living in resentment? Become First. Become First in owning how you showed up. Become First in admitting how long you stayed when you already knew it was not right. Become First in recognizing how often you betrayed your own needs to keep others comfortable. Become First in facing the version of you that allowed what your highest self would never tolerate. Not because it is fair. Not because they apologized. But because you have decided to stop being the hostage of your history.

Here is the part nobody wants to say out loud: people do not only get trapped by other people. They get trapped by the version of themselves that still believes survival is love. Survival is not love. Survival is **strategy**. Survival is "how do I keep this from collapsing?" not "is this good for me?" That is why accountability can feel like withdrawal. You are not only leaving a person, a job, a dynamic, a habit. You are leaving an identity. You are leaving a role your nervous system learned to perform because it once kept you safe.

This is where science and lived truth meet: your nervous system will choose familiarity over health if familiarity once meant safety. That is why you can be attracted to what destabilizes you and bored by what is stable. That is why you can call anxiety "chemistry." That is why you can call calm "suspicious." That is why you can call inconsistency "mystery." That is why you can call your own shrinking "maturity."

Accountability is when you stop romanticizing the familiar.

I will give you a small story—not personal, not confessional, not about anyone you know. A composite, a pattern, a scene that happens everywhere.

A man comes into a room like he is carrying a verdict in his chest. He is successful, sharp, fast. He has built things. He knows how to negotiate, how to win, how to make people respect him. He sits down and tells a story about betrayal. A partner who promised and disappeared. A team that failed him. A client who did not value him. He speaks with precision, because he is not lying. Everything he says is true.

But the thing about truth is this: truth can still be used as anesthesia.

As he talks, his body does not soften. His jaw stays tight. His shoulders stay high. He is not telling the story to release it. He is telling the story to **prove** it. Because proving it keeps him from feeling the deeper loss: that his life has become organized around someone else's behavior. That his peace depends on outcomes he cannot control. That he has placed his nervous system in a hostage situation and called it loyalty, patience, professionalism, love, whatever makes it sound noble.

At some point in the conversation, he says something that sounds like strength but is actually surrender: "What else could I do?"

That question is the doorway. Because it reveals the real problem: he believes he has no choices. He believes his only choices are reaction or endurance. Fight or tolerate. Explode or swallow. That belief is not personality. That belief is learned helplessness wearing a suit. It is what happens when you repeat patterns long enough that your brain stops looking for exits. You start treating the cage like a room you own.

So I ask him one question: "If I told you that you are still showing up to the same dynamic in different clothing, would you argue with me—or would you check the evidence?"

He pauses. Not because he agrees. Because something inside him recognizes the truth. He is not only angry at them. He is exhausted with himself.

That is the moment accountability becomes real. Not as a concept. As a confrontation.

Because here is the truth that changed everything for me: the moment you stop waiting for someone to save you is the moment you start leading yourself. That is accountability. That is strength. That is what it means to Become First. And no, it does not mean you will never be hurt again. It means when pain shows up next time, it will not meet the same version of you. Because the one who owns their part, the one who breaks their silence, the one who stops explaining and starts evolving—that one is accountable. And accountability is what separates the people who repeat patterns from the ones who break them permanently.

When you start taking full responsibility for your life, things get very clear, very fast. You stop obsessing over who was more wrong. You stop rewriting the past just to feel justified. You stop needing anyone to give you permission to move forward. And the freedom that comes with that is not loud. It is not dramatic. It is calm. Steady. Unshakable. Because when you know who you are and what you have owned, nothing external can steal your power again.

That calm is not personality. It is physiology. When you stop feeding the loop, your nervous system stops scanning for the next hit. When you stop rehearsing arguments in your head, your body stops living as if it is constantly under threat. When you stop negotiating with disrespect, your chest stops tightening every time your phone lights up. When you stop performing worthiness, you stop needing to monitor whether you are being chosen. You start choosing.

And that is why accountability is freedom: it makes you unbribable. Not by attention. Not by guilt. Not by timing. Not by potential. Not by hope dressed as excuses.

That is the shift most people avoid. They would rather stay stuck in blame than step into responsibility. Because blame is comfortable—it gives you an enemy. Accountability gives you a mirror. And mirrors do not lie. When I look back at my own life, I see the moments I gave my power away and called it loyalty. The moments I stayed quiet and called it maturity. The moments I said "I am fine" just to avoid having to face the truth: I was betraying myself and blaming others for the consequences. It is easier to say, "They hurt me." Harder to say, "I kept showing up after they did." It is easier to say, "They never saw me." Harder to admit, "I never spoke clearly." It is easier to feel righteous in your pain. Harder to admit that your silence, your passivity, or your fear helped it last longer than it should have.

But when you do admit it—when you finally get honest about your role—something unlocks. You stop performing growth. You start living it. You stop needing the apology. You become your own closure. You stop waiting for someone else to make it right. You decide to make yourself whole.

Blame is a Sedative

That decision changes what you can see: blame is not just a reaction. Blame is a drug. It numbs the part of you that does not want to face your own participation. It gives you the illusion of movement while keeping you parked in the same emotional location. Blame keeps you busy. It gives your mind a job: replay it, dissect it, prove it, relive it, rewrite it. And if you have ever wondered why you can think about something for months, even years, and still feel the same tightness in your chest, it is because your brain confuses repetition with resolution. Rumination feels like control, but it is not control. It is a loop. It is your nervous system staying activated, because activation feels safer than silence. Silence would force you to hear the truth you have been avoiding: you cannot build a future out of a case file.

There is a scientific reason this is so sticky. The brain is a prediction machine. It is constantly trying to reduce uncertainty. Blame offers a clean narrative: "I am in pain because of them." That story is comforting, because it keeps the source of your pain outside of you—meaning, in your mind, the fix is also outside of you. The apology. The reversal. The justice. The acknowledgment. The moment they finally see it. But when your peace depends on someone else's self-awareness, you are not healing. You are negotiating with reality. And reality does not negotiate. A client once described it perfectly without realizing how profound it was. He said, "If I stop being angry, it feels like they got away with it." That is the addiction. The anger becomes a form of loyalty to the wound. The resentment becomes the proof that what happened mattered. And if you grew up in a world where your pain was minimized, dismissed, laughed at, or ignored, resentment can start feeling like the only witness you have. So you hold it. Not because you love suffering. Because suffering feels like evidence.

Here is the brutal upgrade: your healing does not require a witness. Your healing requires a decision. And that decision is not, "I forgive you." The decision is, "I will not let what you did become the architecture of my life."

Because that is what blame does. It turns your life into a courtroom. You walk around collecting arguments, building closing statements, preparing for a trial that never gets scheduled. Meanwhile, your actual life is happening outside the courtroom. Opportunities. Peace. New standards. Better people. A calmer nervous system. All of it waiting for you while you stay inside a story that keeps you emotionally employed but spiritually unemployed. You can be right and still be trapped. You can be right and still be stuck. You can be right and still be living below your own potential because you keep outsourcing your power to someone who does not even understand what they did. This is why accountability is freedom. It does not let you stay anesthetized.

Let me give you a scene you will recognize, even if it is not yours. A woman runs a team. Strong, competent, respected. She calls after a project collapses because one partner kept missing deadlines, then the partner blamed the woman who runs the team for "being intense." The story is true. The partner was irresponsible. The partner was manipulative. The partner used charm like a weapon and confusion like a shield. But here is what she could not see until we slowed it down: she had been compensating for that partner for months. Covering. Fixing. Softening the consequences. Explaining away disrespect as stress. Translating immaturity into "they are just overwhelmed." She was not only working on the project. She was working on the partner's emotional comfort. And by the time the collapse happened, she had already trained the system to believe she would carry what they dropped. Her rage made sense. Her disappointment made sense. Her hurt made sense. But the accountability question was the one that freed her: "Where did you confuse your competence with your obligation?" That question ended the loop. Not because it changed the past. Because it changed her future. And that is the difference between blame and accountability. Blame explains. Accountability corrects. The people who Become First are not the people who never get hurt.

They are the people who stop letting pain become a lifestyle.

Ownership is Not Self-Punishment

A lot of people think accountability is a humiliation ritual. They hear "take responsibility" and interpret it as "admit you were stupid." So they resist it with pride, or with shame, or with that polished, intellectual deflection that sounds mature but is really fear in a suit. But accountability is not self-punishment. Accountability is self-respect with teeth. Self-punishment is when you look at your role and use it as a weapon against yourself: I should have known. I am an idiot. I always do this. What is wrong with me? That is not growth. That is violence with better vocabulary. Ownership is different. Ownership is when you look at your role and use it as a key: Now I see it. Now I know what I tolerated. Now I know what I avoided. Now I know what I will do differently. Same facts. Completely different direction.

The human mind has a built-in mechanism that protects identity. We will rationalize discomfort if admitting the truth threatens how we see ourselves. That is why people stay in situations that drain them and call it loyalty. That is why they keep giving access to someone who misuses it and call it compassion. That is why they negotiate boundaries and call it maturity. Because the alternative is terrifying: admitting that you abandoned yourself. And grief lives inside that admission. People do not avoid accountability because they are lazy. They avoid it because accountability forces grief. Grief for the time you wasted. Grief for the standards you postponed. Grief for the version of you that kept showing up hoping this time would be different. Grief for how long you stayed loyal to potential instead of behavior. And the truth is: grief is the bill you pay when you stop running. Pay it once, and you stop paying it monthly for the rest of your life.

I saw this in a founder who built a company from nothing. Brilliant, relentless, charismatic—and trapped in a pattern. He kept choosing "high potential" people who delivered chaos. He would hire someone with spark, tolerate months of inconsistency, then explode, then feel guilty, then rehire them, then call it "believing in people." When we finally named the pattern, he said something that sounded like confession: "I think I am addicted to fixing. If I fix them, it proves I am powerful." That is the sentence right there. Some people do not stay because they are weak. They stay because they want to feel necessary. They want to feel irreplaceable. They want to feel like their love, their patience, their intellect, their giving can transform someone who refuses to transform themselves. That is not love. That is control disguised as devotion.

Accountability is when you stop trying to earn your power by saving people and start using your power to save your life. This is where scientific reality comes in again: intermittent reinforcement. When someone gives you warmth inconsistently—enough to keep you hoping, not enough to make you secure—your brain latches harder. It is the same mechanism that makes people pull a slot machine lever again and again. Random rewards create stronger attachment than predictable rewards. Your nervous system becomes a gambler. You keep showing up because "sometimes" feels like "soon." Accountability is when you stop gambling with your dignity. And it does not require cruelty. It requires clarity. It requires you to say: I am done confusing inconsistency with depth. I am done calling anxiety chemistry. I am done romanticizing what destabilizes me. That is Becoming First.

Boundaries are Not Speeches

If accountability is freedom, boundaries are the daily proof that you meant it. A boundary is not a request for someone to behave better. A boundary is a decision about what you will participate in. That is why boundaries do not need paragraphs. They need enforcement. People who require your explanations are usually not confused. They are resistant. They want you to keep talking because talking buys them time. Time to charm you. Time to soften you. Time to make you doubt yourself. Time to reframe your standards as "too much." Time to move the goalpost. Accountability is when you stop confusing explanation with power. Power is not the speech. Power is the follow-through.

And yes—your body will fight you at first. Not because the boundary is wrong. Because your nervous system has been trained to equate conflict with danger. So the moment you enforce a standard, you feel guilt, anxiety, doubt, loneliness. You feel like you are doing something bad. You are not doing something bad. You are doing something unfamiliar. There is a pattern I have seen with clients over and over: they set boundaries emotionally, then break them behaviorally. They say, "I am done," then reply. They say, "I will not tolerate this," then tolerate it. They say, "I am moving forward," then check the person's social media at 2 a.m. That is not because they are hypocrites. It is because boundaries create an extinction burst. That is a real phenomenon in behavior. When you stop reinforcing a pattern—when you stop rewarding a dynamic with your attention, your availability, your emotional labor—the pattern often escalates before it collapses. The person pushes harder. The guilt gets louder. The loneliness intensifies. The urge to "just fix it" spikes. That surge is not a sign that your boundary is wrong. It is a sign that the old conditioning is dying.

Most people fail right there. They interpret withdrawal symptoms as proof they should go back. Becoming First is staying steady through the withdrawal. A friend once told me about a client relationship that was draining him. Every call was an emergency. Every message was urgent. Every request came with pressure and implication. He kept answering because he did not want to be "unprofessional." He kept absorbing because he was "strong." He kept over-delivering because he feared losing the account. Then he did something simple. He changed one behavior. He stopped responding immediately. Not forever. Not with drama. Just with consistency. He responded during defined hours, with clean, direct communication. He stopped rescuing. He stopped reacting. Within one week, the client escalated. More messages. More urgency. More emotional manipulation. The old him would have panicked and overcorrected. But he stayed steady. And something happened: the client adjusted. The dynamic recalibrated. The "emergency" was never real. The emergency was the system testing whether it could still control him. That is what boundaries expose: what was real versus what was leverage. Accountability is the choice to become unreachable to leverage. And when you do, your life stops being dictated by other people's chaos. Not because you are cold. Because you are clear.

The Quiet Freedom

People expect freedom to feel like excitement. Like victory. Like a triumphant anthem in the background. Real freedom is quieter. It feels like the end of mental noise. It feels like your chest is not tight for no reason. It feels like you can sleep without replaying conversations. It feels like you do not need to strategize your own worth. It feels like you can say no and still breathe. It feels like you can be misunderstood and still remain loyal to yourself. It feels like you stop living as a negotiator and start living as an author.

This is where the science becomes lived experience. When you are stuck in blame, your nervous system stays in threat mode. You scan. You anticipate. You interpret tone like a detective. You read between lines. You rehearse. You prepare. You brace. Even when nothing is happening, your body acts like something is about to happen. Accountability shifts you from scanning to presence. And presence is a form of power that cannot be manipulated. Because once you decide to make yourself whole, you stop needing external permission to move forward. You stop needing the apology. You stop needing the final conversation. You stop needing them to admit it. You become your own closure. That does not mean you pretend it did not hurt. It means you refuse to keep bleeding in the same place.

One more composite scene, because it is common and it matters. A man is trapped in a friendship that is subtly humiliating. Not overt abuse. Not dramatic cruelty. Just constant small disrespect disguised as jokes. Public teasing. Private dismissal. A tone that makes him feel smaller. He laughs along because he does not want conflict. He tells himself he is "not sensitive." He tells himself it is "just humor." Meanwhile, his nervous system is registering the truth: this is not safe. One day he finally says, calmly, "Do not speak to me like that." The friend responds with the classic defense: "Wow, you changed. You are different now. You are acting brand new." That sentence is a trap. It is designed to make accountability feel like arrogance. But the truth is: becoming different is the goal. He pauses, breathes, and says, "Yes. I am different. That is not an insult." That is accountability in real time. That is Becoming First. Not loud. Not dramatic. Clean.

Here is what happens next, and it always happens: some people adjust. Some people leave. Some people expose themselves by refusing to meet the new standard. That is not loss. That is sorting. That is your life finally protecting itself. Accountability does not just change your relationships. It changes your identity. You stop being the person who waits. The person who tolerates. The person who overexplains. The person who negotiates their dignity to keep closeness. You start becoming the person who does not need to be convinced. And once you become that person, everything changes, because your life stops responding to other people's moods and starts responding to your standards.

That is why accountability is freedom. Not because it feels good. Because it makes you real. Because it makes you sober. Because it returns your power to its rightful owner. You do not need everyone to treat you right. You need you to treat you right. You do not need everyone to be fair. You need you to be honest. You do not need everyone to understand you. You need you to stop misunderstanding yourself. You do not need everyone to apologize. You need you to stop waiting. Because waiting is the most socially acceptable way people waste their lives. They wait for timing. They wait for clarity. They wait for the perfect moment. They wait for someone else to go first. They wait until they are angry enough. They wait until they are hurt enough. They wait until they can leave without guilt. Meanwhile, the years move. The body keeps score. The nervous system keeps receipts. The life you want keeps getting postponed.

Accountability is not a realization. It is a decision you keep paying for in behavior. It is the moment you stop treating truth like an insight and start treating it like a standard. Because a standard is not what you believe. A standard is what you enforce when your nervous system begs you to go back to what is familiar. This is where most people fail. They think freedom is a feeling. They wait to "feel ready," to "feel strong," to "feel sure." But the body does not reward change with comfort in the beginning. The body rewards familiarity. It will offer you the old sedative—blame, rumination, the courtroom, the case file—because that loop is predictable, and predictable feels safe. Accountability is when you stop asking your nervous system for permission to evolve. You do it anyway. You stop texting to regulate. You stop explaining to be understood. You stop performing closure and you choose it. You accept the most offensive truth of all: your life cannot be built on what you hope someone will finally realize. If your peace depends on another person's awareness, your peace is not peace—it is a negotiation with reality. And reality does not negotiate.

So here is the clean line: you do not need the apology to move. You do not need the final conversation to be free. You do not need them to admit it, validate it, or see it correctly for it to be true. You need one thing: to stop letting what they did become the architecture of your life. That is what accountability changes. It moves you out of reaction and into authorship. It turns your attention from the person who mishandled you to the version of you who kept handing over access. Not to punish you—never to punish you—but to return your power to its rightful owner. Because the second you own your part, you gain leverage over your future. You stop confusing competence with obligation. You stop confusing patience with self-abandonment. You stop confusing anxiety with chemistry. You stop romanticizing inconsistency. You stop watering dead plants and calling it loyalty. You stop living like your dignity is a debate.

And then something quiet but irreversible happens: you become unbribable. Not by charm, not by guilt, not by timing, not by potential, not by the occasional warmth that used to keep you hoping. You stop gambling with your self-respect. You stop paying for closeness with silence. You stop explaining your boundaries like they are requests. You enforce. You follow through. You let the extinction burst pass without interpreting withdrawal as destiny. You let the discomfort burn without calling it a sign you are doing the wrong thing. You let yourself be misunderstood without rushing to correct it. Because when you have chosen yourself with clarity, you do not need to be agreed with in order to be aligned.

That is the real freedom. Not the loud kind. The sober kind. The kind that feels like the end of mental noise. The kind where your chest is not tight for no reason, where you do not rehearse arguments in the shower, where you do not check your phone like it is a verdict, where you do not keep returning to the same emotional location just to feel justified. You stop needing life to be fair before you treat yourself right. You stop waiting for the perfect moment to leave what is draining you. You stop postponing your own standards until the pain becomes unbearable. You stop living as a passenger in your own story. You take the wheel. You take the pen. And you do not announce it. You do not threaten it. You do not debate it. You just change. You decide to make yourself whole—and then you live like you meant it.

CHAPTER 3

STOP THE WAITING GAME

The Addiction to Delay

Waiting is a drug. It does not look like it. It looks passive. Harmless. Patient. But it is one of the most dangerous habits a person can carry—because it gives you the illusion of progress while pulling you deeper into paralysis. And paralysis is not always dramatic. Most of the time it is quiet. It is the slow acceptance of a life that keeps shrinking while you keep calling it "temporary." It is the way you keep rearranging your standards so the relationship can still fit, the way you keep bending your boundaries so the partnership does not break, the way you keep editing your truth so the room stays calm. Waiting lets you feel like you are still moving, still hopeful, still "working on it," even while your spirit is learning how to tolerate less and call it maturity.

We wait for the pain to pass. We wait for timing to feel perfect. We wait for people to "get it," change, see us, meet us, wake up. But behind all that waiting is a truth most people never admit: we are afraid to move. Afraid to let go. Afraid of being seen as selfish. Afraid of what we will lose if we act on what we already know. That is why waiting feels clean. It gives you a story where you are not the one making the hard choice; you are simply "giving it time." You can keep your hands looking innocent while your life quietly pays the bill. Because the moment you stop waiting, the moment you say what is true, you become responsible for the next step, and that is the part most people are trying to avoid. So, we wait. And in doing so, we convince ourselves that we are not choosing anything… but waiting is a choice. It is the choice to abandon yourself in slow motion.

The tragedy is that waiting can look like loyalty. It can look like love. It can look like grace. But when waiting is really fear, it becomes a form of control: control of the narrative, control of the discomfort, control of the moment you will finally have to face the reality you have been living inside. People call it patience because "fear" feels too humiliating to admit, and "avoidance" feels too harsh, but that is what it is. Waiting is a way to stay attached to an outcome you do not have the power to produce. You cannot wait someone into growth. You cannot wait someone into accountability. You cannot wait someone into meeting you at a level they have shown you they cannot reach. The longer you try, the more you confuse endurance with devotion, and then you start building an identity around being the one who holds on.

I have lived that choice more than once. One night I stared at my phone like it was a courtroom. Their name lit up the screen and my first feeling was not warmth—it was that familiar drop in the stomach, that tiny internal brace. I read the message and my mind immediately started negotiating: maybe they are tired, maybe they did not mean it, maybe I should respond softer, maybe this is not the time. I could feel myself editing my truth before I had even typed a word, shaping my life around the possibility of their reaction. That is when it hit me with embarrassing clarity: I was not waiting for them to understand. I was waiting for myself to stop being afraid of what my honesty would cost.

I have stayed in conversations I outgrew, hoping they would eventually deepen. I have stayed in partnerships—business and romantic—where I was the only one fighting for growth. I have stayed silent when I should have spoken, waiting for the "right" moment to bring truth into the room. And the "right moment" always felt like it was coming, because waiting has a seductive promise built into it: if you just hold on a little longer, it will get easier. If you wait, you will find a cleaner way to say it. If you wait, you will not have to be the one who breaks the spell. But the truth is that the longer you wait, the more the truth starts demanding a price. It does not disappear. It collects interest. And when it finally comes out, it does not come out gentle; it comes out tired, sharp, resentful, and sometimes even cruel, not because that is who you are, but because you delayed it until it rotted inside you.

Truth does not wait. Truth does not soften itself for your timing. Truth is now. And when you delay it, you dilute it—until it starts to rot inside you. You start turning clarity into hints, boundaries into moods, pain into sarcasm, disappointment into distance, and then you wonder why the relationship feels cold. It feels cold because you have been living two lives: the polite life you show, and the honest life you hide. Eventually, those two lives stop being able to share the same body without consequences.

Most people do not wait because they are noble. They wait because they are terrified of what clarity will demand. Because if you say, "This is not working," you might lose someone. If you say, "This is not enough," you might have to start over. If you say, "I deserve more than this," you might have to actually become the version of yourself who does. And that is terrifying. Not because you are weak, but because stepping into that version of you requires leaving the comfort of confusion behind. Confusion is familiar. Confusion lets you keep explaining. Confusion lets you keep hoping. Confusion gives you something to do. Clarity is different. Clarity ends the performance. Clarity exposes the bargain you have been making with yourself. Clarity forces you to admit that what you keep calling "potential" is often just a fantasy you use to excuse a reality that keeps disappointing you.

Because Becoming First means you stop hiding behind "maybe." You stop putting your peace on layaway, hoping someone else will make the deposit. That is what waiting really is: you keep your life in storage while you negotiate someone else's readiness. You keep postponing your own freedom, because you want the story to end in a way that does not hurt. But waiting does not prevent hurt; it just stretches it. It makes it livable. It makes it normal. It trains you to live with a little ache every day until you forget what it feels like to wake up clear.

Here is what I learned the hard way: time is not medicine when you are using it to avoid your own power. You do not heal by watching the calendar. You heal by facing the truth and choosing something different—before you are ready. Ready is the word we use when we want certainty. But life does not give certainty to people who refuse to move. Life gives clarity to those who act with integrity, even while their hands shake. The moment you stop asking, "What if it gets better?" and start asking, "What is this costing me right now?" is the moment waiting loses its charm.

If you want to know what your life will look like a year from now, look at what you are avoiding today. Still waiting for clarity? Still hoping they will change? Still stuck between what you feel and what you are afraid to say? That is the cost of delay. And if you do not interrupt the pattern now, it will quietly shape your entire future. It will become the way you live: postponing, tolerating, adjusting, shrinking, calling it love, calling it patience, calling it growth. And then one day you will look back and realize the years moved while you kept negotiating with a truth you already knew. That is why Become First is not just a phrase—it is a rebellion against waiting. It is the refusal to waste another year hoping someone else becomes the person you have already decided to be.

Waiting feels harmless. But what it really is—is silent self-abandonment. And the longer you do it, the more you disconnect from the version of yourself that is actually ready. The bold one. The clear one. The one who does not negotiate with truth. But that version of you does not appear by watching the calendar. It appears the moment you decide to Become First. That decision is not always loud. It is often private. It is often ordinary. It is you sitting with yourself after another conversation that left you empty, after another promise that did not become action, after another night where you feel the weight in your chest and you realize you cannot keep calling this "temporary." It is the moment you stop being seduced by the idea of "one more chance" and start asking whether you have been living on chances for so long that you forgot what commitment feels like.

We call it patience. We tell ourselves we are giving them time. We say we are "seeing how it goes." But waiting is often fear in disguise—fear of being alone, fear of being wrong, fear of finally having to accept that what we have been holding onto is not holding us back... it is not holding us at all. That is the part that hurts. Because it means the thing you keep trying to save might not even be there to save. You might be holding a ghost, holding a fantasy, holding a memory of how it felt in the beginning, and then you keep confusing that memory with a future you think you can create if you just endure a little longer.

So, we wait. Not because we are calm, but because we are terrified of what clarity will demand. Clarity costs you your comfort. Your denial. The illusion that things might magically shift without you having to do anything. But more than anything, clarity costs you the chance to hide from yourself. Because once you admit you have been settling, you cannot un-know it. Once you admit you have been abandoning yourself, you cannot romanticize it anymore. Once you admit you have been waiting, you cannot keep calling it love without feeling the lie.

I have paid that cost. There were moments when I knew the relationship was dead, but I stayed—out of fear, guilt, hope. It did not revive. There were people I invested everything into, believing that if I held on a little longer, they would finally see their potential. They did not. There were clients and partners I supported far beyond what was reasonable, confusing loyalty with self-sacrifice. It was not loyalty—it was avoidance. Avoidance of the moment I would have to change without them. Avoidance of the moment I would have to face my own attachment to being needed. Because waiting is not always about them; sometimes it is about the identity you built around being the one who stays, the one who forgives, the one who carries, the one who "understands." But understanding without boundaries is not maturity; it is self-erasure.

Waiting is not a pause. It is a performance. And the longer you perform, the smaller you become inside your own life. You start managing other people's comfort while bleeding silently behind your own smile. You tell yourself you are being strong, but strength is not the ability to tolerate disrespect. Strength is the ability to face the truth without flinching and still choose yourself. Waiting turns the opposite into a habit: you learn how to flinch and call it strategy. You learn how to swallow and call it grace. You learn how to lose yourself politely.

When you wait, you shrink your voice so others will not feel overwhelmed. You stretch your boundaries so they do not feel rejected. You edit your truth so they do not walk away. And little by little, you disappear. You start seeing your life from the outside, like you are a supporting character in a story you did not write. You become the person who is always "understanding," always "patient," always "giving it time," while your own needs sit in the corner like a child you keep ignoring because you do not want the adults in the room to get uncomfortable.

And for what? Validation? Closure? Gratitude? You will not get it, not consistently, not in the way you are secretly hoping. Because the people you are waiting on do not even realize how much of yourself you have buried just to keep them close. That is not an insult; it is just reality. If someone benefits from your over-functioning, they rarely notice it until it stops. But you notice. You feel it every day you wake up knowing you are not where you are meant to be. You feel it in your body when you read a message and your first reaction is dread. You feel it when you look at your life and cannot find your own voice. You feel it when the person you used to be—bold, clear, alive—starts feeling like someone you once knew.

That is the real cost of delay: it does not only steal time; it steals identity. It teaches you to live as a negotiator instead of a leader. It teaches you to keep the peace at the expense of your peace. It trains you to accept a life that does not match your knowing, and then it convinces you that your dissatisfaction is just you being "too much."

But you are not too much. You are awake. And waking up hurts because it means you can no longer pretend. That is why this chapter exists. Not to shame you for waiting, but to expose what waiting really is, so you can finally stop calling it something noble and start treating it as what it is: a habit that keeps you from becoming who you already are.

The Performance of Patience

The reason waiting survives for so long inside people is because it can be framed as virtue. You can hide behind it without looking like you are hiding. You can delay a decision and still appear "reasonable." You can stay in something that is breaking you and still sound compassionate when you describe it. That is why waiting becomes dangerous: it gives your fear a respectable costume, and when fear looks respectable, you stop challenging it. You stop interrogating it. You stop noticing how much of your life is being built around not having to face what you already know.

Most of the time, waiting is not the absence of action. It is a very specific kind of action: the action of maintaining an illusion. You are actively maintaining hope. You are actively maintaining access. You are actively maintaining the fantasy that the next message, the next conversation, the next month, the next season will finally become the proof you were missing. It is work. It is a negotiation with yourself—again and again—just to keep the story alive.

We call it patience. We say we are giving them time. We say we are "seeing how it goes." But what we are often doing is trying to control the outcome without having to confront the reality of the present. Waiting is the compromise that lets you keep your desire and keep your denial in the same room. You do not have to say yes. You do not have to say no. You can stay in the fog. You can keep the door half open. Half open feels safer than closed because it does not force you to grieve. But half open is not neutral. Half open keeps you tethered. It keeps you checking. It keeps you hoping. It keeps you emotionally employed by someone else's potential.

And the mind loves that. The mind loves "almost." Almost means the dream is still alive. Almost means you can keep explaining the red flags as temporary. Almost means you do not have to admit you invested in something that is not investing back. Almost means you can avoid the brutal honesty that would force you to rebuild your life with different rules. Almost becomes a lifestyle.

The problem is that "almost" has a price. It costs you clarity. It costs you presence. It costs you energy you do not get back. It costs you the simple freedom of waking up without a knot in your stomach. It costs you the ability to trust your own instincts, because you keep overriding them. Every time your body signals danger and you talk yourself out of it, you train yourself to distrust yourself. Waiting becomes the training ground for self-doubt.

People think waiting is love because it looks like endurance. They confuse suffering with devotion. They confuse staying with commitment. They confuse tolerating with maturity. But love without respect is not love; it is attachment. It is fear of emptiness disguised as loyalty. It is the belief that if you suffer long enough, life will pay you back with a different version of the person. That is not love. That is bargaining with reality. That is trying to buy a future with pain. It does not work.

I learned that the hard way. I have waited in situations where I knew the truth, but I did not want to accept what it would cost me. I was not waiting for information. I was waiting for permission to be strong. I was waiting for someone else to make the decision so I would not have to carry the weight of it. I was waiting for an ending that would make me look good. That is what most people will never admit: part of waiting is image management. You want to leave in a way that keeps you clean. You want to speak in a way that keeps you liked. You want to choose yourself in a way that does not trigger anyone's anger. You want freedom without consequences. But freedom has consequences. Truth has consequences. And the moment you demand consequence-free truth, you are still trying to stay safe inside the lie.

Waiting is also a way to avoid becoming the person you keep claiming you want to be. Because if you stop waiting, you have to act. And action makes you visible. Action makes you accountable. Action reveals your real standards. As long as you are waiting, you can keep talking about what you deserve without having to enforce it. You can keep telling yourself you have high standards while your life remains proof that you have been negotiating them. Waiting lets you stay attached to an identity you have not yet earned.

That is why the cost of clarity terrifies people. If you say, "This is not working," you might have to step into a new life without a map. If you say, "This is not enough," you might have to admit you settled. If you say, "I deserve more," you might have to stop acting like you do not. And that is the moment the ego panics. Because it is easier to be the victim of someone else's inconsistency than the leader of your own change. It is easier to be disappointed than responsible. Disappointment hurts, but it keeps you innocent. Responsibility hurts differently. Responsibility forces you to stop performing.

Waiting is performance, and it has a script. The script says you are the one who understands, the one who forgives, the one who sees potential, the one who holds space, the one who gives time. That script can become an identity that feels noble. But you have to ask yourself: noble to whom? Because the person you are trying to be noble for is often the same person who keeps taking without giving. Your patience becomes their permission. Your understanding becomes their excuse. Your silence becomes their comfort. You start realizing that what you thought was love might simply be you financing their immaturity with your peace.

And then your life begins to shrink in ways you do not notice immediately. It starts with small edits. You change how you speak, not because you became wiser, but because you are trying to avoid friction. You stop bringing up certain topics because you know the reaction you will get. You stop asking for what you want because you learned the pattern: asking makes you feel needy, asking makes you feel rejected, asking makes you feel like a problem. So, you adapt. You begin to practice a quieter version of yourself.

You shrink your voice so other people do not feel challenged. You widen your boundaries so they do not feel pushed away. You lower your expectations so they do not feel pressured. You start managing their comfort, their moods, their fragility, their defensiveness. And what you call "being considerate" is often you being terrified of the backlash that comes when you stop playing small.

This is not theoretical. You feel it. You feel it when you read their message and your first emotion is not excitement but tension. You feel it when you spend hours rehearsing what you are going to say, trying to make your truth sound gentle enough to be accepted. You feel it when you walk into a conversation already preparing to be misunderstood. You feel it when you realize you are more honest in your head than you are in your life. That gap between internal truth and external performance is where anxiety lives.

Waiting also creates a specific kind of emotional debt. Because you keep investing, you keep giving, you keep trying, and you tell yourself it will balance out later. You tell yourself the person will eventually repay you with effort, with consistency, with recognition. But you cannot build a life on future repayments. You cannot build a relationship on a debt you keep pretending will be honored. The longer you wait, the more resentment accumulates, not only toward them, but toward yourself. You start resenting yourself for staying. You start resenting yourself for negotiating. You start resenting yourself for knowing better and still choosing the comfortable lie over the uncomfortable truth.

That resentment becomes poison. It leaks into your tone. It leaks into your patience. It leaks into the way you interpret everything. A simple delay becomes proof. A simple mistake becomes a trigger. You become hyper-aware because your nervous system knows the pattern. Your nervous system is not confused. It is exhausted. The mind keeps trying to create new explanations so you can keep waiting, but the body does not have the patience for your rationalizations. The body records what is real.

And then you begin to mistake that exhaustion for personal weakness. You think you are "too sensitive." You think you are "overreacting." You think something is wrong with you. But often what is wrong is that you are living in contradiction. You are living in a life where your standards exist in theory, but not in practice. You are living in a life where you keep betraying yourself to maintain the relationship, the partnership, the dynamic, the role you have been playing.

Waiting teaches you to mistake endurance for strength. But strength is not staying. Strength is facing the truth without decorating it. Strength is admitting, without drama, that what you have been tolerating is not aligned with who you are becoming. Strength is not begging for consistency. Strength is not calling absence "space." Strength is not calling disrespect "miscommunication." Strength is not waiting for someone to meet you at a level they have shown you they cannot reach. Strength is choosing yourself without needing the other person to agree with your reasons.

That is where most people get stuck: they want the exit to be approved. They want the boundary to be respected before they enforce it. They want the person to understand. They want closure. They want the ending to feel fair. But fairness is not guaranteed. Understanding is not guaranteed. Closure is not guaranteed. The only thing that is guaranteed, if you keep waiting for those things, is more waiting.

The moment you start moving, you learn something that changes everything: the world does not reward you for suffering. There is no medal for staying too long. There is no crown for being the one who tolerated the most. There is no applause for your quiet self-erasure. The people who benefit from your waiting will not celebrate when you stop. They will question you. They will test you. They will accuse you of changing. They will call your boundary "cold." They will call your clarity "selfish." They will call your decision "dramatic." That is because your waiting made them comfortable, and your movement disrupts the comfort they got used to.

That is the real test of Becoming First: can you hold your truth when it is not applauded? Can you choose your life when it does not come with permission? Can you stop waiting even when your mind tries to seduce you back into the familiar loop?

Because waiting is familiar. It has a rhythm. It gives you something to do. It gives you a role. Stepping out of it feels like stepping into silence, and silence can feel like loneliness at first. But what you call loneliness is often the clearing. The empty space where you finally hear yourself again. The space where your standards stop being ideas and start becoming law.

This is why waiting feels so hard to break. It is not only emotional. It is identity. When you have been the one who waits, the one who holds on, the one who is always available, stopping the waiting feels like betrayal. But you have to ask yourself honestly: betrayal of whom? If the only way to keep a relationship alive is to keep betraying yourself, then the relationship is not alive. It is being propped up by your self-sacrifice.

Stop calling that love.

Love does not require you to disappear. Love does not require you to shrink your truth so someone can stay comfortable. Love does not demand that you postpone your life until someone else is ready to respect it. If you have to keep waiting to feel safe, seen, valued, or consistent, you are not waiting for love. You are waiting for relief. And relief is not a relationship. Relief is a symptom that you have been holding your breath.

The shift begins when you stop asking for time and start asking for truth. Not their truth. Yours. What is real right now? What have you been tolerating? What have you been pretending is temporary? What have you been calling patience that is actually fear?

You do not need another year. You need a decision that matches what you already know. You need to stop performing patience and start practicing self-respect. That is where the waiting game ends. Not when they finally change, not when they finally understand, but when you stop making your life dependent on someone else's readiness.

And that is what Becoming First actually is. It is the moment you return authority to yourself. It is the moment you stop negotiating with reality. It is the moment you stop hiding behind time and decide that your life will no longer be postponed for anyone.

How You Disappear (Quietly)

Waiting does not usually destroy your life in one obvious explosion. It erodes you in small, almost invisible compromises that feel reasonable in the moment. You adjust the tone of your voice. You soften the edges of your truth. You postpone the conversation, again, because today feels "too sensitive," because they had a hard week, because you do not want to ruin dinner, because you are tired, because you do not want to be the person who is always bringing things up. And at first it feels like wisdom. It feels like restraint. It feels like you are choosing peace. But what you are actually doing is training yourself to live without your own full presence and calling it maturity so you can survive it.

This is how people disappear inside their own lives. Not by being taken. By slowly giving themselves away. One adjustment at a time.

It begins with the way you start negotiating with your instincts. Your body reacts, your gut tightens, your chest feels heavy, your sleep changes, your appetite changes, your mood shifts, and instead of listening, you start translating those signals into excuses. You tell yourself you are overthinking. You tell yourself you are too intense. You tell yourself you are too emotional. You tell yourself you are projecting. You begin to distrust the most honest part of you because the honest part of you threatens the story you are still trying to keep alive. Waiting requires you to disown your own knowing, because if you let yourself know what you know, you cannot keep waiting without feeling like a liar.

So, you keep the story alive by shrinking the truth.

You do not say what is real. You hint. You suggest. You "check in." You bring it up gently, half-smiling, making it sound smaller than it is. You place your own pain inside soft packaging so it will be easier to receive. You do not demand. You request. You do not state. You ask. You do not stand. You negotiate. And then, when nothing changes, you blame yourself for not being "better" at communicating, even though you have been communicating for months, sometimes years, through every possible language except the one that would actually cost you something: clean clarity.

The waiting game turns your life into a performance. You are not just waiting for them; you are performing patience for yourself. You are trying to prove you are not the kind of person who gives up too soon. You are trying to prove you are not the kind of person who leaves when it gets hard. You are trying to prove you are not selfish. You are trying to prove you are evolved. You are trying to prove you are good. And in the process, you quietly become someone who is not honest.

Not dishonest to the world. Dishonest to yourself.

Because you can only perform patience for so long before it turns into quiet resentment. Resentment is what happens when your standards exist in your mind but not in your life. You begin to feel bitter at the very person you keep protecting. You begin to notice that you are giving them the best of you while you keep receiving the bare minimum. You begin to feel angry at their inconsistency, but even more angry at yourself for staying available for it. And because you do not want to face the truth directly, that resentment leaks out in other ways. It leaks out as coldness. It leaks out as sarcasm. It leaks out as distance. It leaks out as a lack of desire. It leaks out as impatience with small things. It leaks out as a nervous system that is constantly on alert, because it is tired of pretending.

This is why waiting is not harmless. It does not preserve love. It mutates it.

You start shrinking in very practical ways. You stop bringing up your real goals because you already know you will not be met there. You stop sharing your excitement because it will be dismissed or ignored. You stop asking for depth because it will be treated as drama. You start choosing smaller topics, safer topics, lighter topics, and you call that "keeping things smooth." But smooth is not the same as real. Smooth can be a form of denial. Smooth can be the surface layer of a life where you are starving and smiling at the same time.

One of the most painful moments in any waiting dynamic is realizing how much of your personality has become strategy. You are not being yourself; you are trying to avoid a reaction. You are not speaking from truth; you are measuring impact. You are not expressing needs; you are managing someone else's comfort. You become an expert at reading their mood, predicting their defensiveness, anticipating their withdrawal, adjusting your words so they do not feel attacked. And you can get so good at it that you forget you were ever supposed to be free.

Waiting teaches you to live as if your needs are a burden. It teaches you that wanting clarity is "too much." It teaches you that wanting consistency is "demanding." It teaches you that wanting respect is "controlling." It teaches you that wanting to be chosen fully is unrealistic. And because you do not want to be the bad one, you internalize it. You start acting like the problem is your standards instead of the reality that they are not being met.

This is the quiet moment where self-erasure becomes normal.

The most deceptive part is that you can still function. You can still work. You can still socialize. You can still appear fine. That is why people around you might not see it. But inside, there is a particular kind of exhaustion that comes from living in contradiction. You are constantly regulating yourself. Constantly monitoring. Constantly adjusting. Constantly trying not to upset the fragile balance. It is like living with a low-grade fever that never breaks. You might not collapse, but you are never fully alive.

And then your body starts making the truth louder.

The body always does.

Sleep becomes shallow. Your mind keeps circling the same questions at night because you refuse to answer them in the day. Your appetite becomes chaotic or disappears, your patience becomes thinner, your chest feels heavy at random moments. Even your posture changes. You become smaller physically. You hold your breath more. You brace. You tighten. You develop habits that are really coping mechanisms: distraction, scrolling, numbing, overworking, over-giving, overexplaining. Anything to avoid the quiet moment where you would have to admit you are not okay.

Waiting is not a pause. It is a slow internal war.

It is also the place where you begin confusing attention with love. You start feeling relieved when they finally show up, even if they show up in a way that is still inconsistent. You start feeling grateful for crumbs, because your nervous system has been trained to treat inconsistency as normal. You start celebrating basic decency like it is a gift. You start lowering the bar so much that you forget what the original promise felt like. And this is the moment you should be honest with yourself: the waiting game is not just about the other person. It is about what you have learned to accept as your baseline.

People do not stay in the waiting game because they love suffering. They stay because the waiting game protects them from the bigger pain of acknowledging reality. As long as you are waiting, you do not have to grieve the dream. As long as you are waiting, you do not have to admit you chose the wrong person, the wrong partner, the wrong dynamic, the wrong story. As long as you are waiting, you can pretend the investment will still pay off. You can keep your pride intact. You can keep your hope intact. You can keep your identity intact.

But that identity is often built on a lie: that you do not have power.

Waiting is what people do when they do not want to face their own authority. Authority means you stop outsourcing your future to someone else's readiness. Authority means you stop asking, "When will they change?" and start asking, "What am I doing by staying?" Authority means you stop making their behavior the central mystery and start making your own choices the central responsibility. That is the shift, and it is not comfortable, because it removes the easiest drug of all: blame. As long as you are waiting on them, you can keep blaming them for your stagnation. The moment you stop waiting, you have to face the harder truth: you were participating.

Not because you wanted pain, but because you were afraid of the consequences of leaving it.

There is a specific kind of sadness that arrives when you realize how much of yourself you have been sacrificing to keep something alive. It is not only sadness about them; it is sadness about you. You start remembering who you were before you began editing yourself. You start noticing how you used to speak with certainty, how you used to move with clarity, how you used to feel joy without having to negotiate for it. You start noticing that you have been living with a constant internal apology, apologizing for existing, apologizing for needing, apologizing for wanting more than what is being offered.

That is not love. That is survival.

And then comes the most sobering moment: you realize you have been trying to be chosen by someone you stopped respecting. Not because they are worthless, but because they cannot meet you. That is a different kind of pain. When you stop respecting someone's level, you begin to resent yourself for staying at it. You begin to feel ashamed, not because you were loving, but because you kept making excuses for what you would never advise anyone you love to tolerate. This is where the internal split becomes unbearable. You can either keep performing patience, or you can finally choose alignment.

That choice is the beginning of Becoming First.

Because Becoming First is not a dramatic exit. It is not a public announcement. It is not a revenge move. It is not proving anything to anyone. It is the internal decision to stop shrinking your truth to fit into someone else's limitations. It is the private moment where you admit that waiting has become a lifestyle, and you do not want to live that way anymore. It is the moment you stop calling your fear "timing" and start calling it what it is: avoidance of your own authority.

When you stop waiting, you start seeing something clearly that you could not see while you were inside it: the waiting game was never going to end on its own. It was never going to resolve itself through time. The person was not going to become consistent because you stayed available. The partnership was not going to become balanced because you carried more. The relationship was not going to become respectful because you tolerated disrespect with grace.

Waiting does not train people to rise. Waiting trains them to stay exactly where they are, because your silence tells them it is acceptable.

That is why the waiting game is not just harmful; it is educational. You are teaching people, and you are teaching yourself. You are teaching them how little it takes to keep you. You are teaching yourself to accept a life where your own truth is negotiable. The longer you do it, the harder it becomes to remember that you were never meant to live like this.

The good news is that disappearance is reversible. But it is not reversed through more patience. It is reversed through clarity. It is reversed when you stop acting like your needs are optional. It is reversed when you stop managing other people's comfort at the expense of your dignity. It is reversed when you decide that your life is not a waiting room.

That is where this chapter is going next. Not to motivate you, not to inspire you, but to bring you to the moment where waiting stops being a habit and becomes unacceptable. Because once you see what it costs you, you cannot unsee it. And once you cannot unsee it, you are one honest decision away from returning to yourself.

Withdrawal: When You Finally Move, Life Tests You

When you finally stop waiting, something unexpected happens. You think the hardest part will be the decision itself, the moment you choose yourself, the moment you step back, speak up, leave, or draw the line. But the decision is often the cleanest part. The mess starts after. The mess is the withdrawal.

Because waiting is not just a habit; it is a system you have lived inside. It is a rhythm your nervous system knows by heart. It is a loop that gives you structure, even when it hurts you. Hope, disappointment, recovery, repeat. A message arrives and your body spikes. A silence follows and you spiral. You tell yourself you are done and then you soften. You draw a boundary and then you doubt it. You want to move and then you remember the fantasy. You want to leave and then you remember the good days. You keep calling it love, but love does not usually create that kind of loop. Addiction does.

That is why the moment you step out of it, you do not instantly feel free. You often feel exposed. You feel like you are floating without gravity. You feel the absence of the pattern, and the absence can feel like emptiness. Not because you made the wrong choice, but because you removed the noise that used to keep you busy. Waiting kept your mind occupied. It gave you a daily project: interpret, anticipate, adjust. When you stop waiting, you are forced to face the quiet truth you have been avoiding: you were using the pattern to avoid being alone with yourself.

This is the part that makes people relapse. Not because they miss the person, but because they miss the familiar emotional choreography. They miss the feeling of being "in it," even when "in it" was painful. They miss the anticipation, the possibility, the chance of being proven right. They miss the hope because hope is stimulating. It is a drug. And when you stop taking it, your brain tries to pull you back to the nearest source of relief, even if the relief is temporary and the price is your dignity.

So the world tests you.

Not with something obvious. Not with a dramatic event. It tests you the way it always tests a change: through the return of the old pattern, wearing a new face. Through the text that arrives at the exact moment you are starting to feel stable. Through the apology that sounds beautiful but changes nothing. Through the friend who suddenly remembers you exist when you are no longer available. Through the person who offers warmth only when they feel your absence. Through the "Hey stranger" message that is not love; it is a temperature check.

This is where most people get trapped, again. Because the return feels like confirmation. It feels like the universe is saying, "See? You mattered. See?

They do care." But often, what is returning is not commitment. It is access. It is the person's discomfort with losing control. It is their reaction to your boundary, not their transformation.

That is why when you stop waiting, you must stop interpreting contact as change. Contact is cheap. Consistency is expensive. Contact can be produced in a mood. Consistency can only be produced by character.

The test is not whether they show up again. The test is whether you become the version of you who can see the difference and act accordingly.

I have watched this play out in my own life with almost embarrassing clarity. People reappear when you stop feeding the dynamic. They reappear not because they suddenly understood your worth, but because they assumed your availability was permanent. They assumed you would always pick up. Always respond. Always forgive. Always hold space. Always wait. Your sudden silence becomes a disruption, and disruption makes people reach for what they think they own.

That is not a compliment. It is a diagnosis.

And here is the brutal part: old you would call that reaching "hope." Old you would call it "a sign." Old you would call it "maybe this time." But the whole point of Becoming First is that you stop building your life around maybe. You stop giving your future to people who have already shown you their ceiling.

When you stop waiting, life also tests you internally. Your mind becomes your enemy for a while. It starts producing memories like propaganda. It plays you the highlight reel. It brings up the good moments. It reminds you of their softness, their charm, their potential, the way they looked at you once, the way it felt in the beginning. It does not bring up the months of confusion, the exhaustion, the knots in your stomach, the way you kept shrinking, the way you kept bargaining, the way you kept postponing your life. The mind does not do fairness when it wants relief. The mind does seduction.

So, you must become an adult with your own memory. You must stop letting your brain cherry-pick the past to justify the relapse. You must stop letting nostalgia override truth.

Because the waiting game does not end when you decide to stop waiting. It ends when you stop being persuadable by the same bait that kept you stuck.

This is where the withdrawal becomes physical. You feel restless. You feel anxious. You feel a need to do something, to reach out, to check, to reopen the door. You feel a craving for contact because contact used to quiet the uncertainty for a moment. Even a disappointing message can feel like relief because at least it is something. At least you are not in silence. At least you are not in the void.

But the void is not punishment. The void is the clearing. It is the space you need in order to rebuild your standards without interference.

Most people misinterpret that space as loneliness. They think, "I am alone. I made the wrong choice." No. You are not alone. You are unhooked. There is a difference. When you have been emotionally tethered to someone for a long time, even an unhealthy tether can feel like home. Removing it feels like falling. It feels like you lost something, even if what you lost was only the fantasy of what you hoped it would become.

This is why you must expect the test. You must expect the mind to bargain. You must expect the person to reappear. You must expect the old story to try to pull you back into the old role.

Because waiting is not only what you did. Waiting is often who you became.

Stopping the waiting means letting that identity die. And identity death feels like grief. It feels like you are becoming cold. It feels like you are becoming selfish. It feels like you are becoming "different." But different is exactly the point. Becoming First means you stop living as the version of you that was built for survival, and you start living as the version of you that is built for truth.

The world will call that selfish because the world loves agreeable people. The world loves people who tolerate. The world loves people who stay available. The world calls you "kind" when you make yourself convenient. It calls you "difficult" when you insist on consistency. It calls you "dramatic" when you refuse to keep pretending. It calls you "cold" when you stop being free labor for someone else's emotional immaturity.

That is not your problem. That is your proof.

If your boundary makes someone angry, it often means your boundary took away something they felt entitled to. If your clarity makes someone defensive, it often means your clarity exposed a pattern they wanted to keep unchallenged. If your self-respect makes someone uncomfortable, it often means they benefited from your lack of it.

So, the question is not whether the world applauds you. The question is whether you can hold the line when it does not.

Because the waiting game is a game of training. You trained yourself to tolerate less. Now you must retrain yourself to demand more. You trained yourself to ignore your instincts. Now you must retrain yourself to listen. You trained yourself to manage other people's comfort. Now you must retrain yourself to protect your own dignity.

That retraining is the real work. It is quiet work. It is lonely work at first. It is the work of not responding to the message that would pull you back into the loop. It is the work of not reopening the door because you miss the feeling of being wanted. It is the work of not giving someone access just because they knocked. It is the work of letting discomfort pass without calling it a sign that you should go back.

And that is how you know you are becoming someone new: you stop confusing craving with truth. You stop confusing contact with love. You stop confusing apologies with accountability. You stop confusing words with behavior. You stop confusing your anxiety with intuition. You stop confusing loneliness with loss.

Because once you stop waiting, the real change is not that your life immediately becomes perfect. The real change is that your life becomes yours. You stop outsourcing your future to someone else's readiness. You stop building your identity around someone else's inconsistency. You stop living as if your standards are negotiable.

And then something else happens: you begin to see people clearly. Not through hope. Not through fantasy. Not through fear. You see them through reality. You start noticing who shows up when it is easy and who shows up when it matters. You start noticing who respects you when you are available and who respects you when you have boundaries. You start noticing who only loved you when you were useful.

This is the gift of the withdrawal. It strips away the fog. It forces you to see that waiting was never love. Waiting was you trying to earn what should have been given freely and consistently.

And that is why the next step is not just to stop waiting. The next step is to become the kind of person who cannot be recruited back into waiting, even when the bait is beautiful, even when the message is sweet, even when the memory is warm.

Because the old you would call that bait hope. The new you calls it a test.

And Becoming First means you pass it.

The Quiet Return

There is a moment that comes after the storm that does not look like victory. It looks almost boring. No fireworks. No dramatic speeches. No public declarations. Just a quieter room inside you. A room you forgot existed because for so long your life sounded like waiting—anticipating, interpreting, hoping, bracing, rehearsing, doubting, starting over in your head.

When you stop waiting, the first thing you notice is not freedom. It is silence. And, at first, silence can feel like loss, because you were used to the noise. You were used to the loop. You were used to living one foot in the present and one foot in the future, trying to pull tomorrow toward you with effort and patience and proof. Now tomorrow is no longer your obsession. Now the only thing that matters is what is true today.

That is what makes the shift irreversible. You are no longer living for the moment they finally become who you hoped they would be. You are living for the moment you finally stop betraying who you already are.

The decision itself is rarely loud. It is a small, exact movement in your nervous system. It is the moment you stop reaching for the phone. The moment you stop refreshing the screen. The moment you stop creating explanations that keep you stuck. The moment you stop needing the story to end kindly in order for it to end. It is the moment your dignity becomes more important than your desire to be understood.

And then, slowly, something returns.

You start hearing yourself again. Not the rehearsed version. Not the edited version. The actual you. The one who knows. The one who has been watching your life from behind your eyes, waiting for you to stop negotiating with reality. That version does not scream. It does not beg. It does not need a crowd. It simply stands up and takes its place back.

You begin to recognize the difference between patience and postponement. Between love and attachment. Between kindness and self-erasure. Between hope and denial. You stop romanticizing inconsistency. You stop calling crumbs "effort." You stop treating basic respect as a miracle. The bar returns to where it was always supposed to be, and you wonder how you ever lived below it for so long.

What changes next is subtle but brutal: your tolerance drops. Not because you became cold. Because you became honest. The things you used to excuse start looking exactly like what they are. The dynamics you used to survive start feeling impossible to live inside. Not because they suddenly got worse, but because you finally stopped numbing yourself enough to call them normal.

This is the real relief. Not the relief of being chosen. The relief of no longer needing to be chosen by people who cannot meet you. The relief of no longer begging for consistency. The relief of no longer twisting yourself into a shape that fits someone else's limitations. The relief of not having to pretend that confusion is love.

You do not get a reward for this. You get something better. You get your authority back.

You start moving differently. You stop explaining so much. You stop chasing. You stop staying in conversations that drain you. You stop over-functioning to keep something alive. You stop calling your instincts "anxiety" just because they are inconvenient. You stop bargaining with what you already know. You begin to live as if your life is not a waiting room.

And here is the quiet miracle: once you stop waiting, you start teaching. Not with speeches. Not with threats. Not with demands. With your posture. With your choices. With what you tolerate and what you do not. With what you answer and what you do not. With what you normalize and what you refuse to normalize.

The world notices. People notice. But more importantly, you notice. You feel the shift in the way you look at yourself in the mirror. You feel it in the way your words start matching your standards again. You feel it in the way you stop needing permission to protect your own peace.

That is the redemption of this chapter. Not that life becomes easy. That life becomes yours.

And when life becomes yours, the waiting game ends. Not because everyone changes. Because you do. You stop living like a guest in your own story. You stop giving time to what keeps costing you your self-respect. You stop postponing.

You become the kind of person whose presence has weight. The kind of person whose boundaries are not negotiations. The kind of person whose silence is not fear, it is decision. The kind of person who does not need to announce anything to be taken seriously.

And once you live like that, something else becomes obvious: people do not treat you based on what you hope. They treat you based on what you allow.

CHAPTER 4

YOU TEACH PEOPLE
HOW TO TREAT YOU

The Standard You Live, Not the Standard You Announce

It is not only what you allow. It is what you model.

We live in a culture that has turned boundaries into content. People post them. People preach them. People weaponize them. People decorate their pain with a vocabulary that sounds healed, while their real life stays exactly the same. And that is the part nobody wants to say out loud because it makes everyone uncomfortable: people do not follow your rules. They follow your energy. They follow what you consistently embody. They follow what you tolerate without consequence. They follow what your life teaches them is safe to do around you.

You can write the most eloquent list of personal standards in the world. You can sound evolved. You can sound self-aware. You can sound like someone who knows their worth. But if your choices do not reflect your standards, those standards are not standards. They are poetry. Pretty words that never become law. And people can feel the difference immediately. Not because they are evil. Because humans are not guided by speeches. They are guided by signals.

How you treat you is how the world learns to treat you.

That is why so many people stay stuck. They think the problem is the other person's behavior. They keep trying to fix the other person's behavior. They keep explaining, negotiating, offering context, asking for understanding, asking for empathy, asking for basic human decency like it is a favor. But the deeper problem is not what the other person does. The deeper problem is what you keep doing after they do it. The repeated permission you keep giving through your silence, your flexibility, your over giving, your smile, your instant replies, your "it's okay," your quick forgiveness, your willingness to carry discomfort so nobody else has to feel it.

You are not only setting expectations. You are training people.

Every compromise you make against your own truth is a lesson. Not a dramatic lesson. A quiet one. A lesson that says: this is what you can do with me. This is how far you can go. This is what I will swallow. This is what I will normalize. This is how many times you can test me before I become real.

And please understand me: this is not about blaming yourself for someone else's character. Some people are reckless. Some people are selfish. Some people will take whatever you give them and call it love. That is true. But your life is not a courtroom where you are trying to prove that they were wrong. Your life is a system. And systems respond to patterns. If the pattern is that you keep staying, keep adjusting, keep forgiving, keep bending, then the system will keep giving you exactly what your pattern teaches it to give.

You say you want love, but you accept indifference. You say you want truth, but you filter yourself to avoid discomfort. You say you want loyalty, but you keep showing up for people who disappear the moment you need them. You say you want respect, but you stay polite in rooms where you are being quietly diminished. That is not a moral failure. It is a pattern. And patterns are not broken by intention. They are broken by behavior. By the moment you stop performing the version of yourself that keeps everybody comfortable and start embodying the version of you that is actually aligned.

This is where most people lie to themselves. They think they are being compassionate. They think they are being patient. They think they are being understanding. They think they are being "the bigger person." But often what they are really doing is avoiding the moment where they will have to become the adult in their own life. Because adulthood is not a feeling. Adulthood is a decision. It is the moment you stop hoping someone will treat you right and start requiring that your life reflects what you claim to deserve.

And yes, people will resist that. Of course they will. Every system resists change. When you change, you disrupt a contract that has been quietly benefiting someone. That is why your growth will sometimes be experienced as betrayal by people who got used to your self-abandonment. Not because you harmed them, but because you stopped harming yourself in a way that made their life easier.

Let me give you a real example, because theory is cheap.

A close friend of mine is a world-renowned Harvard professor. One of the sharpest minds I have ever met. An oncology expert with serious, groundbreaking insight. He speaks around the world about nutrition, about prevention, about what the body needs when it is fighting for its life. He even built a pharmaceutical company. When he speaks, you can feel the weight of intellect. He is not playing. He is not guessing. He is not performing. His science is sound.

And yet he weighs nearly two hundred kilos.

I am not saying this with cruelty. I am saying it with the kind of honesty that forces you to see what you already know. Because there is a psychological law that nobody escapes: when the messenger does not reflect the message, the message weakens. Not because it becomes false, but because it becomes theoretical. It becomes something you can admire intellectually without letting it rearrange your life. You start hearing the words, but you stop feeling the authority behind them. Not because you want to judge him, but because your nervous system reads inconsistency faster than your mind can defend it.

That dissonance does not happen because people are shallow. It happens because humans are built to trust embodiment more than explanation. We believe what we see lived. We doubt what we only hear preached. We are hungry for congruence. We are tired of slogans. We have been lied to too many times by beautiful sentences that never became behavior.

And this is where the chapter turns back to you, because it is not about my friend. It is about the principle.

This is the same in relationships. In leadership. In love. In business. In friendship. If you preach respect but tolerate disrespect, people do not suddenly become respectful because you asked. They become more strategic. They learn where the line is soft. If you say you want honesty but you keep smiling while you are dying inside, people do not suddenly become honest. They learn you can be managed. If you talk about boundaries but you never enforce them, you can call it "peace," but the world will call it "permission."

You cannot teach what you refuse to become.

You cannot ask the world to honor you while you are abandoning yourself.

That does not mean you have to be perfect. It does not mean you have to become a performance of strength. It does not mean you have to turn cold. It means you have to become congruent. To stop saying one thing and living another. To stop calling your flexibility love when it is really fear. To stop calling your silence maturity when it is really self-erasure. To stop calling your over-giving generosity when it is really an attempt to secure a place in someone's life that they keep refusing to grant you freely.

I learned this the hard way, and not as a cute lesson. As a painful one.

For years I was "the understanding one." I gave people grace. I excused inconsistency. I told myself they were doing their best. And maybe they were. But I was not. Because every time I rationalized someone else's behavior, I lowered the standard I was supposed to hold for myself. Every time I stayed silent to keep the peace, I betrayed the chaos inside me. Every time I kept giving after being dismissed, I reinforced the lie that I did not matter.

That is not love. That is self-erasure.

And it begins quietly. That is why it is so dangerous. Not in dramatic betrayals, but in small edits you make to yourself in order to stay connected.

You shrink your truth to avoid confrontation. You laugh at what hurts to stay included. You minimize your needs so nobody labels you "too much." You answer fast because you do not want them to forget you. You apologize first because you do not want conflict. You over-explain because you want to be understood. You soften your standards because you are afraid of being alone. And at the time, each one feels small. Each one feels reasonable. Each one feels like you are being "smart."

But those small edits do not stay small. They accumulate. They become identity. They become the way people know you. They become the curriculum you teach without saying a word: my needs are flexible, my discomfort is private, my standards can be negotiated, my love does not require reciprocity, my presence is guaranteed even if yours is inconsistent.

Then one day you look up and you are angry that people do not respect you. And the hardest truth is not that they do not respect you. The hardest truth is that you trained them that your respect for yourself is optional.

This is why "boundaries" as a topic gets romanticized. People want to talk about them like they are statements. Like they are sentences. Like they are a speech you give one day and then the world changes. But boundaries are not announcements. Boundaries are consequences. They are what you do when someone tests your reality. They are the line you hold even when you would rather be liked than be aligned.

And this is where the tone gets real: if you want to be taken seriously, take yourself seriously. If you want to be chosen, start choosing you when it is lonely. If you want depth, stop building your life around shallow agreements. If you want respect, stop making your needs negotiable just to keep access to someone who has not earned it.

Because people do not rise to your requests. They rise to the energy you hold without wavering.

And when you finally hold it, when you finally stop performing strength and start living it, something shifts. Not because you became louder. Because you became clearer. Your life becomes a signal. Your presence becomes a standard. Your choices start teaching for you. You do not have to convince. You do not have to chase. You do not have to explain your worth like it is a résumé.

You embody it. And embodiment is the language people actually understand.

That is where this chapter is headed next. Not into a lecture about boundaries. Into the part nobody wants to face: the ways we confuse love with rescue, helping with control, and "support" with a role we never should have accepted in the first place.

The Illusion of Helping

Sometimes what we call helping is not help at all. It is anxiety wearing a clean suit. It is emotional control dressed up as kindness. It is the need to manage someone else's life, so we do not have to sit with the discomfort of watching them choose a path we would never choose. On the surface it looks generous, even noble, because it comes with the right words and the right intentions.

But underneath, it often carries a hidden contract: I will keep giving as long as you keep changing. I will keep showing up as long as you keep moving toward the version of yourself that I believe you should become. The moment their progress slows, the moment they resist, the moment they remain who they are, the "help" starts turning into frustration, then into disappointment, then into resentment. That is how you know it was never clean support; it was management. Real help does not require a specific outcome. Real care does not need to be in charge. Real support respects autonomy even when autonomy looks like choices you dislike, even when it triggers your impatience, even when it activates your fear that they are wasting their life. Clean support offers without gripping, shows up without controlling, and knows the difference between standing beside someone and dragging them.

The reason this becomes so seductive is because helping gives you an identity. It gives you a role that feels powerful: the one who saves, the one who believes, the one who pushes, the one who does not give up. And if you are honest, sometimes the role is more addictive than the person. Usefulness can become its own drug. When you are needed, you feel safe. When you are essential, you feel chosen. When you are the solution, you do not have to face the quieter fear underneath: what if I am not chosen when I am not useful? So, you keep advising, correcting, rescuing, carrying, organizing, fixing. You offer solutions nobody asked for. You turn conversations into coaching sessions. You turn love into correction. You turn friendship into responsibility. You turn intimacy into labor. You stop being with the person and start working on the person, and you tell yourself it is love, because calling it control would force you to confront your own attachment to being needed.

But rescue does not stay contained. It leaks into your tone, your patience, your desire, your sleep. It drains you, because you are investing energy into a life that is not yours to run. It makes you resent them for not appreciating what they never requested, and it makes you resent yourself for volunteering for a role you cannot sustain. Resentment grows when you keep giving without reciprocity and keep calling it loyalty. It grows when you keep carrying weight that belongs to someone else and keep pretending it is just what love does. It grows when you realize you are exhausted, not because the person is impossible, but because you have been over-functioning as if their growth is your responsibility. And the brutal truth is this: you cannot love someone into maturity if they are not participating. You cannot wait someone into accountability. You cannot rescue someone from a life they keep choosing. You can offer, you can support, you can be present, but you cannot carry their evolution on your back without slowly disappearing inside your own.

That is why the turning point is not becoming colder. It is becoming cleaner. It is noticing the moment your care shifts into fear, the moment your generosity shifts into control, the moment your empathy shifts into intrusion. It is asking yourself, before you step in, whether you are supporting them or trying to manage your own discomfort by being useful. It is recognizing that unexamined empathy can become the nicest-looking form of interference, and that interference teaches people the wrong lesson. It teaches them to rely on you instead of standing on themselves. It teaches them that your presence is a scaffolding they can lean on without ever learning to carry their own weight. It teaches them that you will absorb the emotional labor of the entire relationship, as long as you can call it love. And it teaches you something even more dangerous: that your worth is measured by how much you can endure.

The invitation in this part of the chapter is simple, but it is not easy: stop confusing love with labor. Stop pouring energy into lives you were never asked to lead. Stop making your care conditional on someone else's transformation. Stop turning yourself into the emotional life raft and then acting surprised when people swim less. You are not the solution. You never were. Your job is not to manage another adult's timeline, to upgrade them, to drag them into clarity, or to finance their avoidance with your nervous system. Your job is to stay aligned with yourself. Because you cannot teach people how to see you while you keep showing them you exist to carry them. You teach people how to see you when you stop performing usefulness and start embodying worth, when you hold your standard without gripping other people's lives, and when you finally let responsibility sit where it belongs.

When You Finally Stop (The Backlash and the Mirror)

The scariest moment is not when you realize you have been over giving. The scariest moment is when you stop. Because the second you stop, the room changes. The dynamic that felt "normal" suddenly exposes itself, and you discover what it was really built on. Some people do not react to your love; they react to your availability. They do not miss you; they miss access. They do not value you; they value what you made easy for them. And the moment you pull your energy back, the reaction is rarely gratitude. It is shock. Confusion. Accusation. A sudden rewriting of who you are, as if your boundary erased your entire history.

This is where most people collapse and relapse. Not because they made the wrong decision, but because they are not prepared for what a healthy move looks like to someone who benefited from their self-abandonment. When you change the rules, you expose the contract. Not a contract you signed, but one your behavior created. The unspoken deal where you carried the emotional weight, you made the first repair, you tolerated the inconsistency, you kept the peace, you absorbed the tension, you forgave fast, you explained yourself into exhaustion. You did it so long that it became your identity in their eyes, and in a strange way, in your own. So when you stop, they do not experience it as growth. They experience it as theft. You took away something they felt entitled to: the version of you that made their life comfortable.

People will say things like, "You changed." They say it with a tone that makes change sound like betrayal. They will call you cold, distant, dramatic, selfish, difficult. They will act like you became someone else overnight, when the truth is you are finally becoming who you were before you learned to survive by shrinking. And you will feel it in your nervous system because you were trained to interpret backlash as danger. Your body will want to apologize. Your mouth will want to soften. Your mind will want to explain. You will want to prove you are still good. You will want to rescue their feelings, so you do not have to sit in the discomfort of being misunderstood. That impulse is the old pattern trying to rehire you. It is the identity that kept you safe trying to pull you back into the role you played so well: the one who carries, the one who fixes, the one who makes it okay.

This is why becoming first is never just a decision. It is a withdrawal. You are detoxing from the need to be approved while you protect yourself. You are detoxing from the belief that love must be proven through endurance. You are detoxing from the habit of managing other people's emotions, so you do not have to face your own. The moment you stop over-functioning, you feel the empty space where the over-functioning used to live. And if you do not understand this, you mistake that emptiness for guilt, and guilt becomes your leash. You return, not because you want to, but because the discomfort of being the "bad one" feels worse than the pain of staying small.

But guilt is not a moral compass. Guilt is often just the nervous system reacting to a new boundary it has never held before. When you have spent years being the one who bends, any moment of firmness will feel like cruelty, even when it is simply accuracy. The first time you do not respond immediately, you will feel like you are abandoning them. The first time you say no without a long explanation, you will feel like you are disrespectful. The first time you stop saving the conversation, you will feel like you are failing. But you are not failing. You are unlearning the lie that your worth is measured by your ability to carry other people's comfort.

Here is what nobody tells you: when you stop, you create a mirror. And mirrors make people furious. Because a mirror is not an attack, but it feels like one to someone who has been living off your silence. When you stop apologizing for needing respect, you reveal how often they asked you to betray yourself. When you stop giving endlessly, you reveal how little they have been giving. When you stop playing small, you reveal the size of the space they were trying to keep you inside. The reaction you get is not always about you. It is about what your boundary forces them to see. Some will rise. Some will run. Some will try to guilt you back into your old role. That is the test: not whether they understand your boundary, but whether you can hold it even when they do not.

A lot of people mistake being respected for being liked. They think the goal is harmony. They think the goal is to keep everything smooth. But "smooth" is often just avoidance in a nicer outfit. Smooth can be the surface of a dynamic where you are bleeding quietly. Real respect is not always comfortable. It has edges. It has consequences. It has standards. And the moment you start embodying standards, you will lose people who only stayed when you were flexible enough to be used. That loss hurts, but it also tells the truth. Because the people who truly value you do not punish you for growing. They do not demand you stay convenient. They may struggle, they may adjust, they may need time, but they do not weaponize your boundaries against you.

This is why the phrase "You teach people how to see you" is not a motivational quote. It is a diagnosis. It explains why your life keeps repeating the same characters in different bodies. If you teach people that your needs are negotiable, you will attract people who negotiate them. If you teach people that you will stay through inconsistency, you will attract people who offer you inconsistency and call it love. If you teach people that you forgive quickly, you will attract people who apologize easily. Not because the universe hates you, but because systems respond to what works. Your tolerance becomes the training manual. Your patterns become the instruction set. People learn the version of you that you keep demonstrating, not the version you keep describing.

And here is the part that is hard to admit: sometimes the reason people do not show up for you is not that they do not care. Sometimes it is because you taught them you do not need anything. You taught them you are always fine. You taught them you handle everything. You taught them you have no limits. You trained them to see you as the strong one, the solution, the stable one, the one who does not require care. You might hate hearing that, but it matters because it explains the loneliness that comes from being overly capable. People cannot meet needs you never allow yourself to express. They cannot respect boundaries you never enforce. They cannot give you reciprocity when you keep acting like reciprocity is optional.

That is not a reason to blame yourself. It is a reason to wake up. Because once you wake up, you can change the lesson.

This is also where a deeper truth appears: you are not only teaching people how to treat you; you are teaching yourself who you are allowed to be. Every time you swallow something, you train your own psyche that your discomfort is not important. Every time you stay silent, you teach your own nervous system that your truth is dangerous. Every time you overextend, you tell your own body that rest is not allowed until everyone else is okay. That is why this is not just a relationship issue. It is an identity issue. Over time, you become someone who is always negotiating with yourself, always editing, always delaying, always choosing the version of you that keeps the room calm instead of the version of you that keeps your soul intact.

Then one day you wake up and you cannot recognize yourself. Not because you lost your strength, but because you used your strength to disappear.

When you finally stop, you will feel a strange kind of quiet at first. The quiet is not emptiness. It is the sound of your own life returning. It is the space where you start hearing your instincts again without immediately translating them into excuses. It is the space where your body starts unclenching. It is the space where your standards stop being ideas and start becoming law. But that space will be challenged. It will be challenged by guilt, by nostalgia, by fear, by the urge to fix, and by the people who show up the second you become less available.

Do not confuse their sudden attention with change. Attention is cheap. Access is easy. A text is not character. A warm message is not consistency. An apology is not accountability. People can miss you and still not respect you. People can want you back and still not be capable of meeting you. This is where a lot of people get trapped again, because they interpret the return as proof. They say, "See? They care." But what you need is not care in a mood. What you need is a pattern you can trust. If you are going to become first, you have to stop confusing emotion with structure. Emotion is real, but it is not reliable. Structure is what builds a life. Structure is what builds a relationship. Structure is what allows love to become something you can live inside, not something you keep hoping will stabilize.

This is the moment you stop negotiating with reality. The moment you stop needing to be the "good one" at the expense of your own truth. The moment you allow people to feel whatever they feel about your boundary without rushing to manage it. That is where the new identity forms. Not in your speeches. Not in your explanations. In your restraint. In your refusal to perform. In your willingness to let discomfort exist without treating it as an emergency.

The most powerful thing you can do sometimes is not to defend your change. It is to let your life prove it. To let your consistency speak for you. To let your absence teach what your words never could. Because when you stop doing what made people comfortable, you start finding out who is capable of meeting you in reality, not in fantasy. The relationships that are real adjust. The ones built on imbalance either fight, manipulate, or fade. That is not tragedy. That is sorting.

This is the hard gift of finally stopping: you discover that your presence was a drug for some people. Your attention, your labor, your forgiveness, your emotional availability. They were used to it. They relied on it. They built their comfort around it. And when you remove the supply, you see the withdrawal. They accuse you, they test you, they try to bait you back into the old role. That is not proof you are wrong. That is proof the old dynamic was never fair.

If you can hold the line through that phase, you do not just change what you allow. You change what you are. You stop being recruitable. You stop being the person who can be pulled back into old patterns with a sweet message and a familiar feeling. You become the kind of person who does not need to announce standards because your life already enforces them. And once you become that, you stop needing to teach anyone with words. Your example becomes the lesson. Your presence becomes the filter. Your consistency becomes the boundary.

That is when people begin to see you differently. Not because you demanded it, but because you finally stopped contradicting yourself. You stopped asking for respect while tolerating disrespect. You stopped asking for depth while rewarding shallow behavior with unlimited access. You stopped asking for truth while living in performance. You stopped asking the world to honor you while quietly abandoning yourself. And the moment you stop doing that, you do not just teach people how to see you. You teach yourself that you are worth seeing clearly.

When Love Becomes a Project

When you finally stop, you do not just stop an action. You stop a role. And people do not react to the boundary as much as they react to the structure your presence provided suddenly disappearing. The role you never officially accepted but performed so consistently that it became part of the architecture of the relationship. The one who holds it together. The one who pushes the conversation forward. The one who carries the emotional weight. The one who "cares more." The one who keeps the story alive when reality is trying to end it.

That is why the backlash is rarely about the boundary itself. It is about the loss of what your energy made possible. Some people do not miss you; they miss access. They miss the scaffolding, not the soul. And when you pull back, they do not say, "I relied on you too much." They say, "You changed." They do not say, "I got comfortable." They say, "You stopped caring." They do not say, "I never carried my share." They say, "You abandoned me." The accusation is not always cruelty. Sometimes it is panic. Panic is what happens when someone realizes the version of you they leaned on is no longer available.

This is where helping turns dangerous—not because helping is wrong, but because uninvited rescue trains people to outsource their own growth. And it trains you to confuse love with management. You start believing that if you just explain it better, if you just support harder, if you just stay consistent enough for both of you, they will finally rise. But when your love depends on their upgrade, it stops being love and becomes a project. A quiet arrangement where your nervous system works overtime, and their life stays exactly where it is, because your effort makes their stagnation comfortable.

I learned this in the most humbling way—inside my own home, with the person I love. He wakes up around 4:30 a.m. and trains clients before most people have even opened their eyes. He is grounded, reliable, disciplined. He shows up. He gives fully. And, for a long time, I could not understand why someone like that was not trying to build an empire.

To me the path was obvious. Talent plus discipline plus story equals scale. Brand it. Build it bigger. Make it global. With me beside him, we could have taken it to the ceiling. And the part that stings to admit is this: I framed that vision as love. I framed it as support. I framed it as believing in him. But I did not ask the only question that matters when you claim you are "helping" someone: "do you even want what I am pushing you toward?"

Because what he wanted was not an empire. It was a life. Time. Peace. Connection. Meaningful work in the day, and an evening that still belonged to us. He did not crave millions. He did not seek spotlight. He did not need to scale himself into exhaustion in order to feel worthy. He had already defined success—quietly, precisely—on his own terms. And I fought that. Internally. Silently. Sometimes not so silently. I mislabeled his contentment as fear. I called it complacency in my mind. I treated his peace like wasted potential. I made a judgment, disguised as concern, because his definition of fulfillment did not match my hunger.

That is the moment you realize how easily love becomes a project.

Because the truth is: what I was pushing was not only his growth. It was my definition of growth. My nervous system's relationship with "more." My restlessness. My need to see expansion as proof. Proof that we are not wasting time. Proof that we are doing life "right." Proof that we are becoming something impressive enough to silence an old insecurity. And this is the part most people avoid because it exposes them: sometimes helping is not service. Sometimes helping is control with good manners.

Control does not always look like dominance. Sometimes it looks like constant encouragement that never stops. Advice that keeps arriving even when it is not requested. A subtle disappointment when the person chooses calm over conquest. A quiet impatience with a life that is not optimized, scaled, branded, maximized. It can look like devotion, because it is delivered with intensity, but intensity is not always love. Sometimes intensity is anxiety trying to manage an outcome.

And here is how you know it has crossed the line: you stop seeing the person. You start seeing a blueprint. You stop listening to what they value. You start listening to what they could become. You stop loving who they are. You start loving a version of them that exists mostly in your imagination, and you call that "belief." But belief that cannot respect autonomy is not belief. It is attachment to an outcome.

That energy is poison. Not because growth is bad, but because it turns love into a performance review. It turns partnership into a silent pressure. It makes the other person feel studied, measured, evaluated, and not fully safe. Even if you never say it out loud, the energy says it: you are not enough as you are, because I can see what you could be.

At some point I had to accept a sentence that rearranged me: fulfillment does not always look like expansion. Sometimes it looks like presence. Sometimes it looks like being whole. Sometimes it looks like someone who knows exactly what matters to them and is not willing to sacrifice it for applause. And once I saw that, I was forced to look at myself with a sharper honesty. How often was I calling "alignment" what was actually ambition? How often was I calling "potential" what was actually projection? How often was I confusing hunger with truth?

That realization humbled me—and freed me. It freed me from the arrogance of thinking my pace was automatically the right pace. It freed me from the habit of upgrading people to quiet my own discomfort. It freed me from the subtle violence of judging someone's peace as passivity, just because it did not match my hunger. And it showed me what becoming first means at a deeper level: it is not only about drawing boundaries with other people. It is about drawing boundaries with your own tendencies. Your savior reflex. Your need to manage. Your addiction to "more." Your fear of stillness.

Because here is the hard truth: you do not get to love people and also control their outcome. You can do one or the other. If you choose control, you will eventually poison the love, because control always carries disappointment. Love that respects autonomy carries something else: peace. It lets the other person remain sovereign. It lets their life be theirs. It lets their definition of success be valid, even when your mind can see a bigger headline.

So here is the invitation, and it is not sweet. It is clean. Stop pouring your energy into lives you were never asked to lead. Stop making your care conditional on someone else's transformation. Stop trying to stretch people who are not asking to be stretched. Stop turning love into a project and then calling the resistance "betrayal." Sometimes they are not resisting growth. They are resisting your projection.

And start listening to yourself with the same honesty. Ask yourself where you are trying to manage someone else because you do not want to face something in you. Ask yourself where your need to help is actually a need to feel safe. Ask yourself where you call it love, but the truth is you are trying to control the narrative, so you do not have to sit in uncertainty. Because that is how you become first here: you stop abandoning yourself in the name of rescuing, and you stop rescuing in the name of avoiding your own clarity.

Becoming first in this section does not mean you become cold. It means you become accurate. It means you recognize where your effort ends and someone else's autonomy begins. It means you hold your truth without trying to recruit everyone into your pace. It means you stop needing to be understood and start living in a way that simply reveals the distance—without cruelty, without drama, without chasing.

And when you do that, you teach people something stronger than any speech: your love is not control, your care is not pressure, your presence is not a service, and your standards are not negotiable. You become the lesson instead of the lecturer. You stop trying to convince. You simply live in a way that either resonates—or exposes. That is not punishment. That is clarity. That is how you teach people how to see you. That is Become First.

When you finally understand this, you stop asking the wrong question.

You stop asking, "Why do they keep treating me like this?" and you start asking, "What have I been teaching with my silence?" You stop asking, "Why do I keep attracting this?" and you start asking, "Where am I still leaving the door unlocked?" Not because you are responsible for anyone's character, but because you are responsible for access. You are responsible for what stays. You are responsible for what you normalize. You are responsible for the standards your life quietly enforces.

This is the part where most people want comfort. They want a soft ending that lets them keep their dignity without changing their behavior. They want to be told they are innocent and the world is cruel. But this book is not a lullaby. Become First is built for the moment you stop decorating reality and stop negotiating with what you already know.

Because the truth is simple and unforgiving: people do not rise to the standards you post. They rise to the standards you embody. They do not learn who you are from what you say you deserve. They learn who you are from what you tolerate when it costs you. They learn from the version of you that keeps returning after disrespect. They learn from the version of you that keeps explaining. They learn from the version of you that keeps forgiving without change and calling it growth.

Every time you swallow something that wounded you, you teach the room your pain is optional. Every time you overextend to keep a relationship alive, you teach them your effort has no limit. Every time you minimize your needs to appear "easy," you teach them your comfort is negotiable. Every time you reward inconsistency with access, you teach them they do not have to earn you. And they believe you. Not because they are monsters—because you modeled it.

So if you want a different life, stop waiting for different people to become better versions of themselves. Become the standard. Become the consequence. Become the clarity. Not loudly. Not dramatically. Not as a performance. In the quiet way that changes everything: by removing access to what does not honor you.

This is where your life stops being a conversation and starts being a decision.

Because you are not just teaching people how to see you. You are teaching yourself whether you are safe with you. Whether you are loyal to you. Whether your word means anything when it is only you in the room. And the day you become loyal to your own standard, the entire dynamic reorganizes—without negotiation, without begging, without speeches.

Some people will adjust. Some people will disappear. Some will accuse you of changing as if change is an insult. Let them. Their reaction is not your assignment. Your assignment is the part nobody can do for you: to stop granting intimacy to behavior that requires you to betray yourself.

And that is the real shift. Not that you become harder. That you become clean. You stop confusing attention with accountability. You stop confusing apology with repair. You stop confusing chemistry with character. You stop confusing history with future. You stop confusing "potential" with a pattern you can live inside. You stop calling tolerance "love" when it is really fear.

The moment you stop abandoning yourself, you stop being at the mercy of other people's behavior—not because they suddenly become better, but because you stop offering your life as a place where self-abandonment is required.

Not as a burden. As power.

And once you own that power, you are ready for what comes next—because the next chapter is not about what they did. It is about what you do now, when you finally see the truth clearly and you refuse to unsee it.

CHAPTER 5

YOU'RE NOT TOO MUCH.
YOU'RE HONEST.

They Didn't Call You Too Much. They Called You Accurate.

They have called you intense, too emotional, too direct, too sensitive. They have said you overthink, over feel, overreact, as if your nervous system is a defect instead of a signal. They have tried to make your honesty sound like a personality issue, because that is what people do when they do not want to meet what is real. The world has a habit of labeling clarity as confrontation, depth as drama, and truth as threat, not because truth is dangerous, but because truth removes the hiding places that make people feel safe. When you name what is happening, you interrupt the performance. When you speak cleanly, you collapse the fantasy that everyone can keep pretending. And when you refuse to dilute what you know, you become "too much" only to the ones who built their lives on avoidance.

Here is what no one tells you early enough: "too much" is not a diagnosis. It is a confession. It is the language of people who cannot hold the mirror you bring into the room. It is the vocabulary of those who want the benefits of connection without the responsibilities of intimacy. They want your warmth, but not your standards. They want your loyalty, but not your boundaries. They want your insight, but not your precision. They want your love, as long as your love does not require them to grow up. So, they frame your truth as a problem and your intensity as instability, because if you are "too much," then they do not have to face the fact that they have been offering too little.

Most people do not fear your volume. They fear your accuracy. They fear that you notice patterns they are hoping you will ignore. They fear that you can feel the shift in the air before anyone says a word. They fear that you can hear the subtext under the sweet sentence. They fear that you will ask the question that makes everything honest. And people who have survived by staying vague will always experience precision as aggression. That is why they call you "difficult" when you stop being manageable. That is why they call you "dramatic" when you refuse to normalize what hurts. That is why they call you "intense" when your presence exposes their absence.

But your honesty is not the enemy. Dishonesty is. Dishonesty is what forces you to live in a constant state of translation, turning your intuition into softer language so nobody feels threatened. Dishonesty is what makes you rehearse sentences in your head like a hostage negotiation, trying to say the truth in a way that does not trigger abandonment. Dishonesty is what teaches you to keep your needs minimal, your tone sweet, your standards flexible, because you were trained to believe that being loved requires being digestible. And if you have lived long enough in that training, you start confusing comfort with connection. You start believing that if the room is calm, the relationship must be healthy, even if your soul is quietly suffocating.

Comfort and connection are not the same thing. Comfort is what you get when everyone agrees to keep the surface smooth. Connection is what you get when truth is allowed to exist without punishment. Comfort is a temperature that can be controlled. Connection is a reality that has to be respected. Comfort is often purchased with silence. Connection is built with honesty. And if you are the one who keeps speaking truth, who keeps asking the question nobody wants to answer, who keeps naming the energy that feels off, you are going to be resisted by people who treat emotional avoidance like a lifestyle. Not because you are wrong. Because you are inconvenient to their denial.

This is the part where many people betray themselves. They start asking, "Am I really too much?" They start editing their personality, lowering their temperature, dimming their instincts. They start performing calm as if calm is the same as maturity. They begin apologizing for their own aliveness. They speak less, feel less, ask less, and call it growth, when it is actually survival. They learn how to be agreeable at the expense of being real, and the world rewards them for it. "You are so easy." "You are so understanding." "You are so chill." People praise the version of you that requires the least from them, and you confuse that praise with love.

There is a specific kind of loneliness that comes from being praised for disappearing. You are admired for being "low-maintenance," but what they really mean is you do not disturb their comfort. You are celebrated for being "mature," but what they really mean is you do not demand accountability. You are thanked for being "patient," but what they really mean is you tolerate inconsistency. Over time, the compliments become a cage, because once people get used to your silence, your clarity sounds like a threat. And then you start doing the cruelest thing you can do to yourself: you begin policing your own truth before anyone else has to.

That is why this chapter matters. Not as motivation, but as release. Because if you have been told your whole life to tone it down, dial it back, soften it, let it go, be reasonable, be easier, be smaller, then the problem was never that you were too much. The problem is that you were asked to live in rooms built for people who do not want to feel. And if you keep accepting those rooms as home, you will keep mistaking your honesty for a flaw, when it is actually your compass. You are not too much. You are honest. And honesty, in a world addicted to silence, will always look like disruption.

The Peace You Paid For

I have a friend—let's call him Mark. He is kind, thoughtful, smart, the kind of man people describe as easygoing. He has the type of temperament that makes others feel calm, because he rarely makes a scene and rarely raises his voice. For years, Mark treated that temperament like a virtue and used it as a strategy. In his marriage, he avoided conflict, minimized needs, said yes when he meant no, and swallowed irritation the way people swallow medicine: quickly, with a grimace, convinced it is necessary. He believed being a good partner meant being flexible, and being flexible meant being silent. He thought peace was proof of love.

But time does not reward silence. Time magnifies it. The more Mark avoided small truths, the more his life became built on quiet compromises. At first it was harmless: letting something go, picking his battles, choosing harmony. Then it became a habit: apologizing first to prevent tension, adjusting his preferences to avoid "drama," withholding opinions because it felt safer to be agreeable than to be real. He would say things like, "She has a lot going on," or "It is not worth upsetting her," or "It is not a big deal," and those sentences sounded mature until you listened closely and realized what they were really saying: my truth is not allowed here.

Over time, he began to feel invisible in his own relationship. Not because he was being abused in obvious ways, but because he was no longer fully present as himself. He had trained his own nervous system to stay quiet, to stay easy, to stay acceptable. He had become fluent in disappearing. He did not notice it at first, because the disappearance was gradual, and gradual losses are the most dangerous losses. They do not trigger alarms. They just slowly relocate your identity until you wake up and you cannot recognize your own life.

The scariest part was that no one else noticed. From the outside, things looked stable. Mark was still nice, still agreeable, still helpful, still reliable. He still showed up, still smiled, still handled responsibilities. In other words, he kept performing the role that had been rewarded his whole life: the man who does not make things complicated. But inside, something was rotting. The version of him that used to laugh easily began to feel hollow. His affection started carrying resentment. His patience started turning into quiet contempt. And because he never allowed conflict, he never allowed repair. He did not realize that avoiding conflict does not protect love. It protects dysfunction.

Eventually, Mark did what many people think they want, but few people can actually do. He spoke up. Calmly. Honestly. Without blame. Without a threat. He did not scream. He did not insult. He did not weaponize the past. He simply said the truth about what mattered to him, about what he had been holding, about what he needed to feel like a partner instead of a ghost. It was not dramatic, but it was real, and real is always louder than performance.

His partner did not say thank you. She did not say, "I did not realize." She did not say, "I am sorry, tell me more." She said, "Who do you think you are?" And that sentence revealed everything. Not because she was evil, but because Mark's silence had trained her. When you train people to expect your compliance, your clarity feels like rebellion. When you teach someone that your needs are negotiable, the day you stop negotiating feels like betrayal. When you build a dynamic on one person shrinking, the moment that person expands will be experienced as an attack, even if it is delivered with calm.

That is the cost of shrinking. It does not only harm you. It also trains the people around you into a version of relationship that cannot survive honesty. They get used to the architecture of your self-abandonment. They learn your softness as a guarantee. They begin to rely on you as a stabilizer. And then, when you finally return to yourself, they experience it as instability because the old structure depended on your silence.

Mark's moment was not about dominating or winning. It was about reclaiming his presence. It was about ending the quiet lie that he was fine with a life that did not fit him. It was about choosing something stronger than peace: truth. And it took courage, because truth always risks loss. It risks being misunderstood. It risks being labeled. It risks being punished by people who benefited from your compliance. But it also offers something that performance never will: a life you can actually inhabit.

This is where we need to get something straight. The person who tells the truth is not the one breaking the peace. The person who lies to keep things calm is the one preventing healing. If you have been trained to think honesty is rude, then you have been trained into a life that will punish you for being real. Because real life is not built on calm. It is built on alignment. It is built on agreements that can hold weight. It is built on respect that does not require you to disappear.

Becoming First here means you stop translating your intuition into softer language just to avoid sounding "difficult." It means you stop blaming yourself for other people's avoidance. It means you stop apologizing for the truth of your experience. And no, it does not mean you become a bully or a tyrant. It means you become congruent. You become the same person in private that you pretend to be in public. You stop selling the world a calm version of you while your nervous system pays the price in private.

The moment you stop shrinking, you will learn something sharp and freeing: the people who are capable of love will adjust. They may need time, but they will not punish you for becoming real. And the people who were only capable of comfort will resist. They will label you. They will act confused. They will try to re-negotiate your boundaries back into softness. They will accuse you of changing as if change is a moral failure. But the truth is, you did change. You changed from someone who was recruitable into self-betrayal to someone who is no longer available for it.

The Line

When people tell you that you are "too much," it rarely arrives as cruelty. It arrives as a suggestion. A small social correction wrapped in concern. A tone. A look. A gentle dismissal that carries an unspoken instruction: reduce yourself. Make it easier. Make it smoother. Make it less real. And if you have spent your life being rewarded for being agreeable, you will treat that instruction like wisdom. You will begin translating your clarity into softer language. You will add disclaimers to your needs. You will apologize before you even speak, not because you are wrong, but because you are trying to prevent the discomfort of being seen too clearly. That is how a person becomes "digestible." Not by evolving. By editing themselves down, until they stop triggering anyone's conscience.

This is why "too much" is such an effective weapon: it sounds like feedback about your personality, but it is really a containment strategy. It is how people manage what they cannot meet. It is how they keep depth from entering a room built for performance. It is how they punish the nervous system that refuses to lie. Because honesty does not simply reveal your feelings; it reveals their avoidance. It makes passive aggression visible. It makes inconsistency measurable. It makes excuses sound thin. It makes emotional laziness look like what it is. And people who have built their identity around ambiguity will always experience accuracy as aggression. They will not say, "I am unwilling to match you." They will say, "You are intense." They will not say, "I do not want accountability." They will say, "You overthink." They will not say, "I benefit from your silence." They will say, "You are too emotional." The label is almost never about your volume. It is about your precision.

The tragedy is that you begin cooperating with the label. You start doing their work for them. You soften the truth until it loses its shape. You turn clear boundaries into long explanations, hoping if you sound gentle enough, no one will accuse you of being difficult. You tell yourself you are being mature, diplomatic, emotionally intelligent. But internally it does not feel like maturity; it feels like a small betrayal repeated so often it becomes a lifestyle. You can feel it physically when you do it: that subtle brace in the stomach, that tightening in the chest, that moment your body realizes you are about to abandon it again. The world applauds you for it too. "You are so easygoing." "You are so calm." "You are so understanding." They praise the version of you that exists only when you silence the real one. And that is when the confusion becomes dangerous, because you start believing that peace is the same as connection. It is not. Peace without truth is just a ceasefire you pay for with your identity.

This is also why your honesty can feel lonely. When you are the one who notices patterns, names contradictions, and refuses to pretend, you will often feel like the problem in the room. Not because you are wrong, but because you disrupt the agreement everyone else is maintaining: the agreement to keep things "fine" at the cost of what is real. People will want your insight but not your boundary. They will want your depth but not your standard. They will want you present, but only if you are willing to keep translating your truth into something they can tolerate. That is the subtle bargain: stay close, but stay smaller.

And here is what most people do not understand about that bargain: it does not only shape your relationships. It shapes your self-trust. Every time you swallow what you know, you teach your nervous system that truth is unsafe. You train your body to associate clarity with consequence. You start living as if honesty is an emergency. Not because you are weak, but because you learned—often early—that truth has a price. That is why the label "too much" works so well. It does not only try to control your mouth; it tries to control your courage. It tries to make you question your own perception. It tries to make you treat your clarity as a flaw instead of recognizing it as a form of integrity.

But there comes a point where the cost of shrinking becomes heavier than the cost of being misunderstood. It happens quietly. You do not announce it. You simply stop bargaining. You stop cushioning everything. You stop apologizing for your reality. You stop performing softness as a way to earn safety. And you realize something that changes the entire chapter: you were never "too much." You were simply too honest for rooms built on pretending. Your clarity was not the problem. It was the mirror. And mirrors always offend people who have been relying on shadows.

So, this is the line you learn to draw, not out of arrogance, but out of survival: honesty is not something you practice when it is convenient. It is something you become when you finally decide you are not going to abandon yourself to be easier to hold. Not because you want conflict. Because you want congruence. Because you are tired of relationships that require your self-editing as the entry fee. Because you have learned that the "peace" you were protecting was never peace; it was a performance. And the moment you stop performing, you do not become too much. You become real. And real has a cost, yes—but it also has a gift: it filters your life down to what can actually meet you.

The Body Keeps the Receipt

They never tell you how early it starts, this quiet training to become smaller. You are a child and someone tells you to lower your voice. You are a teenager and someone tells you to stop overreacting. You are an adult and someone tells you to be reasonable, which often means be quiet. You learn, slowly and repeatedly, that your truth is inconvenient, that your feelings are excessive, that your needs are burdensome. And if you grew up in environments where love was conditional on being easy, you learn to treat yourself like a negotiable object. You learn to survive by becoming palatable.

By the time you reach your thirties, your forties, your fifties, you are already fluent. You know how to smile through discomfort. You know how to swallow words that could change the room. You know how to laugh at what hurts. You know how to make your needs small enough to fit inside other people's limitations. You learn the art of disappearing without leaving. You stay physically present while emotionally evacuating, and you call it maturity. The world applauds you for it. "So composed." "So strong." "So calm." They praise the version of you that requires the least from them, and you start believing that being loved means being low-impact.

But your body does not believe that lie. Your body does not congratulate you for being digestible. Your body keeps the receipt. You can feel it physically when you betray yourself. It hits the chest first, then the gut. A tightening, a drop, a subtle nausea, like your system whispering, you just lied. Not to them. To yourself. And the more often you do it, the more your nervous system learns a terrifying lesson: truth is dangerous. Truth costs. Truth risks abandonment. So, your body begins protecting you from truth by numbing you, by making you tired, by making you anxious, by making you overthink, by making you hesitate. Eventually, you are not only silent with others. You become silent with yourself.

This is why the honest ones often look "intense." They are not intense because they want drama. They are intense because they can no longer tolerate the internal fracture of living one life outside and another life inside. They are intense because their system is done paying for performance. They are intense because they have felt what it costs to swallow truth for years, and they are done financing other people's comfort with their own health. Honesty becomes a survival instinct when silence becomes a slow death.

There is also a particular loneliness that comes with being emotionally fluent. You notice what others ignore. You sense shifts in energy like weather changes. You hear what is not said. You catch the pattern, the avoidance, the contradiction. People want the benefit of your perception, but they do not always want the responsibility of meeting it. They want you to see them, but not to name what you see. They want your intuition when it helps them, but they resent it when it exposes them. So, they call you "sensitive" as if sensitivity is weakness, when it is often intelligence. Sensitivity is the ability to detect reality early, before it becomes disaster. But in a world that rewards numbness, sensitivity gets treated like a flaw.

At some point, you start wondering if you should speak softer, feel less, hide more. Self-doubt grows quickly when you are surrounded by people who benefit from your silence. You begin negotiating your own identity to keep a seat at tables that do not even feed you. You become cautious with truth. You start asking permission to exist. You start explaining yourself more than you live. And that is how your honesty becomes a burden instead of a blueprint.

Then comes a moment that shifts everything. It is rarely dramatic to others, but it is irreversible to you. Someone says, "You are too intense," not in anger, but in dismissal, and you laugh it off the way trained people do. But later, alone, it lands differently. It reveals the truth you were avoiding: you have been living in rooms that require you to justify your own temperature. You have been apologizing for your realness. You have been treating your honesty like a social error. And something in you finally refuses.

That refusal is not ego. It is recovery. It is your identity returning. It is the part of you that used to be alive before you learned that love is safer when you are easy. It is the part of you that cannot go back to sleep once it has seen the cost of pretending. Because once you recognize that "too much" is often just "more than they are willing to meet," you stop asking the wrong question. You stop asking, "What is wrong with me?" and you start asking, "Why am I trying to be loved by people who require me to disappear?"

When you stop shrinking, dynamics reveal themselves. You begin noticing who was benefiting from your silence. You see who only loved you when you were agreeable. You recognize who depended on your self-abandonment to feel comfortable, superior, stable. And without bitterness, you outgrow them. Not through a speech, but through a shift. You stop entering conversations where authenticity is punished. You stop staying in rooms where truth feels like a threat. You stop accepting emotional crumbs from people who consume your generosity. You start choosing what your nervous system can actually live with.

The first phase can feel lonely. Of course it can. You are shedding identities. You are breaking contracts you never agreed to sign. You are withdrawing from the addiction of being liked at the expense of being aligned. But that loneliness is not a void. It is a clearing. It is space being created for relationships that do not require translation, for people who do not call your honesty an attack, for connections where your truth is not an inconvenience but a foundation.

The Polite Cage

They did not silence you by screaming. They silenced you with manners. With smiles. With that civilized tone that pretends to be wisdom while it drains your spine. They did not say, "Do not tell the truth." They said, "Say it nicer." They said, "Not like that." They said, "Do not make it a thing." They said, "Be mature." They said, "Be reasonable." And you heard what they meant, because your nervous system is not stupid. You heard the translation under the sentence: be smaller so I do not have to feel anything.

This is how people learn to disappear without leaving. This is how an honest person becomes a polite ghost. Not because they lack courage, but because they have paid the price of truth before, and their body remembers. They remember the look that hardens the moment they speak plainly. They remember the way people suddenly become "confused" when clarity removes their exits. They remember how quickly truth gets reframed as attitude. Not because the truth is wrong, but because the truth is inconvenient to the fantasy everyone is maintaining.

A lot of people do not fear your emotion. They fear your accuracy. They fear that you see what they are doing without them having to confess it. They fear that you can hear the subtext under the sweet words. They fear that you notice the pattern, not the excuse. They fear that you will make the room honest. And when a room is built on social performance, the person who brings reality feels like a threat. So they label you. They call you intense. They call you dramatic. They call you too sensitive. They call you too direct. It is not feedback. It is a containment strategy. It is how emotionally lazy people keep the intelligent ones quiet.

"Be reasonable" is the cleanest weapon in modern relationships because it sounds fair. It sounds adult. It sounds like peace. But most of the time it is not a request for calm. It is a demand for compliance. It is a way to move the conversation away from what happened and into how you reacted, because reactions are easier to criticize than behavior. If they can put your tone on trial, they can avoid their impact. If they can make you defend your feelings, they can escape accountability. If they can make you look "too much," they can keep being too little.

And if you are someone who cares, you will cooperate at first. You will try harder. You will soften. You will add disclaimers. You will give context. You will perform emotional diplomacy, as if love requires you to translate your pain into a language that does not disturb anyone. You will start speaking as if you are asking permission to exist. You will start apologizing before you even say what is true, not because you are wrong, but because you are trained. Trained to believe that truth is only acceptable if it is served with a smile and no consequences.

That is the polite cage. It is not made of cruelty. It is made of social approval. It is reinforced every time someone praises you for being easy when what they really mean is that you do not ask them to grow. "You are so calm," they say, while you are choking. "You are so understanding," they say, while you are erasing yourself. "You are so mature," they say, while you are swallowing disrespect to keep the vibe smooth. And the worst part is that the cage feels like love at first, because it comes with compliments. It comes with belonging.

It comes with access. Until you realize the access is conditional: you can stay close as long as you stay quiet.

This is why so many people confuse comfort with connection. They think if the relationship is smooth, it must be healthy. They think if nobody is upset, it must be love. But comfort and connection are not the same thing. Comfort is what you get when everyone agrees to keep the surface clean. Connection is what you get when truth is allowed to exist without punishment. Comfort is often bought with silence. Connection is built with honesty. Comfort keeps the story intact. Connection forces the story to match reality.

And here is the ugly truth that no one wants to admit: some people prefer your politeness over your peace. They want you regulated, not respected. They want you quiet, not whole. They want you calm, because calm makes you manageable. Calm makes you predictable. Calm makes you easy to keep around without having to change. So, when you start telling the truth, they do not respond to the content. They respond to the threat. They say you changed. They say you are harsh. They say you are cold. They say you are making it bigger than it is, because if they can shrink the event, they can shrink your right to react to it.

The reason this hurts is because you start doubting yourself. You start wondering if your honesty is the problem. You start thinking maybe you are too sharp. Too emotional. Too intense. And that is how the cage becomes internal. At first they police you. Then you start policing yourself. You begin editing your own instincts before anyone else has to. You begin softening your truth until it loses its shape. You begin turning boundaries into essays, hoping if you explain enough, they will finally understand, when the problem was never understanding. The problem was willingness.

This is the moment you need a brutal, freeing sentence: people who are committed to avoiding reality will always experience truth as aggression. You cannot convince them otherwise by being nicer. Nicer does not make them accountable. Nicer just makes you smaller.

So here is where you choose. Not the dramatic kind of choice. The quiet kind that changes your entire life. You stop worshipping politeness. You stop treating "nice" as the highest moral achievement. You stop making your truth optional just to keep a seat at a table that never feeds you. You stop confusing your ability to tolerate with your obligation to tolerate. You stop paying for access with self-erasure.

Because you are not here to be easy. You are here to be real. And real does not fit inside cages built by other people's comfort.

Clean Truth

There is a version of honesty that is just pain throwing furniture. It feels powerful for five minutes and then it costs you everything. People confuse that with truth because it is loud, but loud is not the same as clean. Clean truth is different. Clean truth does not beg. It does not chase. It does not punish. It does not perform. It lands like a fact, and then it stands there, unshaking, because it is not trying to win. It is trying to stop the self-betrayal.

This is where most honest people get trapped: they think the goal is to be understood. So they over-explain. They add context. They pre-apologize. They soften. They rehearse sentences in their head like they are negotiating with a hostage-taker, hoping they can say the truth in a way that does not trigger abandonment. They work so hard to sound gentle that their message becomes fog. And then, when nothing changes, they blame themselves for "not communicating well enough," when the real issue is that the other person has no interest in honoring what is true.

Over-explaining is rarely communication. It is bargaining. It is you trying to buy safety with words. It is you trying to manage the other person's reaction, so you do not have to feel the terror of being seen clearly. But every time you do it, you teach a dangerous lesson: your truth is negotiable. Your boundaries are open for debate. Your standards are flexible if someone applies enough pressure. And pressure is exactly what you will keep receiving, because the system learns what works.

Clean truth is not a speech. It is a line. A line you can live with. A line your body can trust. Because here is what your nervous system wants more than sweet words: congruence. It wants to know that you will not abandon yourself again the moment the room gets uncomfortable. It wants to know that your "I cannot do this anymore" is not a mood. It is a decision. It wants to know that you are safe with you.

That is what Becoming First looks like here. Not the performance of strength. The practice of consistency. You say what is true, and then you stop negotiating with reality. You stop trying to make the truth pleasant enough to be accepted. You let it be what it is. You let the discomfort exist without treating it as an emergency. That is the part most people cannot do. They can speak a boundary. They cannot hold it through the backlash.

Because the backlash is the test. Not whether you can name the truth, but whether you can stay loyal to it when someone does not like it. This is where the old identity tries to come back. The fixer. The peacekeeper. The one who repairs first. The one who apologizes for having needs. The one who rescues people from the mirror. You will feel the impulse to soften. To clarify. To send one more message. To explain your intention. To prove you are still good. To show you are not "too much." That impulse is not love. It is the cage calling you back.

Clean truth does not prove itself. It lives. It does not recruit. It reveals. It does not threaten. It simply removes access. That is why consequences matter. Not as punishment, but as integrity. A boundary without consequence is not a boundary. It is an invitation for the same behavior to return with better timing.

And this is the part that will feel brutal to the version of you that was trained to be liked: some people will not rise to meet you. They will try to lower you. They will call you selfish because they benefited from your selflessness. They will call you cold because they were used to your warmth being free. They will call you dramatic because drama is a convenient label for anything that forces accountability. They will accuse you of changing as if change is betrayal, because your growth exposes how comfortable they were with your silence.

Do not let that confuse you. The people who are capable of love will adjust. They may struggle, but they will not punish you for being real. The people who were only capable of comfort will resist. They will want the old deal back. The deal where you kept things smooth while your insides paid the bill. Your job is not to convince them. Your job is to stop signing that deal.

Clean truth does something sacred when you commit to it. It gives your body relief. Not the relief of everything being easy, but the relief of not living divided. You stop splitting yourself into two people, the public version who looks calm and the private version who is bleeding. You stop living as an employee in your own life, constantly managing other people's emotions. You become the owner again. And ownership is quiet. Ownership is steady. Ownership does not argue for its right to exist.

Then, and only then, the last part of your chapter becomes redemption instead of motivational language. Because "The Return to Your Real Size" is not a nice idea after these two sections. It is the only possible outcome. Once you break the polite cage and you learn clean truth, you cannot go back to performing smaller without feeling obvious self-betrayal. That is the point. That is the evolution. That is the line you will not cross again.

Access Is Not a Human Right

There is a moment in every honest person's life when truth stops being language and becomes law. Not a law you impose on others. A law you finally agree to live under yourself. And once that shift happens, the world gets strangely loud. Not because you are making noise—because you are removing the discount people have been getting on you for years.

Most of your life, access to you was treated like a human right. People spoke to you however they wanted, disappeared whenever they felt like it, returned with casual excuses, and expected your warmth to be waiting like a well-lit porch. Your presence became the place they came to recover from their own choices. Your patience became the loophole. Your understanding became the escape hatch. You did not mean to teach that. But when you keep giving the same response to the same disrespect, the system learns you are not a person—you are a resource.

This is the part nobody prepares you for: the first time you make access expensive, people will call you "different." They will say you are "cold." They will accuse you of "holding grudges," as if your boundaries are emotional immaturity instead of evidence that you finally woke up. They will try to turn your self-respect into a personality flaw because it is easier to criticize you than to confront the fact that they have been enjoying you without earning you.

And it happens in small moments. A message that arrives with fake sweetness after months of silence. A sudden invitation that has nothing to do with repair and everything to do with convenience. A familiar name reappearing the moment you look stable again, as if your stability exists for their comfort. They do not return because they have changed. They return because they assume you have not.

The old version of you would have answered quickly, gently, with a bridge in your hands. You would have translated their absence into a story that made them look human and made you look noble. You would have offered grace as if grace means unlimited access. You would have pretended you were fine, because being fine kept you chosen. But the new version of you hears the subtext. The new version of you can feel the entitlement behind the sentence. The new version of you is no longer interested in emotional recycling.

So you do something that feels almost unnatural at first: you respond in a way that matches reality. Not with cruelty. Not with a lecture. With consequence. You let the gap remain. You do not rush to smooth the tension. You do not rescue them from discomfort. You do not rescue yourself either. You say one clean sentence and you stop. You leave space for their character to show itself.

And this is where the truth reveals people. Some will step up. They will ask real questions. They will own the impact. They will adjust without you begging for it. They will treat your boundary like a doorway, not a wall— because they respect you enough to knock. But others will do what they always do when access is no longer free: they will try to renegotiate the price.

They will bargain with nostalgia. They will bring up history as if time equals intimacy. They will remind you of old versions of you, hoping you feel obligated to perform them. They will act offended that you are no longer available on demand. They will call you "changed" with a tone that really means, "Come back to the version of you that made my life easier." And if you have been trained to be liked, that accusation will hurt. It will activate the old reflex: explain, soften, prove you are good, prove you are not too much. That is how people get you back into the cage—by making you defend your humanity.

But there is a deeper truth underneath all of this: access is not something people deserve because they feel familiar. Access is something people earn because they are safe. And safe does not mean perfect. Safe means accountable. Safe means consistent. Safe means they do not make you pay for being real. Safe means they do not punish your clarity. Safe means your nervous system can stand down when they are in the room.

That is why consequence is not revenge. It is hygiene. It is how you protect the part of you that used to bleed in silence. It is how you stop teaching people that love means endurance. It is how you stop confusing loyalty with self-abandonment. Your boundaries are not there to control them. They are there to keep you from disappearing.

This is where grief enters. Because when you make access expensive, you lose the people who were only present for the discount. And that loss can feel like failure if you still believe connection is measured by how many people stay. But losing what could not honor you is not failure. It is clarification. It is the moment your life stops being a charity for emotionally careless people and becomes a home you protect.

You will also notice something else: the calmer you become, the more certain people panic. Because your calm is no longer compliance. Your calm is final. Your calm is not the calm of someone trying to be good. It is the calm of someone who finally believes themselves. And there is nothing more threatening to a manipulative dynamic than a person who can say no without anger and then actually live as if no means no.

This is the quiet power most people never reach. Not the power to make others behave. The power to stop making your life available to those who keep proving they cannot hold it. The power to remove access without a speech. The power to leave the door locked without standing guard over it every day. The power to be consistent enough that your boundaries become reality, not conversation.

And once you do that, something shifts in you that is almost spiritual in its simplicity: your nervous system stops bracing. You stop anticipating disappointment as a normal part of love. You stop rehearsing explanations.

You stop editing yourself to avoid conflict. You stop being the translator between truth and comfort. You become loyal to your own experience. Not as ideology. As practice.

That is what Becoming First looks like in real life. Not slogans. Not bold statements. Not dramatic exits. Just a quiet refusal to keep offering full access to people who only show up for the parts of you that cost them nothing.

Because when access has a price, the wrong people call it cruelty. The right people call it clarity. And clarity is what brings you back to your real size.

The Return to Your Real Size

There comes a point where honesty stops being something you occasionally practice and becomes the only way you know how to breathe. Not because you want to be bold, not because you want to provoke, but because anything less than truth feels like suffocation. The cost of silence becomes heavier than the fear of speaking. You hear yourself say "It is fine" when it is not fine, and you can no longer tolerate the hollowness behind your own voice. You feel the split between your inner world and your outer performance, and your system refuses to keep paying.

This is the moment you stop explaining yourself. Not because you are cold. Not because you are tired. Because you finally understand that explaining is what people do when they believe they need permission to exist. Honesty does not ask for permission. Honesty is permission. It is you granting yourself the right to be real without negotiating with other people's comfort. It is you choosing clarity over approval, alignment over access, truth over performance.

When you anchor into that, you see everything differently. You see that the people who called you "dramatic" were often terrified of accountability. You see that the ones who said you "overreacted" were hoping your silence would protect their convenience. You see that the ones who told you to "be reasonable" were often asking you to be smaller than your own reality. And you stop hating them for it. You just stop arranging your life around their limitations. You stop trying to be understood by people who do not want to understand. You stop auditioning for acceptance you no longer want.

Honesty does something remarkable when you let it become your baseline. It does not just change what you say. It changes who you are available to be. Your presence becomes steadier. Your boundaries become quieter and stronger. Your standards become natural instead of performative. You stop rushing to rescue other people from the discomfort of your truth. You stop cushioning reality to keep the room calm. You allow tension to exist without treating it as an emergency. And in that restraint, something heals. You begin trusting yourself again.

You also begin attracting differently. You stop being surrounded by people who love the version of you that is convenient for them. You begin attracting people who feel safe enough to tell the truth themselves, because truth recognizes truth. You start meeting humans who do not require you to dilute your feelings, who do not treat your standards like a threat, who do not call your depth "too much," because they are living at a depth where they can breathe. And you realize that what you used to call intensity was simply the normal temperature of a real life.

This is not about becoming harsh. It is about becoming clean. Clean honesty does not insult. It does not escalate. It does not need theatrics. It is direct, precise, and calm, because it is not trying to win. It is trying to be true. It does not beg. It does not chase. It does not bargain with reality. Clean honesty says, this is what is true for me, and then it lives accordingly. And when you do that, you stop being trapped in other people's opinions. You stop living as a tenant in a life built on external approval. You become the owner again.

You may still feel deeply. You may still sense everything. You may still be moved by life in ways others are not. That does not make you fragile. That makes you alive. Emotional depth is not a liability when it is paired with boundaries. Sensitivity is not a weakness when it is paired with self-trust. Honesty is not "too much" when it is paired with self-respect. The combination is power, not because it dominates others, but because it returns you to yourself.

So here is what I want you to understand, in a way that lands not as a slogan but as relief. You were never too much. You were simply in rooms that could not hold you. You were speaking a language of truth in environments that survived on performance. You were asking for intimacy among people who confuse comfort with love. And yes, that made you feel like the problem, because the honest one always looks disruptive in a room full of pretending. But the disruption was not your character. It was your clarity.

When you stop shrinking, life does not become perfect. It becomes real. And real is lighter than performance, even when it is hard. Real is cleaner than negotiation, even when it costs. Real is calmer than numbness, because numbness is not calm. Numbness is pressure locked inside the body. Real may create moments of discomfort, but it also creates a steadiness that no amount of people-pleasing ever will. Because steadiness comes from living in alignment, not from being liked.

This is the redemptive truth at the center of this chapter. Your honesty is not your burden. It is your blueprint. It is the way your life tries to bring you back to your own standards, your own instincts, your own dignity. The people who can meet you will meet you. The ones who cannot will label you. Let them. Labels are what people use when they do not want to do the work of seeing you clearly. You do not owe anyone a smaller version of yourself so they can remain comfortable.

And if you have spent years believing you were too much, I want you to consider the simplest possibility. Maybe you were not too much at all. Maybe you were just done lying. Maybe your nervous system refused to keep pretending. Maybe your depth was the evidence of how seriously you take love. Maybe your intensity was the sign that you are no longer willing to live half-alive. Maybe the discomfort you create in others is not proof you are wrong. Maybe it is proof you are awake.

That is not a curse. That is a gift.

Because once you stop apologizing for your honesty, your life starts opening in quieter ways. You begin sleeping better. You begin breathing deeper. You begin feeling less fractured. You begin trusting your intuition without putting it on trial. You begin choosing relationships that do not require you to perform. You begin building a world that can hold you. You begin experiencing a new kind of peace, not the peace of silence, but the peace of integrity.

And that is what Becoming First looks like here. Not louder. Not harsher. Not more dramatic. Just more true.

You are not too much. You are honest. And the moment you stop treating honesty like a flaw, you stop living like you owe the world a smaller version of your soul. You return to your real size. You stop negotiating your identity. You stop translating your truth into comfort. You stop asking permission to exist. You simply live in a way that is congruent, and congruence is what finally feels like freedom.

That is the relief. That is the redemption. That is the point. And you do not negotiate your size ever again.

CHAPTER 6

WANT RESPECT? EARN IT INTERNALLY

The Standard Before the World

Everyone wants respect. We post about it. We demand it in relationships. We complain about it at work. We keep private lists of moments we were dismissed, spoken over, minimized, taken for granted. We treat respect like a resource other people are supposed to provide, and when they do not, we call it injustice, bad luck, bad people, bad timing. But the truth is cleaner than all of that: you do not get the respect you ask for. You get the respect you reflect. And what you reflect is not your résumé, your followers, your charm, your ability to be "strong," or your talent at surviving. What you reflect is your internal standard—the rule you live by when no one is watching.

Most people confuse respect with recognition. Recognition is applause. Recognition is being acknowledged, praised, noticed, invited, validated. Recognition is social, visible, and fragile. Respect is structural. Respect is the invisible architecture that forms around a person who has decided what is acceptable and what is not, and who lives as if that decision is real. That is why you can have recognition and still be treated casually. That is why you can be admired and still be dismissed. Because people can applaud you and still not take you seriously. People can "like" you and still not adjust their behavior around you. Respect is what makes behavior adjust.

A standard is not what you say in a speech when you are fed up. It is what you enforce in silence when you are afraid. It is not the boundary you announce once. It is the boundary you hold the third time someone tests it with a smile. It is not the confident sentence you practice in your head. It is the decision you keep when you feel lonely, when you feel guilty, when you feel tempted to go back to what is familiar, just because familiar feels safer than change. Your standard is your private constitution. It is the law your nervous system learns to trust.

This is why internal respect matters more than external respect. External respect is a reflection. Internal respect is the source. If the source is weak, your reflection will always flicker. If the source is unstable, your world will treat you as negotiable. And negotiable is exactly how most people end up living— negotiating their dignity for belonging, negotiating their boundaries for connection, negotiating their needs for approval, negotiating their truth for peace. They call it maturity. They call it love. They call it being a good person. But it is not maturity when it requires self-betrayal. It is not love when it demands your disappearance. It is not kindness when it turns you into an employee in your own life.

Internal respect begins with a brutal, but freeing, question: "where am I asking the world to treat me well while I keep treating myself as optional?" "Where am I demanding that others take me seriously while I keep taking my own needs lightly?" "Where am I begging for a different experience while I keep repeating the same compromise?"

Because your self-talk is a blueprint. The way you speak to yourself in private becomes the posture you bring into public. If you talk to yourself like you are a burden, you will tolerate people who treat you like one. If you treat your time like it is disposable, you will attract people who fill it with their urgency. If you treat your boundaries like they are negotiable, you will attract people who negotiate them. If you treat your exhaustion like it is normal, you will attract relationships that feed on your stamina. The world does not disrespect you randomly. It responds to the negotiations you keep making with your own value. This is not a punishment. It is a mirror.

That mirror can feel offensive because it removes excuses. It forces you to look at patterns instead of personalities. It forces you to admit what you already sense but keep avoiding: a lot of what you call "being disrespected" is the consequence of you not defending your own dignity early enough. Not because you are weak. Not because you are stupid. Because you were trained.

Most of us were trained to be liked before we were trained to be respected. We were trained to be agreeable. We were trained to keep things smooth. We were trained to lower our tone, soften our needs, "be reasonable," which often means be quiet. We learned, early, that truth has a price. That needs create tension. That boundaries risk abandonment. So we became smart. We became socially fluent. We learned how to read rooms. We learned how to anticipate moods. We learned how to deliver truth in a way that does not trigger anyone's defensiveness. We learned how to become digestible.

And the world rewards digestible people. It praises them for being "easy." It calls them "mature." It calls them "understanding." It calls them "calm." But calm is not always healthy. Sometimes calm is compliance. Sometimes calm is a freeze response dressed up as wisdom. Sometimes calm is just the absence of your truth. And when your truth is absent, your respect cannot be present. You cannot earn respect while you keep editing yourself into silence.

The most dangerous thing about this training is that it feels moral. You feel proud of your patience. You feel proud of your flexibility. You feel proud that you can "handle it." You feel proud that you do not "make things complicated." But there is a difference between strength and self-erasure. There is a difference between humility and self-minimization. There is a difference between kindness and fear. And internal respect is the moment you stop confusing fear for virtue.

Here is the cleanest line in this entire chapter: you do not rise into respect by performing goodness. You rise into respect by enforcing reality. Reality is what you can live with. Reality is what you will tolerate. Reality is what you will no longer negotiate. That is why respect does not live in your words. Respect lives in your patterns.

People are always watching patterns. They watch what you forgive without repair. They watch how quickly you answer after they disappear. They watch whether your boundaries have consequences or whether your boundaries are just speeches. They watch whether you keep showing up the same way regardless of how they treat you. And if you keep showing up with the same access, the same availability, the same warmth, even when they disrespect you, your nervous system is sending a message louder than your mouth ever will: I will stay. You can treat me casually and I will remain.

So let us make this precise. The reason people can keep disrespecting you is not because you are "too nice." It is because your standard is unclear. Or worse, it is clear in your mind but not enforced in your life. You can feel disrespected and still keep giving access. You can feel used and still keep answering. You can feel minimized and still keep auditioning. That is not because you like pain. It is because you are afraid of what happens when you stop. You are afraid that boundaries will cost you love. And sometimes they will. But what you call love that disappears the moment you respect yourself was never love. It was permission disguised as intimacy.

Internal respect is not a threat. It is not a weapon. It is not you becoming harsh. It is you becoming congruent. Congruence is the end of begging. It is the end of negotiating your identity. It is you becoming the same person in private that you pretend to be in public. The same person with yourself that you are with others. The same standard in the dark that you claim in the light.

This is why the chapter title is not a cute phrase. Want respect? Earn it internally. Earn it with the way you keep promises to yourself. Earn it with the way you stop abandoning your needs because someone else is uncomfortable. Earn it with the way you stop treating your body like a machine that exists to serve your schedule. Earn it with the way you stop making your truth optional so you can stay close to people who only tolerate you when you are small.

Internal respect begins where nobody applauds. It begins in the tiny decisions that look boring from the outside but change your entire life. The decision to rest when your body asks instead of proving you can keep pushing. The decision to say no without adding a paragraph to justify your existence. The decision to delay your response not as punishment, but as a signal to your nervous system that urgency does not own you. The decision to stop laughing at jokes that cut you. The decision to stop explaining what should be obvious to an adult. The decision to stop offering the same access to people who keep proving they cannot hold it.

And yes, this will create friction. Your life has been built around certain contracts, and contracts do not dissolve politely. When you raise your standard, people will notice. Not because you announced anything, but because the discount is gone. The speed you used to answer is gone. The forgiveness you used to offer without accountability is gone. The emotional labor you used to provide automatically is gone. The version of you who could be used as a cushion is gone. And some people will react like you betrayed them, when all you did was stop betraying yourself.

Expect it. It is not proof you are wrong. It is proof you changed the terms.

This is where the fear shows up: "If I respect myself, I will end up alone." That fear is loud because it has history. It brings up every time you lost someone after you spoke the truth. It brings up every silence, every withdrawal, every abandonment, every punishment disguised as distance. But listen carefully: you are already alone when you are surrounded by people who only recognize you when you are convenient. The loneliness of self-betrayal is heavier than the loneliness of self-respect. One empties you. The other rebuilds you.

Internal respect is not a destination. It is a discipline. And like any discipline, it does not feel natural at first. At first it feels like you are being "mean." At first it feels like you are being selfish. At first it feels like you are withholding. That is the old conditioning fighting back. You were trained to earn your place by being useful, by being available, by being agreeable. So, the first time you treat yourself like you matter, it feels wrong. It is not wrong. It is unfamiliar. And unfamiliar is not danger. It is growth.

When you internalize this, your entire approach to respect changes. You stop chasing it like a prize. You stop arguing for it like a lawyer. You stop demanding it from people who have no interest in giving it. You become the kind of person whose energy does not negotiate. Not because you are superior, but because you are finally clear. Clear about what you will live with. Clear about what you will no longer tolerate. Clear about who has access to your time, your body, your attention, your emotional world.

This is the only way respect becomes real. Not by asking the world to treat you better, but by treating yourself well enough that the world has to adjust—or lose access. That is the standard before the world. The standard before the relationship. The standard before the conversation. The standard before the apology that may never come.

And once that standard exists, everything else in this chapter becomes inevitable. Because once you stop living like your dignity is optional, you start seeing where you have been leaking it. You start noticing the habits you called "being nice" that were actually self-erasure. You start noticing the ways you try to buy belonging by shrinking. You start realizing that respect is not something you demand when you are finally angry enough. Respect is something you practice until it becomes impossible to ignore.

That is what we are building here. Not a louder voice. A stronger spine. Not a harder heart. A cleaner standard. Not a dramatic exit. A quiet refusal to keep living at a discount.

The Respect Leaks You Call "Being Nice"

Most people imagine respect as something you either have or you do not, as if it arrives fully formed the moment someone "recognizes your value." That is not how it works. Respect is built—quietly, relentlessly—through what you permit, what you reinforce, and what you refuse to normalize. It does not collapse because of one catastrophic moment; it erodes through a hundred small concessions that feel reasonable at the time. You do not feel it as disrespect in the beginning. You feel it as social pressure. A tone you ignore. A comment you swallow. A last-minute request you accept because you do not want to be "difficult." And then you look up and realize people speak to you with a casualness that would have been impossible if your standard had been visible from the start.

Here is what makes it tricky: the tests rarely look like tests. They come disguised as familiarity. They come wrapped in humor, urgency, stress, "I'm going through a lot," "you know I didn't mean it like that," "be reasonable," "do not make it a thing." They come in the form of someone changing the plan and expecting you to rearrange your life as if your life is flexible by default. They come as small digs masked as jokes that leave you tight in the chest, then make you feel guilty for being affected. They come as people disappearing and returning with warmth but no repair, expecting your emotional availability to be a permanent subscription they can activate whenever they feel lonely. And if you have been trained to be good, you will respond with what you think is maturity: you will smooth it over, minimize it, explain yourself, and keep the vibe stable. You will call it kindness. You will call it being the bigger person. You will call it love. But often, what you are really doing is teaching people that your boundary is a suggestion and your dignity is negotiable.

This is why "nice" becomes dangerous when it is not anchored in self-respect. Because nice is easy to exploit. Nice is predictable. Nice will tolerate ambiguity. Nice will accept partial effort and translate it into intention. Nice will keep the peace while the soul pays the bill. And the world loves a person who keeps the peace—until that person finally asks for something real. Then the same people who benefited from your softness suddenly call you "changed," "cold," "dramatic," "too much." Not because you became wrong. Because you became expensive. Because you stopped offering a discount on your time, your attention, your emotional labor, your availability. That is the moment you learn a hard truth: the more you protect your dignity, the more clearly you see who was only present for the access.

Respect does not live in your words. It lives in your patterns. People do not memorize what you say you deserve; they adapt to what you repeatedly accept. They learn from the way you respond when something feels off. They learn from whether you hesitate before speaking, whether you smile to soften your truth, whether you laugh when you are hurt, whether you rush to reassure when someone disappoints you. They learn what they can get away with, not because they are always malicious, but because human beings follow the path of least resistance. If your boundary is always a long conversation, they will keep turning it into a conversation. If your "no" comes with guilt and an apology, they will keep expecting you to be bendable. If your discomfort is always managed quietly by you, they will keep living as if your discomfort is irrelevant. That is how the standard drops—not with a declaration, but with your silence becoming their permission.

Leak #1: Over-explaining your boundaries

Over-explaining is one of the most common ways people leak respect while believing they are being emotionally intelligent. It looks polite. It looks considerate. It sounds mature. But when you are honest with yourself, most over-explaining is not communication—it is fear management. It is you trying to control the other person's reaction so you do not have to face the possibility that your boundary might cost you approval, access, or attachment. You write the paragraph. You add context. You justify. You soften. You make sure you do not sound harsh. You try to be "fair." And what you are really doing is treating your own boundary like it needs a defense attorney in order to be valid.

A clean boundary is simple: it is a decision stated without begging for permission. The more you explain, the more you quietly suggest that your boundary is negotiable if they can find the right argument, the right guilt, the right "but." People who respect you do not need your essay. They need your clarity. People who do not respect you will use your essay as an opening—something to debate, reinterpret, exhaust, or manipulate. They will ask more questions than necessary. They will act confused. They will frame your boundary as "hurtful," "dramatic," "unfair." And if you are used to being liked, you will go right back into explaining, because explaining feels like you are being good. But a boundary that requires you to be good is not a boundary. It is a request.

The standard is this: your "no" is not rude. Your "no" is information. Your "no" is self-respect in action. If someone needs you to suffer in order to feel comfortable, that is not a relationship problem—that is a character problem. You cannot explain your way out of someone else's entitlement. You can only remove its access to you. And when you stop over-explaining, something powerful happens: you stop auditioning for your own dignity. You stop speaking as if your needs are a burden. You stop treating your time like it is less valuable than other people's emotions. Your voice becomes calmer because it is no longer trying to convince. It is simply stating reality. That is where respect begins—when your boundaries are not a performance, but a posture.

Leak #2: Saying "yes" when you mean "no," then calling it loyalty

There is a specific kind of "yes" that is not generosity. It is fear. It is the yes that comes out of your mouth while your body tightens. It is the yes you say because you do not want someone to be disappointed in you, to leave you, to label you, to withdraw affection. It is the yes you offer because you would rather exhaust yourself than risk conflict. And it is one of the fastest ways to train people to disrespect you, because it teaches them that your limits are not real. They are theatrical. They exist only until pressure arrives.

When you agree to things you do not want, you do not only betray your time; you betray your self-trust. Your nervous system keeps score. It learns that your own needs are not protected by you. And once you teach yourself that, you become easier to push. Not because you are weak, but because you are divided. Part of you wants to be real, part of you wants to be safe, and safety has been defined as being liked. So you keep choosing comfort over alignment. You keep choosing approval over truth. And then you wonder why people treat you casually. They treat you casually because you keep showing them that you will rearrange yourself to keep them close.

True loyalty does not require self-abandonment. Real devotion is clean; it does not leave resentment behind. If your "yes" is creating a debt inside you, it is not love—it is a loan you expect to be repaid, and it rarely is. That is why so many people feel disrespected: they keep giving what was never requested, then feel furious that it is not honored. They keep being "understanding" in situations that require boundaries, then feel shocked that the other person took advantage of that flexibility. But people do not respect what you give away under pressure. They respect what you protect on principle. And the day you stop saying yes out of fear is the day your life stops being organized around other people's convenience.

Leak #3: Laughing off disrespect to keep the atmosphere comfortable

Many people do not lose respect because they are too intense. They lose respect because they are too accommodating. They make jokes about themselves first. They laugh when something stings. They swallow the comment, smile, change the subject, and tell themselves it is not worth it. They do it because they want to be easy to be around. They do it because they have learned that tension is dangerous. But the problem is this: when you laugh off disrespect, you are not neutral. You are consenting. You are telling the room, "This is acceptable." And once you set that rule, it becomes very hard to change it later without backlash.

Disrespect does not need to be loud to be real. It can be subtle. A dismissive tone. A sarcastic remark. A "joke" that repeatedly targets your sensitivity, your appearance, your intelligence, your ambition. And if you keep absorbing it, you train people into comfort at your expense. You also train yourself to confuse humiliation with belonging. You learn to tolerate being minimized as the entry fee for connection. That is not connection. That is a social contract where you pay for access with your dignity.

The correction is not drama. It is clarity. Sometimes it is as simple as not laughing. Sometimes it is a pause and a calm sentence: "Do not speak to me like that." Sometimes it is removing yourself. The point is not to punish. The point is to stop normalizing what your body registers as disrespect. Because every time you override that signal, you weaken your internal authority. Every time you honor it, you strengthen it. And internal authority is what people respond to before they ever respond to your words.

Leak #4: Allowing inconsistency, then calling it "understanding"

A lot of people pride themselves on being understanding. They call it compassion. They call it maturity. They call it having a big heart. But what they are actually practicing is tolerance of inconsistency, and inconsistency is where respect dies quietly. The person shows up when they feel like it. They communicate when they want something. They disappear when accountability is required. They offer sweetness when they return, not responsibility. And because you want to believe the best, you translate their pattern into a temporary phase. You tell yourself they are busy, stressed, healing, complicated, misunderstood. You keep rewriting their behavior into a story that protects your hope. Meanwhile, your nervous system is learning the truth: you are not safe in a dynamic that changes based on someone else's mood.

Respect requires consistency because respect is a form of reliability. If someone cannot be consistent with effort, presence, and accountability, then they are not offering you respect. They are offering you convenience. And convenience always comes with a hidden message: "I will engage when it benefits me." If you accept that message repeatedly, you will eventually feel disrespected, because you are being used as an emotional resource rather than met as a person.

This is where internal respect becomes visible. You stop rewarding inconsistency with access. You stop responding to minimal effort as if it is extraordinary. You stop confusing words with character. You begin measuring people by pattern. You begin respecting yourself enough to require basic adult behavior: follow-through, clarity, responsibility, repair. Not perfection. Repair. Because respect is not the absence of mistakes. Respect is the presence of ownership.

Leak #5: Treating your time like it is flexible by default

Time is one of the clearest signals of self-respect because time is the only resource you cannot earn back. Yet many people treat their time as if it is communal property. They say yes to things they do not want. They answer messages immediately out of anxiety. They keep their schedule open "just in case." They allow other people's urgency to become their priority. And then they wonder why nobody takes them seriously. It is difficult for the world to treat your time as sacred when you treat it as available.

Respect begins to shift when your time gets protected before anyone asks for it. When your default is not access, but intention. When your calendar reflects your values, not other people's moods. When you respond on your timeline, not out of panic. When you stop making yourself constantly reachable in order to feel chosen. The irony is that constant availability rarely creates love. It creates consumption. People take what you keep giving. They assume it will remain unlimited. And when you finally need space, they act shocked—as if your humanity is a surprise.

You do not need to become cold to protect your time. You need to become accurate. Accurate about what you have. Accurate about what costs you. Accurate about what you are no longer willing to pay for with your peace. That accuracy is not harshness. It is maturity. And mature people are respected because they are clear.

The Turning Point: From "Good" to "True"

The most dangerous part of these respect leaks is that they feel normal. They feel like being a good partner, a good friend, a good son, a good leader, a good person. But goodness is not measured by how much you can endure. It is measured by how congruent you can stay. If your goodness requires you to betray yourself, it is not goodness. It is conditioning.

Internal respect is the moment you stop asking, "How do I get them to treat me better?" and start asking, "Why have I been available for less?" That question is not self-blame. It is self-ownership. It returns your power to the only place it can actually live: your choices. Because you cannot control whether people behave with respect. You can control whether disrespect has access to your life. You can control whether your boundaries are spoken as a suggestion or held as a reality. You can control whether your kindness has a spine. You can control whether your peace is protected or continuously donated.

When you close these leaks, your life changes in a way that feels almost unfairly simple. Not because everything becomes easy, but because everything becomes clear. You stop negotiating with obvious patterns. You stop translating entitlement into need. You stop mistaking familiarity for safety. You stop treating disrespect like a misunderstanding that needs another conversation. You begin responding to reality as it is, not as you wish it would become. And that is the moment respect stops being something you chase and becomes something you embody—quietly, steadily, without needing to announce it.

The Private Standard

Self-respect does not start in public. It starts in the unglamorous minutes nobody witnesses—the minutes where you decide what you will tolerate from yourself. That is why so many people think they want respect but cannot hold it when it arrives. They want the mirror without changing what the mirror reflects. They want to be treated with gravity while living with excuses. They want to walk into a room and feel authority, but they keep abandoning themselves in small, daily ways that teach their nervous system they are optional.

I learned that the hard way, because for a long time my identity was built on endurance. I mistook survival for strength. I thought if I could carry more than everyone else—more pressure, more responsibility, more pain—then I was winning. I thought that was what "high value" looked like. I did not realize I was training people to approach me like a service counter. I will handle it. I will fix it. I will absorb it. I will smile. I will make it look easy. And if you make yourself look endlessly available, people stop seeing you as a person. They start seeing you as a system.

There is a private moment that happens before the public disrespect. It is always quiet. It is always small. It looks like answering a message you do not want to answer because you feel guilty. It looks like taking a call when your body is exhausted because you do not want to seem "difficult." It looks like laughing at a comment that stung because you do not want tension. It looks like swallowing a boundary because you do not want to lose someone. In that moment, you do not think you are doing anything dramatic. You think you are being kind. Mature. Flexible. But your body knows what you just did. Your body knows you negotiated your worth again.

People do not suddenly disrespect you out of nowhere. They adjust to the version of you that keeps proving you will tolerate less than you deserve. That is not an insult. That is the physics of human behavior. The world is not philosophical. The world is patterned. And once a pattern is established— once your nervous system becomes the place where other people drop their mess—your life will fill with people who treat your kindness like an unlimited credit line.

I used to think respect was something you earn by being impressive. By working harder. By becoming more accomplished. By making yourself undeniable. But I have met plenty of impressive people who are still treated casually. And I have met people who are not loud at all, not famous, not flashy, yet the room treats them differently. Not because of what they say. Because of what they will not accept. Their standard is not a speech. It is a posture. They are not performing self-respect. They are living inside it.

When my health collapsed, I discovered something humiliating and liberating: you cannot fake a standard when your body is the one keeping the books. In that era—there were days where I could feel my self-respect physically. Not as confidence. As something more primal: the question of whether I would keep abandoning myself to keep the world comfortable.

I remember the heaviness of it. Not just the weight on the scale. The weight in my mind. The weight of being "the strong one" while quietly panicking. The weight of showing up to life like a soldier while my body was sending distress signals I kept translating into "Just push through." That translation cost me. It cost me physically, emotionally, spiritually. Because every time you push through what you should listen to, you teach yourself you do not matter. And that lesson does not stay internal. It leaks into your relationships, your business, your choices, the way you let people talk to you, the way you let them show up late, disappear, return, demand, and act entitled to your energy.

The most dangerous disrespect is the one you normalize. The small kind that does not look like abuse. The kind that looks like "That is just how they are." The kind you defend to your friends because you do not want to admit you are accepting crumbs. The kind you tolerate because the alternative is loneliness, and loneliness scares you more than betrayal. But that is how you slowly become a person who begs for basic treatment. Not because you are weak. Because you have trained yourself to believe that your needs are negotiable.

And once you train yourself that way, you carry that posture everywhere. You carry it into friendships. Into partnerships. Into rooms where you should be treated with respect. You carry it into business. You start over-delivering to compensate for a lack of internal authority. You start saying yes too quickly, discounting too quickly, explaining too much, responding too fast, being too available, because you are trying to manufacture respect with output. But respect does not come from output. Output can bring admiration. Respect is different. Respect comes from your inner boundary being real.

The moment that changed me was not a highlight reel moment. It was not applause. It was not a public victory. It was a private sentence: I will not abandon myself again. And it did not arrive as a motivational quote. It arrived as survival.

Because when you have been through enough pain—real pain, body pain, identity pain—something becomes clear: you cannot heal while living in self-betrayal. You cannot rebuild your life while still negotiating your dignity. You cannot demand that people treat you better while you are still treating yourself like an afterthought. At some point, the cost becomes obvious. The cost is your health. Your sleep. Your nervous system. Your sense of who you are.

Here is what I mean by "earning respect internally." It is not about arrogance. It is not about acting superior. It is not about becoming cold. It is about becoming consistent. Consistent with your time. Your boundaries. Your values. Your body. Your truth. When you are consistent, you stop broadcasting confusion. And when you stop broadcasting confusion, the world stops testing you as much. Not because people become saints. Because you stop offering loopholes.

Most people do not realize how much they negotiate themselves. They do it in micro-moments all day. They say, "It is fine," when it is not fine. They say, "No worries," when it absolutely worries them. They say yes when their body says no. They stay in conversations that drain them. They tolerate subtle disrespect and call it "being chill." Then they wonder why they feel invisible. They wonder why they feel used. They wonder why they feel like the room does not take them seriously. But the room is responding to the contract you keep signing with yourself.

My body forced me to look at that contract. And while all of that was happening, my weight spiraled into something that felt like a public confession. People think weight is only about food. Sometimes it is grief. Sometimes it is cortisol. Sometimes it is a nervous system living in survival mode for so long that the body starts building a bunker around the soul. I did not just gain weight. I gained evidence. Proof that something inside me was collapsing while I kept smiling like nothing was wrong.

Then came the diagnosis that cracked whatever pride I had left: a pituitary tumor. Hormones turned into chaos. Testosterone dropped to zero. Prolactin went through the roof—high enough that the jokes write themselves, except I was the one living inside the punchline. It did not only disrupt my body. It attacked my sense of identity—masculinity, mood, energy, libido, self-image, the basic feeling of being myself.

This is where most people either disappear or harden. I did neither. I did what I had always done: I kept going. I kept being the reliable one. The responsible one. The strong one. The one who does not fall apart. Because that was my brand long before I had a brand. And if you have lived like that long enough, collapsing starts to feel like betrayal—not to others, but to the story you built about who you are.

You can put on the face for a while, but your system does not care about your image. Your system cares about truth. And that is where self-respect becomes non-negotiable. Because you realize you are not dealing with theory. You are dealing with consequences. There is a kind of self-respect that is built in pain—not because pain is noble, but because pain strips away the lies. Pain makes you stop performing. Pain makes you stop trying to be liked. Pain makes you ask a brutal question: "am I living in a way I can actually sustain?" And if the answer is no, then you do not need inspiration. You need a new standard.

A standard is what you do when nobody is clapping. It is what you do when you are tired. It is what you do when you are lonely. It is what you do when you are scared. It is what you do when the old you would have folded. Self-respect is not a feeling. It is a behavior. And behavior is where the entire world gets trained.

This is why I do not romanticize "being nice" anymore. Niceness without boundaries is not a virtue. It is a strategy. And sometimes it is a trauma strategy. It is the strategy of someone who learned that conflict is dangerous, that being disliked is unsafe, that silence keeps you close to people, even when those people are draining you. But that strategy does not create respect. It creates access. It creates familiarity. It creates a version of relationship where your comfort is always last.

When I was in that season of my life—I could feel how much I was still trying to earn my place by being useful. I could feel the addiction to being needed. Because being needed feels like value. But being needed is not the same as being respected. Sometimes the more you are needed, the less you are respected, because need can turn you into a tool. Respect requires boundaries. Respect requires that your value is not dependent on your availability.

This is where people get scared. Because the moment you stop being endlessly available, certain relationships get tested. The moment you stop over-explaining, certain people get uncomfortable. The moment you stop responding immediately, certain dynamics start shaking. And that is the point. Not to punish anyone. To reveal what is real.

If someone only feels close to you when you are exhausted, that is not closeness. That is consumption. If someone calls you selfish the first time you protect your time, that is not love. That is entitlement. If someone withdraws the moment you stop over-giving, they were not attached to you. They were attached to your discount.

Internal respect means you stop offering the discount.

I did not become this way because I read it in a book. I became this way because my body and my life made the lesson unavoidable. All of it did something to me: it stripped away the fantasy that I could keep paying for everyone else's comfort with my own wellbeing.

At some point, you realize there is nothing heroic about self-abandonment. There is nothing spiritual about tolerating disrespect. There is nothing mature about swallowing your truth until it turns into resentment and illness. That is not maturity. That is slow self-erasure.

Respect is built when you stop erasing yourself.

It begins with the way you treat your own time. The way you speak to yourself. The way you move when nobody is watching. It begins when you stop rehearsing your boundaries like you are asking permission. It begins when you stop negotiating your "no." It begins when you stop explaining what should be obvious to someone who actually respects you. It begins reminder by reminder, decision by decision: I am not available for what dishonors me.

That is not ego. That is alignment.

And once alignment becomes your baseline, respect stops being a war you fight with other people. It becomes a reality you live in. People feel it. Not because you are louder. Because you are clearer. Not because you are harsher. Because you are consistent. Not because you demand more. Because you finally stopped accepting less.

Most people think a "standard" is something you prove in big moments— breakups, confrontations, public wins. It is not. A standard reveals itself in the smallest minutes: what you tolerate, what you excuse, what you absorb, what you smooth over so nobody feels uncomfortable. That is why the private standard matters. It is the only part of your life that is not negotiated with an audience.

But here is the uncomfortable truth: you can understand all of this intellectually and still fail the test when it counts. Because the nervous system does not follow your philosophy. It follows your conditioning. And when pressure rises, you do not rise to your ideas—you return to your default.

I learned that in the most literal way possible. Not in a relationship argument. Not in a business room. On a hospital gurney, minutes before a high-risk surgery, with my body shaking and my life being reduced to signatures and probabilities. That was the moment my "standard" stopped being theory and became a verdict.

When the Room is on Fire, Who Do You Save First?

UCLA. Pre-op. That fluorescent light that makes everyone look slightly unreal, as if the body has already been converted into a file. I was on a gurney, for pituitary tumor surgery (a noncancerous growth on the pituitary gland), shaking so hard it felt like my bones were in debate with reality. Not mild nerves. Not "a little scared." Full-body fear—the kind that narrows time into a corridor with no exits and no negotiation.

It was not a simple procedure. It was a complex operation that demanded an entire orchestra of specialists— neurosurgery coordinating with ENT and endocrinology, with microsurgical precision where millimeters are the difference between a life that returns to itself and a life that never feels the same again. A pituitary tumor is not only a medical problem; it is an identity problem. It is chemistry, yes, but also mood, energy, libido, sleep, masculinity, self-image, sanity. It is the quiet terror of realizing that what you thought was "you" can be disrupted by something that does not care about your willpower.

Before a single incision, my body was already in rebellion. Stress had swollen my stomach so much I looked visibly distended—like fear had taken a physical form. The fear had a visible shape. And still, a part of my mind kept trying to perform control—like "strength" means you are obligated to be calm while your life is being placed on a table.

Then the nurse came in with paperwork. Not a few pages—an institutional document thick enough to feel like a warning in physical form. Complications. Disability. Death. The system protecting itself with language that does not ask how you feel; it only tells you what can happen. The nurse read it out loud with the steady tone of someone who has said these words too many times to carry their weight. It was not cruel. It was procedural. But procedure can be brutal when your nervous system is already screaming.

My partner stood beside me, and I watched the shift in real time—his face, his breath, his eyes widening with that specific panic that comes when control evaporates. He spiraled. He said we should leave. Now. He tried to grab an alternative with both hands: medication, shrinking the tumor pharmacologically, "like most people," another path, another plan, anything that removed this moment and this risk from the room. He was terrified. And here is the truth that exposes the pattern: I was the one on the gurney. I was the one shaking. I was the one carrying the tumor. But the second he broke, I forgot myself.

I looked at him—still trembling inside—and I smiled. Not because I felt safe. Because I needed him to feel safe. I performed calm so he could breathe. "Look at me," I told him. "Everything is perfect. Everything is excellent. I am not afraid." I became the caretaker of the room while the room prepared to gamble with my life. I protected his nervous system with my own body on the line. In the most critical moment of my survival, I defaulted to what I had been trained to believe love looks like: soothe first, stabilize first, manage everyone else first.

That is not romance. That is conditioning. It reveals a version of me who measured love by how well I could handle other people's fear, a version of me who believed being "strong" meant never needing anything in public—not even in a hospital, not even minutes before a life-altering operation. Real strength would have been brutally simple: "I am terrified. Hold my hand. Stay with me. Let me be human." I did not do that. I went straight into service, because service had become my safest identity. If everyone else is okay, then I am safe. That is the lie that keeps people leaking their dignity while calling it loyalty.

This is why respect is earned internally. Self-respect is not a quote you post when you are angry, and it is not an attitude you weaponize at other people. It is the private standard that shows up when you are exposed—when you are not performing maturity, not strategizing, not impressing anyone. It is what you do when your survival instinct is activated. In that room, I learned something humiliating and clarifying: I did not have a confidence problem. I had a standard problem. My standard—my internal contract—still said, "I will take care of everyone else first," even when I was the one on the table.

That day at UCLA did not teach me medicine. It taught me identity. It showed me the cost of an identity built on being the one who never needs anything: you can keep everyone calm and still lose yourself. You can be loved for what you carry and still never be held. You can be praised for your strength and still feel privately abandoned—by others, and by you. And the bill always comes later: in fatigue, resentment, bitterness, illness, and the quiet sense that your life is organized around rooms you did not create but keep saving at your expense.

That is why this chapter cannot stay a lecture. It has to be a confession. Because until you see your pattern clearly, you keep calling it "circumstance," "bad luck," "other people." Sometimes it is simpler and harder than that: you built a life where your dignity is negotiable, and your nervous system learned to treat self-erasure as virtue. Life does not reveal that to punish you. It reveals it to wake you up.

The correction is not dramatic. It is disciplined. It begins with one brutal adjustment: when the room is on fire, you stop running to save everyone else while you burn. You hold your own line. You let your fear exist without translating it into performance. You stop protecting people from the truth of your humanity. And that is where your respect starts to return—quietly, privately, in the only place it can ever become real.

The surgery worked. The tumor came out—successfully—and it happened right before the world shut down for COVID: February 14, 2020. A Valentine's Day I will never forget, not for romance, but for what it did to my definition of love. Love, I realized, is not the story you tell when everything is easy. Love is what happens when fear is real and the body is on the line. And in the weeks that followed, as the planet went into lockdown and my nervous system tried to recover from a war I had been carrying for years, one truth became impossible to ignore: I could not go back to the same pace, the same pressure, the same performance—like nothing happened. The body does not negotiate with denial. So, when the noise of the world rose and the space to breathe disappeared, my partner and I made a decision that was not an escape. It was an emergency. We went to Greece. I needed distance from the machine so I could hear what I had been avoiding for a long time: that my problem was never only the tumor, or the weight, or the injuries. My deeper problem was a private contract that kept making my dignity negotiable.

The Masterpiece Under the Broken Glass

"After surgery, I could not go back to the same pace or performance—so we went to Greece, and that is where the deeper lesson finally surfaced."

One day, walking with my physiotherapist—still swollen, still healing, still trying to feel human again—he offered a gentle compliment. Nothing dramatic. Nothing therapeutic. Just something sincere about my progress, my effort, my strength. It should have landed like encouragement. Instead, my mind went to the place it had been living for years: an internal courtroom where I was always both defendant and judge.

And I replied with a story.

I told him there once was a painting. Not just any painting—the painting. A divine, unique piece of art. People would stop and marvel at it. Admire it. Desire it. Whisper about its depth, its colors, the emotion it evoked. Some even envied it, because it was irresistible. It had a magnetism that could not be ignored.

I could see his face shift as he listened—polite at first, uncertain where I was going. But once you start telling truth through metaphor, the truth moves faster than your pride can stop it.

And then, I said, something happened. A fall. A crack. A shatter. The glass was destroyed. The frame splintered. And now, nobody looks at it. Nobody sees it. It has been cast aside like garbage—forgotten, unwanted, covered in dust and judgment. As if the beauty was never real. As if the moment it cracked, it stopped mattering.

I stopped walking. My voice got quieter. And then I said it—almost ashamed of the honesty.

That is how I feel.

That sentence did not come from confidence. It came from exhaustion. From the part of me that had been trying to hold the image of strength while privately experiencing myself as a broken object. Because when you spend a lifetime being admired for capacity—output, composure, performance—you start believing respect is something you lose the moment you show damage. You start believing people love you when you function.

He stopped too. Turned toward me. Looked at me with eyes that did not flinch—blue eyes that felt like still water. No pity. No performance. Just presence. He placed his hand on my shoulder and said something I will never forget, not because it was poetic, but because it was accurate.

"Mr. Vitali," he said, "you have misunderstood everything. The masterpiece is still there. It was always there. You just need to take, one by one, the broken pieces of glass away, and let it shine again. The frame may have broken. The glass may have shattered. But what is behind it is still you. Unruined."

In that moment, something returned. Not my shoulder. Something deeper. The part of me that had confused damage with identity. The part of me that had treated pain as proof I was less valuable. The part of me that had accepted the world's reaction as a final verdict.

Because what he did, in one sentence, was separate the core from the covering. He separated art from glass. Truth from distortion. And I stood there, stunned and exposed, because for the first time in a long time, I believed it—maybe not perfectly, not magically, but enough to feel the shift.

Enough to recognize the hidden policy my nervous system had been enforcing for years: if I crack, I lose my worth. And when that policy is running, you negotiate everything. You tolerate tone you should not tolerate. You accept half-effort because you fear abandonment. You over-explain boundaries because you are trying to earn permission to have them. You keep giving and smoothing and forgiving because being needed feels safer than being respected. Meanwhile your dignity leaks out in a thousand small moments— and you call it maturity.

That day, I made a decision I did not announce. I did not post it. I did not turn it into a slogan. I simply decided: I will not abandon myself again.

That is what internal respect actually is. Not ego. Not attitude. A private vow that becomes a standard. And a standard is not proven in speeches. It is proven under pressure, when your old reflex would be to disappear. That is the real work: removing the broken glass. Piece by piece. The excuses. The performative strength. The addiction to being useful. The fear of being disliked. The reflex to negotiate your dignity to keep the room comfortable.

And this is where the chapter lands, cleanly: the world cannot treat you as sacred if you keep treating yourself as replaceable. It cannot be trained to respect what you keep discounting. But when you stop discounting—quietly, consistently—something changes. Not because people suddenly become better. Because access becomes more expensive. Because disrespect stops being "a misunderstanding" and becomes what it always was: information.

That is the standard before the world.

And once you have it, you do not need to beg for respect. The room adjusts—or it loses you.

CHAPTER 7

THE COST OF NOT CHOOSING YOURSELF

The Invisible Accumulation

There is a cost to not choosing yourself, and it does not announce itself. It does not arrive with collapse or crisis, but with adaptation. The human system is extraordinarily good at adapting. That is both its greatest strength and its quietest danger. When something hurts but remains tolerable, we do not remove ourselves from it; we adjust to it. When a situation slowly erodes us, we do not rebel; we normalize it. The nervous system is not designed to seek happiness. It is designed to seek familiarity. And familiarity, even when painful, feels safer than the unknown.

This is how the cost begins to accumulate. Not through dramatic betrayal, but through repetition. You stay. You endure. You learn how to carry something that does not belong in your hands, and eventually your hands forget what it feels like to be empty.

There is a principle deeply embedded in human physiology: what is carried long enough becomes part of posture. Muscles adapt to load. Hormones adapt to stress. Neural pathways adapt to expectation. This is not philosophy; it is biology. When you live in a state of constant accommodation—managing emotions, anticipating reactions, holding space without receiving it back—

your system calibrates around that demand. It tightens. It braces. It holds. And because the change is gradual, you do not feel the moment when holding becomes your default state.

This is why so many people wake up one day inside a body they do not recognize. The weight did not come from food alone. The exhaustion did not come from work alone. The inflammation did not come from age alone. The body was doing what it always does: adapting to an environment that never felt safe enough to soften. Holding becomes protection. Extra weight becomes insulation. Chronic tension becomes armor. You are not broken. You are trained.

What makes this training brutal is that it does not feel like a decision while you are inside it. It feels like being "reasonable." It feels like being the bigger person. It feels like being stable. You do not wake up and choose self-erasure. You choose what keeps the day smooth. You choose what prevents the argument. You choose what avoids the look on someone's face that makes you feel like you did something wrong for having a need. And because the consequence is immediate when you do not comply—tension, coldness, guilt, drama—you start obeying the fastest route back to peace. Your body learns that peace is not a state. Peace is something you earn by shrinking.

That is how people end up living in a permanent "almost." Almost rested. Almost okay. Almost free. Almost themselves. Almost. And the word "almost" is expensive because it keeps you investing. Almost is the currency of people who have not admitted that they are paying for connection with their nervous system. Almost is what you accept when you are afraid that demanding the real thing will cost you the relationship, the job, the identity, the story you have been telling yourself to make the pain feel purposeful.

The invisible accumulation is not only stress. It is self-editing. You begin to edit your tone, your timing, your needs, your truth, your standards, your face. You begin to edit your excitement so you do not look foolish. You begin to edit your sadness so you do not look needy. You begin to edit your anger so you do not look "too much." And slowly you become an expert at presenting a version of yourself that is easy to be around but expensive to inhabit. People call that maturity. Sometimes it is. But when it is chronic, it is not maturity. It is a survival skill that overstayed its purpose.

This is the part no one prepares you for: when you edit yourself long enough, you stop knowing what you actually think. Your preferences become negotiable. Your instincts start whispering and you start answering them with logic. Your own internal signals become something you debate instead of something you respect. You become the kind of person who does not ask, "What do I want?" but "What will cause the least disruption?" You become the kind of person who can read a room perfectly and cannot read themselves. And because the skill is impressive, everyone benefits. Everyone—except you.

Over time, the cost shows up as a particular kind of exhaustion that has nothing to do with hours and everything to do with friction. Internal friction. The friction of smiling while bracing. The friction of saying yes while resenting. The friction of staying loyal to what is draining you and calling it character. The friction of treating your own boundaries as negotiable information and other people's comfort as law. That friction is not dramatic. It is constant. And constant friction creates heat. That heat becomes irritability, insomnia, cravings, numbing, emotional distance, a short fuse, a low-grade rage that feels "out of character," until you realize it is not out of character at all. It is the backlog speaking.

There is a reason anger becomes confusing in people who do not choose themselves. Anger is designed to protect. It is a biological boundary marker. It tells you what is unacceptable. But when your entire identity is built around being agreeable, anger has nowhere clean to go. So it gets redirected. It turns inward and becomes shame. It leaks sideways and becomes sarcasm. It disappears for years and then returns as an explosion that makes you feel like you lost control, when what actually happened is simpler: you ran out of storage.

And then comes the cruel distortion: you start blaming yourself for the symptoms of your own adaptation. You call yourself weak for needing rest. You call yourself selfish for wanting space. You call yourself dramatic for finally reacting. You call yourself ungrateful for noticing what is missing. But the body is not moral. The body is accurate. When you live in a pattern of self-deferral, the body does what it can to keep you alive inside the contradiction. It braces. It stores. It tightens. It numbs. It prepares for impact because your life has been teaching it that impact is normal.

This is why so many people cannot relax even when nothing is happening. They sit in silence and the body still scans. They take a day off and still feel guilty. They go on vacation and still feel tense. The problem is not that they do not know how to rest. The problem is that their nervous system does not recognize rest as safe. Their baseline has been urgency, accommodation, monitoring, managing, smoothing. Rest feels like losing control. And losing control feels like danger. That is training. That is not personality.

The hardest truth is this: you can be successful and still be self-abandoned. You can look strong and still be internally negotiable. You can function at a high level while quietly disappearing as a person. That is why this chapter matters. Not because the cost is poetic. Because the cost is real. It shows up in your health, your relationships, your capacity for joy, your tolerance for life, your ability to feel like you are actually living instead of managing yourself through it.

Eventually, something in you starts to revolt—not loudly, but honestly. You stop being impressed by your own endurance. You stop romanticizing your ability to "handle it." You begin to sense, in your body, that what you have been calling resilience may actually be prolonged self-betrayal with better branding. And when that realization arrives, it does not feel like empowerment at first. It feels like grief. Grief for the time. Grief for the energy. Grief for the years you were present but not fully alive.

I learned this earlier than I could explain it. Before I had language for it, I was placed inside a metaphor and asked to carry it with my body. I did not understand why it stayed with me. I only understood the feeling: the strange intimacy people can develop with what hurts them, simply because it is familiar.

That is where the cube begins.

The Cube You Learned to Call Home

When I was very young, I participated in a short film I did not fully understand at the time. I remember the silence more than the script. The kind of silence that is not empty—silence that forces the body to speak. I played a man who carried a cube everywhere he went. A glass cube. Transparent. Heavy. Fragile. It looked clean enough to be harmless. That was the trick.

He held it against his chest the way people hold what they are afraid to lose. Sometimes he caressed it like it was love. Sometimes he clenched it like it was evidence. He could see through it, which made it feel honest. He could be seen through it too, which made it feel exposed. The cube was not simply an object; it was a rule. It was a world with edges. It was a home with no softness. And because it was glass, it carried a particular cruelty: it let you believe you were free because you could still see the outside.

That is the kind of prison people build when they cannot leave. Not iron bars. Not chains. Something polite. Something transparent. Something that looks like "this is fine" from the distance. Something you can explain. Something you can normalize.

In the film, he tried to put it down. He tried to lean it against a wall and walk away like a normal person. But his hands did not know how to be empty. He had been holding it for so long that the absence felt like danger. He tried to give it to someone else, the way people try to hand off emotional weight disguised as "sharing." But when someone reached for it, he resisted. Not because the cube was precious, but because it was familiar. Because he had learned how to breathe inside it. Because even pain becomes a kind of shelter when it is predictable.

There was a moment—this is the part that stayed with me—when the opportunity to break it appeared. Not a dramatic moment. Just a chance. A clean opening. A simple act that would have ended the contract instantly. Others tried to help him. They reached. They offered. They wanted him free. And he panicked. He fought them with a desperation that looked irrational until you understand the real truth: people do not protect what is good. They protect what they know.

That is what you are doing when you do not choose yourself. You are not just enduring discomfort. You are defending the architecture of the life that made your discomfort normal. You are protecting the cube. You are polishing it. You are calling it "my situation," "my responsibility," "my family," "my marriage," "my work," "my loyalty," "my personality," "my fate." And because you have carried it long enough, you stop calling it what it is. You call it home.

A cube is a perfect symbol because it has no mystery. It has corners. It has borders. It has limits. And once you learn those limits, you can survive inside them. You can learn where to move without getting cut. You can learn which truth is too sharp. You can learn which needs create consequences. You can learn the exact version of yourself that keeps the cube from cracking. You can become incredibly skilled at living small while pretending you are being mature.

This is where the damage gets subtle. Not choosing yourself does not always look like tragedy. Often it looks like competence. You become the person who "handles it." You become the person who stays calm. You become the person who smooths, translates, absorbs, forgives, adjusts, and keeps the atmosphere stable. That stability is your cube. It is clean. It is controlled. It is predictable. And because it prevents chaos, everybody benefits from it. Everybody— except the person carrying it.

The cube is also how self-betrayal becomes respectable. You learn to call your suppression "emotional intelligence." You learn to call your silence "strength." You learn to call your exhaustion "work ethic." You learn to call your loneliness "independence." You learn to call your shrinking "humility." You can wrap an entire life of self-erasure in language that sounds noble, and no one will question it, because it makes life easier for them.

What you do not see while you are inside it is that the cube is not just around you. It becomes you. The nervous system adapts to edges. The body adapts to holding. The mind adapts to limitation by making limitation feel moral. You stop asking, "Is this right for me?" and you start asking, "Can I manage it?" That shift sounds small, but it changes everything. Because management is not a life. Management is how people survive a life they are afraid to change.

And here is the ugly part—the part most people avoid because it burns to admit: once you have lived inside a cube long enough, freedom feels suspicious. You can crave peace and still reject it when it arrives, because you do not recognize yourself in a life that does not require bracing. You can dream of love and still flinch when someone offers it cleanly, because your system learned that love is earned through endurance. You can say you want "something better" and still sabotage it, because better has no rules you have memorized yet.

This is why "leaving" is not only logistical. It is neurological. People do not just leave a person, a job, a city, a dynamic. They leave the identity that was built to survive it. And the identity does not walk out calmly. It panics. It bargains. It says: be patient, be understanding, do not overreact, do not be dramatic, do not make it a thing. It says: you have invested too much. It says: you will regret it. It says: you are not the kind of person who gives up. It says: who do you think you are to want more?

That voice is not wisdom. It is the cube speaking.

In real life, the cube is not glass. It is pattern. It is the familiar tension in your chest before you answer a message you do not want to answer. It is the reflex to smile while something in you goes cold. It is the habit of explaining your no until it becomes a yes. It is the way you minimize your own hurt so you can keep the room livable. It is the way you protect other people from the consequences of their behavior by absorbing them into your body.

And because it is familiar, you treat it like safety.

The cube is also why people can stay in the most draining versions of "almost." Almost respected. Almost loved. Almost seen. Almost chosen. Almost safe. Almost. That word is expensive. Almost keeps people loyal to a life that never fully arrives. Almost becomes a substitute for reality because reality would demand a decision. And decisions are what break cubes.

You can hear it in the way people talk when they are still inside it. They do not describe the truth; they describe the management plan. "It is not that bad." "They mean well." "We have history." "They have been through a lot." "I can handle it." "It is complicated." The story is always an explanation that makes leaving look unreasonable. The body tells the truth quietly: tightness, fatigue, heaviness, numbness, inflammation, insomnia, cravings, dread. The body is not poetic. It is precise. It reacts to the environment you keep translating into language.

The cube does not just hold pain. It holds identity. If you have been the one who endures, then enduring becomes your proof of worth. You do not just tolerate because you are kind—you tolerate because it makes you feel necessary. It makes you feel strong. It makes you feel chosen, even when you are not. It gives you a role. And roles are addictive when you do not know who you are without them.

That is why breaking the cube feels like death to the old self. Not because the old self is dramatic, but because it was built for survival. Survival identities do not want freedom; they want predictability. They want to know the rules of the pain. They want to know where the corners are. They want to know what you can tolerate. They want to keep the story intact, because the story is what made the suffering feel purposeful.

But the cube is not purpose. It is containment.

Here is what I know now, with adult eyes and a body that has paid for years of "being fine": the most dangerous cages are the ones you can decorate. The ones you can explain. The ones that do not look like cages to anyone else. The ones that let you keep functioning, because functioning is how people avoid telling the truth.

People do not stay because it is good. They stay because it is known. They stay because the unknown would force them to meet themselves without the role. They stay because leaving would require them to admit that what they called loyalty was fear with manners. They stay because breaking the cube would expose how long they have been living inside something too small.

And if you are honest, you already know your cube. You know the relationship that makes your nervous system brace. You know the environment that demands you be smaller to be loved. You know the place where your truth becomes "too much." You know the dynamic where you are always managing the temperature, always translating the disrespect, always paying the difference.

The cube you learned to call home is not the thing you carry. It is the part of you that believes you have to carry it to deserve your life.

That is why this part matters. Because before you can choose yourself, you have to stop romanticizing what has been containing you. You have to stop calling predictability "safety." You have to stop calling endurance "love." You have to stop calling your adaptation "maturity," when it is actually the slow, elegant erosion of your own authority.

Breaking the cube is not loud. It is not revenge. It is not an announcement. It is a private moment of disgust that finally becomes self-respect. A quiet decision that says: I will not keep living inside what I must constantly justify. I will not keep caressing what cuts me. I will not keep protecting what has been training me to disappear.

You do not need hatred to put it down. You need clarity. You need the willingness to let your hands be empty long enough to remember what freedom feels like.

And that is where the story turns—not when the cube shatters, but when you stop treating it like home.

When the Bill Comes Due

There is a moment when the cost stops being an idea and becomes a fact. Until then, everything can be explained away with respectable language. Fatigue becomes "a busy season." Weight becomes "getting older." Irritability becomes "stress." Numbness becomes "being practical." Distance becomes "needing space." As long as you are still functional, the mind is incredibly talented at protecting the structure. It will keep generating narratives that let you stay where you are, keep doing what you do, keep paying what you have been paying—quietly—without calling it a payment.

That is how people stay trapped for years without realizing they are trapped. Nothing collapses, so nothing feels urgent. Nothing "dramatic" happens, so nothing feels valid enough to act on. You keep telling yourself, one more week, one more conversation, one more adjustment, one more compromise, one more time being the bigger person. And because you are capable, because you can endure, because you can hold your face and keep moving, you confuse capacity with consent. You confuse your ability to survive something with proof that it is acceptable. You confuse "I can handle it" with "I should keep handling it."

But systems have limits. Not moral limits. Biological ones.

The nervous system is not impressed by your intentions. It does not care that you were being patient, loyal, empathetic, professional, forgiving, spiritual, strong. It tracks load. It tracks exposure. It tracks how often you swallow what you want to say. It tracks how many times you override the signal and keep smiling anyway. It tracks how long you live inside contradiction—saying yes while you mean no, staying while you want to leave, explaining what you should not have to explain, making yourself smaller so the room stays smooth. The mind can romanticize that. The body cannot. The body does math.

When the bill comes due, it does not arrive with a letter. It arrives as symptoms. It arrives as resistance. It arrives disguised, which is why people miss it at first. They think it is a motivation problem. They think it is a discipline problem. They think they "fell off." They think they are becoming negative. They think they are becoming difficult. They do not realize they are finally becoming honest—just not with words yet.

It starts quietly. Your tolerance changes. Things that used to be manageable suddenly feel invasive. A simple request feels like a demand. A casual tone feels like disrespect. A delay feels like abandonment. You surprise yourself with how fast you go from neutral to irritated, and then you judge yourself for it. You say, "That is not me." What you mean is: that is not the version of me I have been performing in order to keep everything stable.

This is what nobody tells you: the performance has an operating cost. A high one. And you do not get to opt out of the invoice just because you were trying to be good.

At a certain point, endurance stops being invisible. It becomes visible through friction. The friction shows up in your sleep first. You go to bed tired and wake up tired, like the night did not pay you back. You wake up with a jaw you did not choose to clench. You find yourself holding your breath in rooms that are not physically dangerous. You notice you cannot fully relax even when nothing is happening, because your system is trained to stay ready. Not ready for opportunity—ready for impact. You are always braced for the mood shift, the tone shift, the sudden disappointment, the next little thing you will need to manage.

And because that has been your normal for so long, you do not even call it bracing. You call it "being responsible."

The bill also shows up in your appetite, but not in the simplistic way people love to judge. Not in a lazy morality tale. It shows up as cravings that feel louder than logic, because cravings are often the body's emergency language. The body is trying to stabilize blood sugar, regulate cortisol, create comfort, create ground, create a sense of "enough." When emotional ground has been unstable for too long, the system starts building physical ground. That is why weight gain is not just a food story for so many people. It can be insulation. It can be padding. It can be a subconscious boundary—an extra layer between you and a world you do not trust. It can be the body saying, if you will not protect yourself with your mouth, I will protect you with mass.

People do not like hearing that because it takes the conversation away from shame and into reality. And shame is the drug people use to feel in control. If you tell yourself you are failing, you can keep trying harder and avoid the deeper question: what am I adapting to that is quietly breaking me?

By the time the bill comes due, the mind is still trying to bargain. It will keep offering you "reasonable" compromises so you do not have to face the truth cleanly. It will say, maybe I just need a vacation. Maybe I just need to sleep more. Maybe I just need a new routine. Maybe I just need to communicate better. Maybe I just need to be more grateful. Maybe I just need to meditate. Maybe I just need to stop being dramatic. Anything—anything—except the one sentence that would change the structure: this is not livable.

That sentence is hard because it does not sound like self-help. It sounds like an ending. And endings scare people because endings require accountability. Endings require you to stop negotiating with what has already proven itself.

When the bill comes due, the psyche also changes the way it relates to desire. Desire gets muted, not because you are broken, but because desire is expensive in a life where you do not believe you are allowed to have what you want. When you live in constant self-deferral, wanting starts to feel like a setup. You do not want to want, because wanting confronts you with how much you have been settling. So, the system adapts the only way it can: it lowers the volume. It makes you "fine." It makes you indifferent. It makes you tired. It makes you call it peace. But it is not peace. It is a reduction in aliveness, so you can keep surviving a life that would otherwise feel intolerable.

This is why people can look successful and still feel hollow. They are praised but not nourished. They are admired but not met. They are accomplishing but not living. They are doing everything right on paper and still waking up with a low-grade dread that has no clear object. The object is the contract they have been living under: I will keep it smooth, I will keep it stable, I will keep them comfortable, and I will keep myself manageable.

The bill comes due when your system is done being manageable.

And when that happens, you start withdrawing. Not theatrically. Not as a power move. As a survival reflex. You cancel plans you used to force yourself to keep. You stop returning messages, not because you are rude, but because each reply feels like a new obligation you cannot afford. Conversations feel heavy. People feel loud. Socializing feels like work. You start fantasizing about disappearing—not because you hate your life, but because you crave a nervous system that is not rented out to everyone else.

This is where many people label it "burnout" and move on. They treat it as an occupational issue. Sometimes it is. But very often it is not primarily about work. It is about the role you have been playing everywhere: the stabilizer, the translator, the absorber, the one who makes it easy. You are not tired from doing too much. You are tired from being divided. You are tired from living with internal friction—the friction of acting okay when your body is not okay, the friction of staying polite when something is unacceptable, the friction of smiling while your chest tightens, the friction of being the mature one in rooms that require you to be smaller to keep them calm.

That friction creates heat. And heat becomes anger.

Anger is not your enemy. It is a boundary signal. It is the body's "no." It is the psyche's "enough." But in a life where you learned to survive by being agreeable, anger becomes dangerous. It threatens the role. It threatens the identity. So, it gets managed the way everything else gets managed: it gets swallowed, softened, redirected, delayed, edited. And then people wonder why it comes out sideways—sarcasm, snappy tone, impatience with innocent things, a short fuse, a coldness that feels unlike you. It is not unlike you. It is you after years of compression.

Suppressed anger does not disappear. It accumulates. It becomes a backlog. It becomes a debt. And when it finally surfaces, it carries the weight of every moment it was not allowed to exist cleanly.

This is also why the bill comes due in relationships in a colder way than most people expect. When your identity has been endurance, your relationships are often built around your flexibility. The "peace" you maintained was not neutral. It was purchased. It was paid for with your speed, your softness, your forgiveness without repair, your willingness to keep access constant regardless of behavior. You were subsidizing the dynamic. And the environment does not call it a subsidy. It calls it "how things are." People get used to discounts. They forget the real price.

So when you finally stop paying, dynamics react as if you changed the rules. You did.

You removed the subsidy. You stopped making their inconsistency affordable. You stopped translating their entitlement into "they are just stressed." You stopped absorbing the emotional consequences, so nobody had to feel them. And when you do that, you learn a brutal thing: some people were not attached to you. They were attached to access. They were attached to the version of you that kept everything easy.

That realization can produce a specific kind of loneliness. Not the loneliness of being alone, but the loneliness of realizing how many connections were sustained by your self-editing. You look around and feel unseen, because you were present in a way that did not require anyone to actually meet you. You were functional. You were helpful. You were stable. You were the one who could "handle it." And now you are tired of being a function. You want to be a person.

A person has needs. A person has limits. A person has standards. A person has timing. A person cannot be constantly available without paying internally. And when you finally allow yourself to be a person, certain relationships do not know what to do with you. Not always because they are evil. Sometimes because they were trained by your pattern. Humans adapt to what you repeatedly accept more than they adapt to what you say you deserve.

This is where people often make a mistake that keeps them trapped: they try to get closure from the very dynamic that created the wound. They want the other person to understand. They want the apology. They want the recognition. They want the admission of fault. They want the ending to be fair. And that is where so many people hand their freedom back.

Because the moment your closure depends on someone else's comprehension, you are still negotiating your dignity. You are still living as if resolution is something other people grant.

When the bill comes due, the mind tries to regain control by turning it into a courtroom. It starts rehearsing arguments. It starts writing speeches. It starts organizing evidence. It wants a verdict. It wants to be "right." But being right is not the same as being free. The body does not calm down because you won a case. The nervous system does not soften because you made a perfect point. Your system wants something more basic: a change in exposure. A change in pattern. A change in how often you betray yourself in small ways and call it maturity. The bill is not asking you to think harder. It is asking you to stop lying with your behavior.

Here is what makes this chapter uncomfortable, but necessary: by the time the bill comes due, you usually do not feel empowered. You feel ashamed. You feel behind. You replay the years and wonder why you tolerated what you tolerated. You get angry at yourself for not leaving earlier, speaking earlier, choosing yourself earlier. You feel stupid for giving so much. You feel disgusted that you normalized what you normalized. You feel humiliated that your body is now forcing you to face what your mouth avoided. That shame is understandable. And it is also useless. Shame is a useless accountant. It does not reduce the debt. It adds interest.

The cleaner truth is: you did what you had to do when you did not believe you had a choice. You survived with the tools you had. You found a way to endure. You became consistent. And what you did consistently, you can now interrupt.

That is the real pivot: not blaming yourself for adapting but recognizing when adaptation has overstayed its purpose. There is a difference between being resilient and being trapped. There is a difference between being patient and being postponed. There is a difference between being understanding and being negotiable.

When you are honest, you can feel the difference in the body. Flexibility expands you. Self-erasure constricts you. Flexibility leaves you with more life. Self-erasure leaves you with less access to yourself. The bill comes due when your margin disappears—when your system can no longer pretend that "handling it" is the same as living.

And here is the part that should land like a punch and a relief at the same time: the bill is not punishment. It is evidence. Evidence that something in you is still alive enough to refuse the lie. Evidence that your system is done subsidizing a life built on self-deferral. Evidence that the cube you learned to call home has become too small to breathe in.

If you read this part and you feel exposed, good. Exposure is what happens when you stop living under the old armor. It does not mean you are weak. It means you are no longer sedated. It means you can finally see the invoice clearly.

Because until you see the invoice, you keep calling it "life."

And once you stop calling it life, the next part becomes inevitable: you face the only question that matters now. Not "How do I cope better?" Not "How do I endure longer?" Not "How do I fix myself so I can keep paying?" The real question is simpler, and it is the beginning of the exit:

"What would I do if I stopped negotiating with what has been costing me my life slowly?" That question is where the bill stops being the end of you and becomes the start of you.

That is where you choose differently.

The Moment You Stop Living Second

The most humiliating part of not choosing yourself is not the pain. Pain, at least, has honesty. The humiliating part is how normal it starts to feel. You do not wake up one morning and announce, "Today I will become a smaller version of myself so the room stays calm." You just do it. You do it once, and nothing explodes, so you do it again. You do it because you are intelligent enough to read consequences and sensitive enough to feel responsibility for other people's moods. You do it because you have history, because you have hope, because you have a stomach that turns when conflict gets close, because you have been taught—directly or indirectly—that your truth is expensive. Then one day, without a clear turning point, you realize you have been living with your hand on your own throat, calling it maturity.

That is why the real turning point rarely looks like empowerment. It looks like refusal. Not the dramatic kind. The exhausted kind. The kind that happens when the body has carried enough, when the psyche is tired of negotiating, when the part of you that keeps justifying finally gets outvoted by the part of you that can no longer pretend. People think the turning point is when you finally love yourself. It is often when you finally stop disrespecting yourself. It is when you cannot keep paying the bill and still call your life your life. It is when you reach a private clarity that does not need anyone's agreement to be true: I am done living second.

This is where the book title stops being a concept and becomes a line in the sand. Become First is not branding. It is not confidence coaching. It is not a cute slogan you put on a mug and ignore in real life. Become First means your life stops being a negotiation where everyone else's comfort gets final approval and your needs get placed in a waiting room with no appointment time. It means you stop treating your own nervous system as collateral for keeping things "smooth." It means you stop confusing your ability to survive something with proof that you should. It means you stop performing stability while your inner life is quietly collapsing behind the curtains. Become First means you become the first person you consult before you give your time away, your truth away, your body away, your years away.

You have to understand what you are actually doing when you do not choose yourself, because the mind loves to make it sound noble. It calls it patience. It calls it loyalty. It calls it being understanding. It calls it being the bigger person. It calls it professionalism. It calls it grace. And sometimes, in short seasons, those words are real. The problem is when those words become a permanent strategy for avoiding the truth. The problem is when you keep calling self-erasure "love," because it sounds better than admitting you are afraid. Afraid of being judged, afraid of being abandoned, afraid of being misinterpreted, afraid of losing access, afraid of losing the story you built to justify staying. The human system does not just fear change; it fears the identity collapse that comes with change. It fears the moment when you have to look at yourself and admit: I stayed where I shrank because shrinking was familiar.

That is why the cube matters. Not as a clever metaphor, but as a mechanism. The cube is not simply what you carry; it is what you have learned to call home. It is an environment with rules you memorized. Corners you learned not to touch. Edges you learned to respect. Limits you learned to treat as morality. You learned exactly how to move inside it without bleeding too much, and after a while you confused that skill with strength. But the cube was never strength. The cube was containment. It kept you functional. It kept you predictable. It kept you safe from the chaos of honest consequences. It gave you a role, and roles are addictive when you do not feel anchored in who you are without them. You became the one who endures. The one who absorbs. The one who smooths. The one who can handle it. And the world applauded you for being easy to live with while you paid the price privately, with your body.

The moment you Become First is the moment you stop protecting the cube. Not because you become cruel, but because you become clear. You stop polishing what cuts you. You stop explaining what is unacceptable as if your intelligence can make it livable. You stop calling predictable pain "safety" just because it is familiar. You stop treating your own discomfort as a minor inconvenience compared to everybody else's comfort. You stop walking into a room and instinctively shrinking before anyone even asks. You stop editing your tone, your timing, your face, your needs, your truth, so that you can remain "lovable." You stop paying for belonging by disappearing.

This is where people panic, because there is a myth that choosing yourself is selfish. That myth exists because when you start choosing yourself, certain people lose benefits they were receiving without paying for. Your "yes" was a discount. Your flexibility was a subsidy. Your patience was a shield. Your self-editing was the reason other people did not have to improve. And when you remove that subsidy, the dynamic reacts. Not always violently. Sometimes politely. Sometimes with confusion. Sometimes with guilt trips that sound like concern. Sometimes with that subtle tone that says, "Who do you think you are?" People call it "you changed," as if the goal was to remain a convenient version of yourself forever. They say, "You are acting different," as if you were born to be manageable. They say, "This is not like you," when what they really mean is: this is not like the version of you I knew how to access.

This is why Become First is not a single decision. It is a sequence of decisions made in the face of your own conditioning. Because the first wave after you choose yourself is not peace. It is discomfort. It is guilt. It is that internal alarm that goes off when you violate an old rule that once kept you safe: do not cause disruption, do not be difficult, do not need too much, do not say no without a full explanation, do not disappoint people, do not risk being misunderstood. When you begin to Become First, you will feel selfish even when you are simply being sane. That does not mean you are wrong. It means your nervous system is recalibrating.

Here is the truth that most people do not say out loud because it is uncomfortable: you have been trained. Trained to associate peace with compliance. Trained to associate belonging with self-deferral. Trained to confuse love with endurance. Trained to confuse being needed with being valued. Trained to believe that if you are kind enough, patient enough, good enough, someone will eventually treat you the way you deserve. And sometimes that works, temporarily, with healthy people who are capable of receiving. But with unhealthy dynamics, your goodness does not heal them; it enables them. It becomes the reason they do not change, because you keep making the consequences affordable. Your body, however, never agreed to this arrangement. Your body kept track. Your body kept receipts. Your body kept escalating because your mouth kept negotiating.

So what does it actually look like, in real life, to Become First? It does not look like a motivational speech. It looks like a boundary you enforce before you feel ready. It looks like an uncomfortable pause where you do not rush to soothe someone's reaction. It looks like allowing your needs to exist without immediately turning them into a problem you must solve quietly so nobody is inconvenienced. It looks like being willing to be temporarily disliked in order to remain permanently intact.

That is what scares people. Not that they will lose a person. That they will lose the version of themselves that was built around being chosen by others. That is the deeper addiction behind so many patterns: the addiction to external approval as proof of worth. When you have lived second for a long time, being chosen becomes a substitute for choosing yourself. You learn to feel alive when someone wants you, needs you, approves of you, validates you. You learn to feel safe when you are useful. You learn to calm your anxiety by making yourself necessary. And then you call that love. But love is not the relief of being needed. Love is being met without self-erasure. Love is being held without being handled. Love is having your truth survive the room.

This is where Become First becomes unforgiving—in a good way—because it exposes the difference between love and attachment to familiarity. People do not stay in draining situations because they are good. People stay because they are known. The known has rules. The known has corners. The known has a predictable way you can suffer while still believing you are in control. The unknown requires you to meet yourself without the role. It requires you to learn a new identity that is not built around endurance. It requires you to tolerate the emptiness that comes when you stop performing. And that emptiness is not emptiness. It is space. But if you have never lived in space, space feels like danger.

So, the first stage of becoming first is not confidence. It is tolerance. Tolerance for the discomfort of being a new version of yourself before it feels natural. Tolerance for guilt that is not true guilt, but conditioned guilt. Tolerance for other people's reactions without rushing to manage them. Tolerance for being misinterpreted without defending yourself into a nervous breakdown. Tolerance for the awkwardness of not knowing exactly who you are yet outside the cube. That stage is ugly. It is quiet. It is not photogenic. It is where most people go back, because going back is familiar, and familiar feels safe, even when it is killing you slowly.

But if you stay with it—if you keep choosing yourself even while you feel guilty—you start to notice something that should feel like a relief and a punch: your body begins to respond. You sleep differently. Not perfectly, but differently. Your breath changes. You stop holding your stomach the way you have been holding it for years. Your jaw relaxes. Your cravings lose some of their desperation because your system is no longer constantly trying to create comfort through emergency measures. Your anger becomes cleaner because it is not being stored and compressed; it is being listened to earlier. Your sadness becomes softer because it is not being denied; it is being acknowledged. Your joy becomes possible again because it is not having to fight through layers of bracing.

This is not magic. This is physiology. When you stop living in contradiction, the nervous system does not have to spend so much energy managing internal war. When your outer behavior begins to match your inner truth, your body stops screaming for attention. The bill stops compounding because you stop accumulating interest. Your system was not weak. It was overloaded. It was doing what systems do when the environment is not safe: it adapted. And what adapts can change. Not overnight, but over time, with consistency. The same consistency that built the cage can dismantle it.

This is where the book title needs to be said plainly, because people love to turn it into something inspirational and vague. Become First is not "put yourself first" like you are choosing a restaurant. Become First is a refusal to keep living as a supporting character in your own life. It is the decision that your body will no longer pay for what your mouth refuses to say. It is the decision that your time is not a charity you distribute to earn approval. It is the decision that your love is not a currency you use to buy security. It is the decision that your standards are not negotiable depending on who is watching. It is the decision that you will not keep calling survival "stability" and pretending that is enough.

And yes, you will lose some things when you do this. Let us be honest, because a premium book does not lie to the reader. You may lose certain relationships, or at least the version of those relationships that was built around your self-editing. You may lose your role as the one who always accommodates. You may lose your reputation as the easiest person in the room. You may lose the illusion that if you just explain one more time, they will finally understand. You may lose the fantasy that patience will turn someone into a different person. You may lose the comforting identity of the one who endures. You may lose access to people who only loved you when you were manageable. That is real loss, and it deserves grief.

But there is also something you gain that makes the trade worth it: you gain yourself back. Not a motivational version of yourself. The real one. The one with limits. The one with preferences. The one with standards. The one with timing. The one with truth that does not need permission. You gain the ability to be coherent. You gain the ability to live without constantly negotiating your own existence. You gain the ability to be present without performing. You gain the ability to say no without shaking. You gain the ability to rest without collapsing first. You gain a nervous system that is not rented out to everybody else.

This is where the reader needs to be confronted, because the whole point of Chapter 7 is that the cost is not theoretical. You can read this and still keep your cube. You can read this and still go back to your old pattern. You can highlight a sentence, share it, nod, feel seen, and then return to living second. People do that all the time. They turn insight into decoration. They decorate the cage with language and call it growth. They become fluent in self-awareness and still refuse to make a decision. They use understanding as a substitute for action. They use compassion as a way to delay boundaries. They use "I am working on it" as a way to remain in the same life indefinitely.

This is where Become First draws blood, because it does not let you hide behind insight. It asks you a question that is not spiritual, not philosophical, not cute: what are you still tolerating that you would never advise someone you love to tolerate? What are you still calling love because you are afraid to call it what it is? What part of your life requires constant explanation in order to remain acceptable? What part of your life makes your body brace before it makes you feel safe? What relationship, what environment, what pattern, is training you to disappear?

If you are honest, you already know. Your body knows. Your sleep knows. Your appetite knows. Your shoulders know. Your irritability knows. Your numbness knows. Your low-grade dread knows. The tension in your chest before you answer knows. The way you rehearse conversations in your head knows. The way you keep waiting for the right moment knows. The way you keep hoping for a version of someone that they have not proven they can be knows.

The only thing that does not know is the part of you that is still bargaining. And bargaining is how people die slowly. They bargain with time. They bargain with health. They bargain with truth. They bargain with their own life as if they have unlimited years to keep "figuring it out." They tell themselves, not now, later, when it is calmer, when I have more energy, when they are in a better mood, when the timing is right, when I am less tired, when it is easier. But the years move while you negotiate. The nervous system keeps receipts while you negotiate. The body keeps score while you negotiate. The cost compounds while you negotiate.

The reason the reader needs a hard mirror here is because the book is called Become First, not Become Aware. Awareness is not the finish line. Awareness is the beginning of responsibility. Responsibility is where your life changes. Responsibility is where you stop waiting. Responsibility is where you stop asking for permission to exist. Responsibility is where you stop saying you want peace while choosing the same war inside your body every day.

So let us make it brutally simple, because simplicity is often what saves people: if your life requires you to consistently betray yourself in order to keep it, it is not your life. It is a life you are renting. It is a life you are managing. It is a life you are surviving. And survival is not shameful, but it is not the destination. Survival is the phase you outgrow once you stop romanticizing it.

This is why the ending of this chapter cannot be a pep talk. It has to be a line you cross. The cost of not choosing yourself was never paid all at once; it was paid daily, in small compromises that felt reasonable in the moment and cruel in hindsight. Become First is not a single dramatic act. It is the decision to stop paying in small betrayals. It is the practice of choosing coherence over comfort. It is choosing truth over familiarity. It is choosing your body over the room. It is choosing your life over your role.

And now comes the part that should leave the reader breathless, because it is the part people avoid: you do not need to hate anyone to choose yourself. You do not need to vilify them. You do not need a villain to justify your boundary. You do not need to prove you are right. You do not need their apology, their understanding, their agreement, their closure, their confession. You do not need the ending to be fair. Fair endings are rare. Clean endings are earned.

What you need is clarity.

Clarity that says: I will not keep living inside what I have to constantly justify. I will not keep calling endurance love. I will not keep calling predictability safety. I will not keep calling my shrinking maturity. I will not keep paying for connection with my health. I will not keep waiting for someone to become a person they keep refusing to be. I will not keep making my life smaller so that somebody else can keep their behavior the same.

Because here is the truth that changes everything: the moment you choose yourself, you do not just change one relationship or one job or one pattern. You change the standard by which you will live. You change what you will tolerate. You change what you will call normal. You change what you will call love. You change what you will call a life.

That is why Becoming First is terrifying at first, because it removes the lies you used to survive. It removes the soothing narratives that made staying feel noble. It removes the comfort of being the good one. It removes the identity that was built around being needed. It leaves you with something raw: a direct relationship with yourself. And in the beginning, that relationship will feel unfamiliar, because you have been living in other people's eyes for so long that your own eyes feel too honest.

But then—if you keep going—something happens quietly that feels like redemption: your life begins to feel like yours. Not perfect. Not easy. Not free of difficulty. But yours. Coherent. Aligned. Real. You stop being a passenger in your own story. You stop waiting for a crisis to justify your truth. You stop postponing the part of you that was always meant to lead. You stop living with your own life on hold.

And if there is one final sentence this chapter must leave under the reader's skin, it is this: the cost of not choosing yourself was never the pain. The cost was the years you spent being present but not fully alive. The cost was the life you kept delaying while you tried to make the cube comfortable. The cost was the version of you that you kept sacrificing so the room stayed stable.

Become First is the moment you stop delaying. It is the moment you stop negotiating with what has been costing you your life slowly. It is the moment you stop making your body pay for your silence. It is the moment you put the cube down, not loudly, not as revenge, not as an announcement, but as a clean private decision: I am done living inside what makes me smaller. And the moment you do that, you will feel something that is both terrifying and holy in its simplicity: your hands are empty. Empty enough to finally remember what freedom feels like. Empty enough to finally hold your own life with two hands.

Empty enough to finally Become First.

CHAPTER 8

THE QUIET COST OF BEING THE STRONG ONE

The Role You Never Officially Accepted

There is a kind of strength that does not register as strength while you are living inside it. It does not feel like power, or confidence, or victory. It feels like constant internal management: calibrating your tone, editing your reaction, swallowing the first honest sentence before it reaches your mouth. You are not "strong" in the cinematic way. You are strong in the structural way, like a beam that holds up a ceiling nobody even looks at—until it cracks.

People rarely call you "the strong one" as a form of love. They say it as a label that sounds flattering but functions like an assignment. They mean, without ever saying it directly, that you will handle it, you will understand, you will not make this complicated. And the most dangerous part is that somewhere along the way you agreed—not with a signature, but with repetition. You did not become the strong one because you enjoyed being strong. You became the strong one because, in a room where need was punished and emotion was inconvenient, being stable was the safest position available.

This is not a personality trait. It is training. You learned to stop your feelings at the border and only let in what could be useful. You learned how to translate pain into competence because competence kept you included. You learned to keep your face aligned with the version of you people preferred: calm, capable, reasonable, unbothered. Over time, the world read your self-control as proof that you had no needs worth attending to, and you let that misunderstanding stand because correcting it felt like risk.

At first, the role can feel rewarding. People rely on you. They trust you. They come to you because you do not scare them. When you have been emotionally underfed for long enough, being needed can start to feel like being loved. So you stay available. You stay rational. You stay steady. You become the person who does not break—not because you are invincible, but because breaking was never allowed to be part of your story.

Then the system learns. The system always learns. It learns that your stability is guaranteed, that your capacity is renewable, that your calm will be there tomorrow, even if it costs you everything today. It is rarely cruelty; it is convenience. People do not necessarily intend to drain you. They simply behave according to what you have demonstrated you will tolerate. They bring their storms to your chest because you have mastered the art of looking like shelter.

This is the first quiet cost: invisibility of the kind that hurts. They see your output, not your depletion. They see your competence, not your loneliness. They see the way you show up, not what it took to make you show up. And because you have always been "fine," they build their expectations on that word as if it is a permanent condition, rather than a performance you have been funding with your nervous system.

Another cost follows, and it is more intimate. You start believing your own reputation. You begin living as if your value depends on endurance, as if rest is indulgence, as if softness is danger. You confuse suppression with maturity because from the outside they look similar; both are quiet, both are controlled, both are socially acceptable. But maturity is choice. Suppression is prohibition. One expands you. The other cages you—often with excellent posture and a clean public image, so nobody thinks to ask whether you are okay.

And because you are intelligent, you justify it. You call it discipline. You call it standards. You call it leadership. You tell yourself you are above the chaos, that you refuse to stoop, that you are not like the people who fall apart. But there is a moment where you have to be precise with yourself: how many times did you "stay strong" when what you actually did was disappear? How many times did you "let it go" when what you did was swallow it? How many times did you "keep the peace" when what you really did was betray your own instinct, so you could remain easy to be around?

This is not about blaming you. It is about naming the mechanism, because if you cannot name it, you cannot stop paying for it. The strong one does not collapse on schedule. The strong one delays. You do not grieve when the wound happens; you grieve later, in a car, in the shower, in the wrong week, or not at all—and then your body starts grieving for you through fatigue, tension, insomnia, appetite, inflammation, a quiet sense that you are functioning while someone inside you has filed a missing-person report with your name on it.

Here is the first clean truth of this chapter: "You are the strong one" is not only a compliment. It is a contract written in other people's relief. Once they believe you are a guarantee, they start taking risks with your nervous system. They borrow your clarity as if it replenishes overnight. They load you, not always to harm you, but because you have convinced them you cannot be harmed by weight.

The problem is not that you can handle it. The problem is that once you prove you can, you become the person who always will—unless you interrupt the story. And that interruption begins with a question you may have avoided for years because it threatens the role you have been using to survive: how much of what you call strength is actually strength, and how much of it is fear—fear that if you stop holding, you will not be held?

When Strength Became Currency

At some point, strength stops being something you have and becomes something you spend.

That is the shift most people miss. They think the strong one is simply built differently—more resilient, more composed, more capable. But that belief is not only wrong; it is convenient. It allows people to admire you without having to care for you. It lets them imagine you are made of different material, exempt from the same needs that make everyone else human. As if resilience means you do not ache. As if composure means you do not worry. As if capability means you do not get scared.

The truth is more precise and far more uncomfortable: the strong one has the same needs as everyone else. The same hunger for reassurance. The same fear of being left alone with their thoughts. The same desire to be held without having to earn it. The difference is not the absence of emotion. The difference is where emotion is forced to live. The strong one still cries; it just does not look like crying to the outside world. It looks like staying productive while the chest is tight. It looks like answering messages while the body is begging for silence. It looks like making decisions with a steady voice while something inside is shaking.

And it stays buried for one reason: the strong one is watched. Once people have invested in you as "the strong one," you begin to feel responsible for their belief. You start guarding your own humanity, so you do not disappoint the audience that relies on your stability. You keep grief disciplined, panic quiet, softness private—not because you do not need it, but because you learned, directly or indirectly, that your vulnerability would cost other people their comfort. And the strong one, by definition, is the person who refuses to cost anyone anything.

That is why the transaction stays invisible. Because the strong one does not announce the price. The strong one pays quietly, up front, and then shows up as if nothing was charged.

They do not see the transaction happening underneath.

So strength became my currency. Not as a philosophy, but as behavior. I used it to buy peace, to buy acceptance, to buy time, to buy a version of love that did not have the courage to call itself love. I paid with self-erasure and called it maturity, because the alternative felt like risk.

I remember learning, in a very ordinary moment, that calm could purchase safety. Not a dramatic scene, not a life-altering speech—just a familiar room where tension had already settled into the air, voices moving too fast, and me noticing, almost automatically, that one honest sentence would make everything worse. So I edited myself in real time. I lowered my tone. I replaced emotion with logistics. I offered a solution instead of telling the truth about how I felt. The room softened. The temperature dropped. People relaxed, grateful for the stability they did not have to create themselves. Nobody said, "Thank you for paying for this." They simply moved on, relieved. And that relief became the reinforcement that shaped me.

If I stay composed, the room stays safe. If I stay useful, I stay included.

This is where the strong one starts losing track of themselves, because the reward is immediate and the cost is delayed. You are praised for your steadiness and penalized for your need. You are welcomed when you regulate the environment and quietly punished when you make the environment confront you. Over time, you learn that the fastest way to be loved is to be low-maintenance. You learn that the fastest way to be accepted is to become easy. And "easy" becomes your brand.

There is a moment that repeats in the life of the strong one, and it rarely looks dramatic from the outside. Someone shows up carrying more than they should be carrying. They do not ask if you have room; they assume you do. They begin speaking as if your capacity is a public utility—available on demand, always on, always steady. They are not necessarily cruel. Often, they are simply relieved to have found a place where their chaos will not be rejected.

And you do what you always do. You take it. You stabilize it. You translate it. You make it coherent. You give them back a cleaned-up version of their own life. You say the right thing at the right temperature, with the right level of restraint. You carry the weight in your chest so they can walk away lighter.

Then they look at you with admiration—sometimes even affection—and that is how the role locks in. Admiration is a dangerous substitute for care. It does not nourish you, but it makes you feel valuable enough to keep starving. It makes you feel chosen while you are being used. It turns your endurance into something people applaud instead of something people protect.

I have been that person in more than one chapter of my life. In personal relationships, I became the calm inside someone else's storm so consistently that people stopped recognizing my calm as effort. They treated it like my natural climate. And I reinforced the misunderstanding, because I liked what the identity did for me: it gave me status, it gave me control, it gave me a moral high ground. I became the person who "does not overreact," the person who "keeps things stable," the person who "understands." It is seductive because it makes you feel above the mess, as if you have transcended what breaks other people—when in reality you have simply learned to break in places nobody can see.

And there is a private loneliness that comes with that. Because when you are always the regulated one, people do not approach you with gentleness. They approach you with expectations. They do not ask what you are carrying; they add to it. They do not check whether you have space; they assume you do. They interpret your silence as capacity, and your capacity as permission.

In business, the transaction becomes even cleaner, almost brutal in its logic. The strong one becomes the one who absorbs panic so others can keep performing. I have sat in rooms where I could see people unraveling—voices tightening, faces hardening, decisions turning sloppy—and I watched myself step into the familiar costume. I made myself colder than I felt. I made myself clearer than I was. I chose language that would calm the room instead of language that would tell the full truth. The room left with confidence. I left with a quiet nausea I could not explain, because it was not about the meeting. It was about the pattern: once again, I purchased collective comfort with private cost.

And what does the strong one receive in return?

Not rest. Not tenderness. Not the kind of protection that would allow you to soften without consequences.

You get access. You get reliance. You get the privilege of being the person people call first when something breaks. You get praised for being "solid" as if solidity is an endless resource rather than a daily decision you are making against your own fatigue. You become the one who can hold the weight—and the more you prove it, the less anyone imagines you might need help holding your own.

That is the paradox: strength attracts dependency, and dependency quietly repels care.

Because once people label you "the strong one," they unconsciously reorganize around your endurance. Their urgency becomes your responsibility. Their emotional overflow becomes your "maturity." Their inability to self-regulate becomes your "gift." They do not think of it as exploitation because you do not present it as pain. You present it as competence.

Over time, you start participating in the misunderstanding in ways that are difficult to admit. You time your honesty. You delay your needs. You keep your requests small and polite so nobody feels burdened. You become skilled at asking for almost nothing. And then you feel offended when people give you exactly what you trained them to give you: almost nothing.

This is the part most strong people do not want to see: you teach people how to treat you by the price you pretend you are not paying. You teach them that you can handle more by handling more. You teach them that you do not need tenderness by never requesting it. You teach them that you are okay by being okay in public every time you are not okay in private.

And at some point, the currency you have been spending stops buying what you think it buys.

It buys stability, not intimacy. It buys approval, not being known. It buys admiration, not being held. It buys a smooth surface, not a safe depth. It buys a life that looks controlled while your interior becomes a storage unit of unprocessed emotion that nobody is allowed to enter—not even you, sometimes.

Here is where it gets personal in the way that exposes the whole economy: the strong one often mistakes endurance for love. You prove love by staying. You prove loyalty by absorbing. You prove devotion by regulating yourself, so the other person does not have to. You carry what they refuse to carry and call it partnership. It can look noble. It can even be beautiful. But without reciprocity, it becomes emotional bankruptcy disguised as virtue.

And then one day—quietly, not dramatically—you notice the imbalance. You notice that you are the person everyone turns to, but nobody is turning toward you. You notice that your competence has made you valuable, but not necessarily cared for. You notice that your steadiness has made you reliable, but not necessarily protected. You notice that people love the version of you that costs you the most.

At some point you have to tell the truth: you did not only become strong to survive. You stayed strong because the world rewarded you for it. The reward was never what you deserved, but it was enough to keep the pattern running— enough to keep you performing stability while something inside you kept waiting for the moment someone would notice you are a person, not a function.

This is where the chapter turns. Because the next question is not whether you are strong. You already proved that. The next question is what strength has been costing you—and how long you plan to keep paying a price nobody has agreed to reimburse.

The Invisible Drain

The cost of being the strong one rarely arrives as a catastrophe. It arrives as erosion.

That is why it is so easy to dismiss at first. You do not wake up one day and collapse in a dramatic scene that finally "proves" you have been carrying too much. You keep functioning. You keep delivering. You keep being the person people depend on. And because you are still standing, everyone—including you—assumes you are fine. But what is actually happening is quieter: the strong one starts losing life in small withdrawals that do not look like danger until the account is empty.

The drain begins with time, because time is the first resource you stop protecting. You become the person who is always available "just for a minute," and your life becomes a series of minutes that do not belong to you. You learn to answer things immediately because you do not want anyone to feel abandoned. You learn to respond fast because silence makes other people anxious, and you have trained yourself to treat other people's anxiety as your responsibility. Before you realize it, your day has been spent mostly in service of managing other people's emotional weather.

I have watched this happen in my own life in ways that were almost embarrassing in their simplicity. Not a dramatic sacrifice. Just patterns: answering calls I did not have the energy for, writing back when my body was telling me to stop, taking on "one more thing" because I was afraid of what would happen if I said, "I cannot." And then, at the end of the day, realizing I had not lived my day—I had administered it. I had been efficient, responsible, impressive. And still, something in me felt faint, like I was leaving myself behind in small installments.

The drain continues with intimacy, because intimacy requires presence, and presence requires that you are not performing stability. The strong one is always performing, even in love. You do not enter relationships as a raw human being; you enter as a regulated system. You become the person who can handle moods, handle stress, handle the difficult weeks. You become the one who knows what to say, who de-escalates, who carries the emotional load without making the other person feel guilty for dropping it on you. And over time, you confuse being useful with being loved.

This is the part people do not want to admit: sometimes your strength becomes your substitute for closeness. It is easier to be the dependable one than the vulnerable one. It is easier to be the one who fixes than the one who asks. It is easier to show loyalty through endurance than to show trust through exposure. But the bill comes anyway, because a relationship where you are consistently the container is not intimacy. It is a service.

There is a particular loneliness that appears when you are always the strong one. You can be surrounded by people and still feel emotionally undocumented. People know your competence. They know your reliability. They know your ability to hold. They do not know your private fear, your private fatigue, your private need to be held without having to deserve it first. And sometimes, even when someone tries to get close, you do not let them, not fully—not because you are cold, but because you are trained. You are trained to keep the machine running. You are trained to keep the image intact. You are trained to protect other people from your reality.

Then the drain moves into the body, because the body is the last place you can lie without consequences. Your mind can rationalize. Your voice can stay steady. Your calendar can look full and successful. But the body keeps score in a language you cannot negotiate with.

The strong one's body often becomes a storage unit for what the strong one refuses to feel on time. Tight shoulders that do not release. Sleep that does not restore. Appetite that becomes chaotic—sometimes absent, sometimes urgent, sometimes oddly disconnected from hunger. A nervous system that lives in mild emergency as if calm is not safe. You might not call it anxiety. You might call it "high standards," "drive," "ambition," "pressure." But your body does not care what you call it. Your body only knows whether you are safe.

I have had seasons where my body was screaming and I kept translating the scream into productivity. I would tell myself I was just tired, just busy, just under pressure. I would fix the schedule, fix the plan, fix the strategy, fix everyone else—while ignoring the obvious truth that the one thing I was not fixing was my relationship with myself. The strong one can spend years treating the body like a tool that should cooperate, instead of a living messenger that is trying to prevent a breakdown you are too proud to acknowledge.

The invisible drain is not only exhaustion. It is the slow disappearance of joy. Not because you become incapable of joy, but because joy requires unguarded presence, and you are rarely unguarded. The strong one can laugh and still feel numb. The strong one can win and still feel empty. The strong one can achieve things other people envy and still privately wonder why none of it lands.

And here is the most dangerous part: when you live in that state long enough, you start normalizing it. You begin to treat depletion as adulthood. You treat emotional hunger as weakness. You treat the inability to rest as "discipline." You start believing that life is supposed to feel like a constant low-grade burden, and anyone who looks relaxed is either irresponsible or lucky.

That belief is poison. Not because it is dramatic, but because it is convincing.

The strong one is often the person who does not allow themselves to receive. You can give, you can produce, you can carry, you can solve. Receiving feels foreign. Receiving feels suspicious. Receiving makes you feel exposed. So, you create a life where you are always the provider of stability, and then you feel resentful that nobody provides it back. But resentment is not the core emotion. The core emotion is grief—grief for how long you have been alone in the role.

This is the moment where the chapter has to tell the truth without softness: the invisible drain is not accidental. It is designed by the role. If you are always the strong one, your system does not get to rest, because resting would mean someone else has to feel what you have been absorbing. And you have been trained to prevent that.

So the cost keeps accumulating. Not as a single event, but as a slow, private taxation of your life.

You start losing spontaneity because spontaneity is not efficient. You start losing desire because desire requires ease. You start losing tenderness because tenderness requires that you stop defending yourself. You start losing your ability to be surprised by life because you are always anticipating what could go wrong.

And that is how the strong one becomes exhausted without permission to call it exhaustion.

Not because you are weak. Because you are human.

And a human being was never meant to function as infrastructure.

The "Contract" You Never Read

There comes a moment—usually after you have carried one thing too many—when the strong one finally understands what has been happening the whole time. Not as an insight that flatters you. As a realization that sobers you. You have not been living inside a relationship, a family, a team, a dynamic. You have been living inside an agreement you never negotiated.

A "contract" written in assumptions.
The "invisible contract."

It was never presented to you. Nobody slid it across a table. Nobody asked, "Are you comfortable with these terms?" It formed the way pressure forms—quietly, repeatedly, invisibly—until one day you realize you have been obeying something you never consented to in plain language.

It was drafted the first time someone leaned on you and you did not step back, because you knew—instinctively—that stepping back would come with consequences. It was reinforced every time you said, "It is fine," when it was not fine, not even close. It was renewed every time you swallowed the sentence that would have protected you, because you were trying to protect the room. And the room, of course, accepted your protection like people accept oxygen: without thinking, without gratitude, without a single moment of awareness that someone is paying for their comfort.

The worst part is not that others benefit from the contract. The worst part is that the contract begins to feel like your identity. You start confusing compliance with character. You start believing you are noble when you are simply trained. You start telling yourself you are "strong" when what you are doing is managing the fear of what might happen if you stop.

I remember the exact type of moment where this becomes obvious. It is never cinematic. It is always ordinary. A phone call that arrives too late. A message that begins with "I just need five minutes," as if five minutes are never five minutes. A conversation where someone unloads their chaos with the casual confidence of a person who has done this before and never been turned away. And you can feel yourself doing it—your body bracing, your mind switching into problem-solving mode, your voice taking on that controlled temperature that makes other people relax. You become the container again, even while a quieter part of you is watching and thinking, with a kind of exhausted disbelief: I did not agree to this tonight. I did not choose this right now. I am simply the default.

That is what the "invisible contract" does. It turns you into the default.

And when you are the default, people stop asking. They stop checking. They stop noticing the difference between your kindness and your depletion. They do not necessarily mean harm. They are simply relieved. They are relieved you exist. They are relieved you can hold. They are relieved you do not demand much. They are relieved you are not "complicated." And you have to be honest: you have encouraged that relief, because relief from others can feel like safety for you.

This is where the strong one usually tries to find a villain, because a villain would make it easier. If there is a villain, you are innocent. If there is a villain, you do not have to look at the part of the story that is hardest to admit: that the "contract" survived because you kept signing it with your behavior.

Yes, some people took advantage of your reliability. Yes, some people treated your capacity like it belonged to them. Yes, some people built their emotional life on the assumption that you would be there no matter what. But the contract did not become permanent because they were powerful. It became permanent because you were consistent. Because you showed up first. Because you answered fastest. Because you made it look effortless. Because you made your boundaries negotiable and then acted surprised when others negotiated them.

That is not an accusation. It is a key.

Because if the agreement was built through repetition, it can be broken through repetition. But the strong one must first admit what they were buying with that agreement. And the answer is never "nothing." The strong one always gets something. It just comes with interest.

You were buying belonging. You were buying a seat at the table. You were buying the right to stay without making anyone uncomfortable. You were buying the illusion that if you remained useful, you would remain safe. You were buying a version of love that did not require you to expose your need.

And maybe—this matters—maybe at some point in your life that was not weakness. Maybe it was intelligence. Maybe it was a brilliant strategy for surviving a room where honesty cost too much. Maybe you learned early that the people around you could handle your competence but not your vulnerability. Maybe you learned that calm made you acceptable, that being "easy" made you lovable, that being strong made you untouchable in the one way that felt like protection.

But then the world did what the world always does: it raised the price.

Because the moment people get used to you absorbing pain without complaint, they begin expecting you to absorb it without limit. The moment they get used to you being "understanding," they begin using understanding as a weapon: if you do not understand today, you are "changing." If you say no, you are "cold." If you ask for care, you are "too much." And because you are the strong one, you start fearing something that sounds irrational until you name it: that your humanity will be treated like betrayal.

That is the clause nobody says out loud. The clause you feel in your bones.

If you do not keep holding, you might not keep your place.

So you keep holding. You keep smoothing the edges. You keep taking responsibility for emotional climates you did not create. You keep translating other people's chaos into a language the room can tolerate. You keep performing strength and calling it loyalty, even when loyalty has quietly turned into self-abandonment.

And then one day, the strong one notices a pattern they can no longer unsee: the more you carry, the less you are held. The more you endure, the more invisible your pain becomes. The more reliable you are, the less anyone thinks to protect you. You get praised in public and depleted in private. You receive admiration instead of support. Respect instead of tenderness. Compliments instead of care.

And then comes the most humiliating part of all, the part that actually sets you free: you realize nobody is coming to rescue you from a role you keep performing.

Not because you do not deserve rescue. Because the role itself teaches people that you do not need it.

So the shift begins the only place it can begin: inside.

Not as a dramatic speech. Not as revenge. Not as a new personality. But as one internal decision so clean it feels almost cold and so honest it feels like oxygen:

I will not keep paying this price to keep my place.

That sentence is the doorway.

Not to a fight. To a return.

Because once you stop signing the "invisible contract," you do not become cruel. You become real. You stop being the infrastructure of everyone else's life and begin becoming a human being, again—one boundary at a time, one refusal at a time, one quiet act of self-respect that finally tells the truth.

The First Refusal

The strong one does not change with a speech. The strong one changes with a refusal. Not a loud refusal, not a public performance, not a moment designed to impress anyone. The first refusal is usually quiet and almost anticlimactic, which is exactly why it is real. It is the moment you stop paying. Not because you suddenly became angry, but because you finally understand that you have been financing other people's comfort with your own life.

Here is the slap: nobody has been coming to save you because you have been too good at surviving. Your competence has been interpreted as consent. Your silence has been interpreted as capacity. Your calm has been interpreted as unlimited. People may not have intended to exploit you, but they absolutely benefited from your self-erasure, and you participated in that economy because being necessary felt like a safer form of love than being fully seen.

That is what you have to grieve—not only what others took from you, but what you kept offering in exchange for belonging. Because the real trap of being the strong one is not the weight itself; it is the identity built around the weight. It is the private story that says: if you stop holding, you will stop being loved; if you need, you will be too much; if you collapse, you will be alone. The strong one lives under that story for so long that it starts feeling like reality. It is not reality. It is conditioning.

The moment you see that clearly, the entire internal economy shifts. Strength stops being performance and becomes ownership. You stop treating your nervous system like collateral. You stop confusing your capacity with your obligation. You understand, with a precision that feels almost brutal at first, that calm is not consent and endurance is not a life purpose. Capacity is simply capacity, and you are allowed to decide what it is for.

So, you do something that initially feels wrong, because it violates the role you have been trained to protect: you allow other people to experience the consequence of their own behavior without rushing in to rescue them from it. You stop managing the emotional temperature of the room. You stop translating chaos into something digestible. You stop offering clarity as anesthesia so nobody has to feel discomfort. You remain present without performing stability, and you let your humanity be visible in real time. Then you say the sentence that changes your life, not as a dramatic declaration, but as a clean boundary that does not negotiate with panic: "I cannot do that." Sometimes it is softer, "Not today." Sometimes it is exact, "That is not mine to carry." And when you are ready to end the pattern instead of managing it, you say it in the only language the "invisible contract" understands: "I am not available for that dynamic anymore."

Something will happen immediately. The system will test you. People who relied on your yes will treat your no as selfishness. People who were comfortable with your self-erasure will suddenly feel "abandoned." They will say you are changing as if changing is betrayal. They will call you cold because they have been using your warmth like a utility. Some will react with guilt, confusion, anger, or that subtle weaponized disappointment that is designed to pull you back into the role.

This is where most strong people fail and return to the old self, not because they lack courage, but because they are trained to reduce discomfort at any cost, including the cost of themselves. Do not miss the lesson here: the discomfort you create by refusing is not harm. It is truth entering the room.

It is reality returning to a space that was being artificially stabilized by your over-functioning.

And here is the release, the part that gives you leverage instead of rage: the reactions you receive become data. A healthy bond makes room for your boundary. An unhealthy bond demands you remove it. A person who loves you will adjust; a person who uses you will punish. Your first refusal becomes a filter, quiet and ruthless, separating what is real from what was convenient.

Then something even more important begins to happen. You start recovering your life in small, unglamorous ways that nobody applauds, but your body recognizes immediately. You stop answering everything instantly. You stop being emotionally available on demand. You stop sacrificing sleep, appetite, and peace just to maintain your reputation. You begin protecting your nervous system the way you would protect something you cannot replace, because you cannot replace it. You learn to let rest exist in your identity without apology, and you learn to let other people manage their own emotional weather without making it your job to rescue them from it.

This is the new strength, and it is not the kind that impresses anyone from the outside. It is the strength to disappoint people who were never going to protect you. It is the strength to be misunderstood while you rebuild your boundaries. It is the strength to lose access in exchange for peace. It is the strength to stop performing stability and start living honestly.

And at some point, almost quietly, the definition of "strong" changes inside you. You stop feeling proud of how much you can tolerate. You start feeling proud of how clearly you can choose. You no longer need to be the strongest person in the room; you need to be the most loyal person in your own life. Because the quiet cost of being the strong one was never only exhaustion. It was self-abandonment disguised as character.

That is the slap. Now comes the liberation. You were never meant to be the infrastructure. You were meant to be a person. And the moment you stop paying for love with your life, the illusion collapses: the thing you keep asking other people for is the very thing you refuse to give yourself. You cannot outsource self-respect. You cannot bargain for peace through someone else's approval. You cannot demand tenderness while denying it to your own nervous system. This is where the pattern ends. This is where you stop negotiating your worth. This is where you come back to yourself—quietly, decisively, without permission.

This is where you **Become First**.

CHAPTER 9

STOP ASKING FOR WHAT YOU REFUSE TO GIVE YOURSELF

The Ask That Sounds Like Longing

It almost always starts the same way: a complaint that sounds reasonable, even tender, because it is wrapped in pain. "Why do they not show up?" "Why do they not love me the way I love them?" "Why can they not just meet me where I am?" On the surface, it looks like longing. Underneath, it is something sharper and far more personal: a demand for an experience you have not made real in your own behavior.

Most people do not like that sentence. They want the problem to stay outside of them, because outside feels cleaner. Outside has villains. Outside has excuses. Outside has timing. Inside has responsibility, and responsibility has no dramatic soundtrack. Inside is simply the mirror.

The truth is not that you should stop wanting love. The truth is that the way you ask often betrays what you claim you want. You say you want tenderness, but your tone arrives like pressure. You say you want reassurance, but your energy communicates investigation. You say you want to be chosen, but your nervous system shows up like a courtroom where the other person is already guilty. Then you call the other person "cold" when they flinch. You call them "avoidant" when they protect themselves from the way you are coming at them. You call it "not being loved," while quietly refusing to admit the possibility that your ask has become a weapon you swing without noticing the blade.

And it is not because you are bad. It is because you are trained. Trained by disappointment. Trained by silence. Trained by environments where love felt conditional, and the only way to keep your place was to become intense, vigilant, precise. You learned to read micro-signals. You learned to detect shifts. You learned that waiting too long to speak could cost you. So your ask became urgent. It became loaded. It became a test. It stopped being "Can you love me?" and started being "Prove that you love me right now, so my nervous system can calm down."

That is not love. That is bargaining.

This is where the title becomes unforgiving: you keep asking for what you refuse to give yourself. Not as an abstract concept, but as a real-time behavior. You ask for calm while you keep flooding your own system with pressure. You ask for patience while you treat your own needs like an inconvenience. You ask for clarity while you keep refusing to say the clean truth out loud because you want the other person to guess it and deliver it perfectly. You are not only asking for love; you are asking for relief from your own refusal to grant yourself the thing you crave most: internal permission to be safe without external proof.

But there is an even harder layer—one you named, and it belongs in the bone of this chapter. Sometimes you are not only refusing it for yourself. Sometimes you are refusing it for them.

That is the part that makes a reader sit up, because it feels insulting until it feels accurate.

A person says, "I need space," and you hear, "I do not care." They ask for a pause, and you interpret it as abandonment. They need an hour to breathe, and you turn it into a moral failure. So you press. You follow. You explain. You demand a resolution on your schedule. You call it closeness, but it is control wearing the costume of love. Then you look them in the eyes and say, "You do not love me," while violating the very thing love requires in that moment: respect.

And you may still be right about your pain. You may still be right that something is missing. But if you want to understand why the pattern keeps repeating, the mirror has to be honest. Are you asking for love, or are you asking for compliance? Are you asking to be understood, or are you demanding a performance that proves you are safe? Are you asking for connection, or are you using connection language to justify pressure?

I have watched this dynamic in myself in moments that were not dramatic enough to deserve their own story, which is exactly why they matter. The scenes were ordinary: a late message that triggered a familiar tightness; a delay that felt like disrespect; an unanswered call that felt like being dropped. And the old reflex rose immediately—my mind building a case, my body bracing for impact, my mouth preparing to demand what I believed I deserved. In that moment, I could have stayed with the raw truth—"I feel scared, and I need reassurance"—but the reflex was faster. I went for precision. I went for control. I went for the tone that sounds strong but is actually afraid. And I remember noticing, even while I was speaking, how the room changed. Not because the other person was evil, but because my ask did not feel like love. It felt like pressure disguised as love. It felt like a contract being enforced.

That is what happens when your nervous system turns the relationship into a courtroom. You stop asking and start prosecuting. You may be right about the facts, but you poison the atmosphere that would have made repair possible. Then you feel even more alone, because now you have added a second wound on top of the first: the wound of realizing you became the very energy you said you could not tolerate.

This is where perfection enters the room, because perfection is the favorite hiding place of unhealed fear. You demand the perfect response, the perfect timing, the perfect tone, the perfect words that will finally make you feel secure. And when you do not get perfection, you punish—sometimes loudly, sometimes subtly, sometimes through coldness, sometimes through relentless "talking it out" that is not talking at all, but pressure. Then you tell yourself you are only asking for basic decency. But the mirror asks a better question: when you demand perfection, do you give it in return? Not your standards. Your behavior. Your tone. Your patience. Your ability to respect space. Your willingness to love in a way that does not require the other person to prove their worth every time your fear gets activated.

Because this is the contradiction most people refuse to see: they want unconditional love, but they communicate with conditions. They want safety, but they create threat. They want softness, but they bring sharpness. They want someone to "hold them," but they do not know how to be held without turning it into a test.

The real tragedy is that they call this "high standards." It is not standards. It is anxiety trying to be in charge.

And anxiety is never satisfied. Anxiety always finds another clause. Another detail. Another thing that "should have been done." Another reason to stay on edge. If you build your relationships around anxiety, you do not get closeness; you get management. You do not get intimacy; you get constant auditing. You do not get love; you get a performance review that never ends.

There is a reason Become First matters here, and it has nothing to do with motivational language. It is a behavioral pivot. If you want love, you embody love first. Not as sweetness. As discipline. As a decision to bring the tone you want to receive. As a refusal to escalate into cruelty just because you are hurt. As a willingness to respect space without interpreting it as rejection. As the strength to stay kind without becoming weak, and the strength to set a boundary without becoming violent.

This is where you said something essential: even the hardest person bends to a good manner, to a loving way of speaking, to a clean tone that does not beg and does not attack. That is true, and it is also dangerous if misunderstood. It does not mean you tolerate harm. It does not mean you stay where you are being "hit," emotionally or otherwise, hoping your kindness will convert cruelty. Become First is not martyrdom. Become First is leadership of your own energy. It is the refusal to become the ugliness you are trying to escape. It is the ability to hold your ground while keeping your soul intact.

Most people underestimate what a loving tone can do when it is paired with boundaries. The world expects you to either collapse or attack. It expects you to either beg or punish. A calm, firm, loving stance is disruptive because it removes the usual game. It removes the drama that people are addicted to. It removes the leverage of chaos. It makes the truth unavoidable.

And that is why this chapter begins here: not with what you want from them, but with what you are practicing through your ask. Because your ask is not only a request; it is a demonstration. It teaches the other person how to treat you. It reveals what you believe you deserve. It exposes whether you are looking for love or looking for control. And if you want your life to change, you cannot keep demanding outcomes while refusing to examine the method.

The pattern does not break when they finally become perfect. The pattern breaks when you stop making your peace dependent on their perfection. The pattern breaks when you stop confusing pressure with love. The pattern breaks when you stop asking for what you refuse to practice—toward yourself and toward the person in front of you.

That is the first cut. Not gentle. Necessary.

And it sets up the next part, where the mirror gets even more specific: the difference between thinking you show love and proving it through behavior, especially in the moment you would rather be right than be real. Because that moment is where everything is decided. That moment is where you either repeat the contract, or you Become First.

The Difference Between Saying it and Being it

Most people think they are clear because they speak. They are not clear. They are loud.

They think love is proven by what they feel, by what they intended, by how intensely they wanted it to land. But relationships do not live inside intention. They live inside impact. They live inside the temperature you bring into the room, the timing you choose, the way your tone tightens when you do not get what you want, the way your kindness disappears the moment your fear gets activated. That is why so many people stay confused: they are convinced they are "showing love," while the other person is experiencing control, pressure, or punishment wearing the costume of connection.

This is the line most people refuse to cross because it threatens their self-image: you do not get credit for love you did not deliver. You do not get credit for respect you did not practice. You do not get credit for patience you only have when everything is going your way. You do not get credit for being "a good person" when your behavior, in the moment that matters, becomes sharp enough to make the other person shrink.

And yes, that moment exists for all of us. The moment when you want reassurance but you reach for interrogation. The moment when you want closeness but you reach for pressure. The moment when you want peace but you reach for being right. That moment is where your real pattern shows itself, because that moment strips the performance. It reveals what you become when your nervous system stops asking politely.

People say, "I do not feel loved," and the sentence sounds pure. But sometimes that sentence hides a private demand: "Love me in the exact shape that calms my fear, right now, with no delay, with no human complexity, with no needs of your own." That is not love. That is an order. And when the other person cannot obey—because they are human, because they are tired, because they need space, because they are not built to perform on command—your tone changes. Your attention becomes conditional. Your kindness becomes a bargaining chip. You call it honesty. It is leverage.

This is why words do not mean what people want them to mean. Words are cheap, because words can be said while your actions betray them. Anyone can say, "I love you," and then punish you for needing an hour alone. Anyone can say, "I respect you," and then violate your boundaries the moment they feel insecure. Anyone can say, "I want peace," and then choose escalation as their default language. Words are currency in a room full of fear. Behavior is the only proof that survives stress.

There is a specific trap here that destroys relationships while everyone stays convinced they are trying: people measure their love by how much they would do, while the other person measures love by what is actually being done. They measure their loyalty by how intensely they feel, while the other person measures loyalty by what happens when it is inconvenient. They measure their respect by their values, while the other person measures respect by the tone, the timing, the boundaries, the space. This is how two people can talk for hours and still feel unheard. They are not discussing love. They are discussing definitions.

But the deeper problem is not definition. The deeper problem is discipline.

Because the truth is brutal and simple: love without discipline becomes entitlement. It becomes "I am allowed to do anything because I feel a lot." It becomes "my pain justifies my tone." It becomes "if you loved me, you would tolerate the way I speak to you." And that is where people cross a line without noticing. They start using the language of love to justify behavior that violates love. They start demanding tenderness while they deliver harshness. They start asking to be understood while they refuse to understand. They start asking for space to be respected while they treat the other person's space like a personal attack.

I have had to confront this in myself in moments I did not want to admit existed. Moments where my mind was convinced I was pursuing "truth," but my body was pursuing control. Moments where I believed I was fighting for the relationship, but what I was actually fighting for was certainty—certainty that I would not be left, certainty that I mattered, certainty that I was safe. And certainty is a drug. It makes you do things you later call "out of character," when, in reality, they were simply out of your performance. They were you, without the costume.

One of the most revealing experiences is how the body knows before the mind admits. You feel it in the jaw, in the chest, in the speed of your words. You feel the moment your tone becomes a tool. You may still say "I love you" in the sentence, but the energy underneath says, "Do not fail me." You may say, "I just want to talk," but the room hears, "I will not let you leave until I feel calm." That is not conversation. That is containment. That is you making the other person responsible for regulating you.

And then you wonder why they withdraw. Of course they do.

This is where Become First stops being philosophy and becomes personal accountability. You do not get to demand the outcome while refusing to clean up the method. You do not get to ask for a loving relationship while communicating like a threat. You do not get to require softness while arriving with a blade hidden inside your words. The tone is not decoration. The tone is the message. The tone tells the truth long before content does.

So, the question is not "Do you love them?" The question is: do they feel loved when you are activated? Do they feel safe when you are disappointed? Do they feel respected when they say no? Do they feel free to be human, or do they feel audited? Do they feel allowed to have a nervous system, or do they feel like they have to manage yours?

Because if you want perfection from another person, you do not get to deliver emotional chaos and call it authenticity. If you want a partner who speaks gently, you do not get to speak like a prosecutor and call it passion. If you want someone who holds space for you, you do not get to invade their space and call it closeness. That is the mirror. It is not polite. It is honest.

And it is also hopeful, because it gives you a lever.

There is a kind of power that does not come from controlling the other person. It comes from controlling what you bring. It comes from refusing to weaponize your pain. It comes from refusing to make your love conditional on your fear being soothed instantly. It comes from practicing the standard you demand.

That is Become First. Not first as in "superior." First as in "I set the tone."

If you want respect, you become first in respect. Not in theory—in behavior. You respect their space even when your anxiety hates it. You respect their timing even when you want immediate relief. You respect their boundaries even when you feel rejected. You respect their humanity even when it inconveniences your desire for certainty. That is what love looks like in real time: not a feeling, but a discipline that refuses to turn fear into force.

If you want tenderness, you become first in tenderness. You speak with love even when you are hurt. Not as performance. As choice. You do not soften your truth; you soften your delivery so the truth can be received. You do not hide your boundary; you remove the poison from your language so the boundary can stand without becoming war. You learn to say hard things without making the person bleed for triggering you. That is a level of strength most people never develop because it requires mastery, not reaction.

Now, the critical line you said needs to live here in a way that does not get misused: a good manner bends even the hardest person. That is true—when good manner is paired with boundaries. When kindness is not begging. When love is not self-erasure. When your tone is clean and your line is firm. Hard people do not bend to pleading. They bend to clarity that stays calm. They bend when the usual game is removed—no drama to feed on, no chaos to leverage, no emotional violence to hide behind. They bend when you refuse to become what they are used to handling.

That is why this part matters. Because it shows the reader the difference between being "nice" and being powerful. Nice is often fear. Powerful is calm. Powerful is a loving tone that does not negotiate with disrespect. Powerful is a boundary delivered without contempt. Powerful is refusing to escalate even when you could destroy the room with your words, because you have done it before and you know what it costs.

And this is where the chapter starts building momentum into the next cut: you cannot keep asking for love while refusing to practice it under stress. You cannot keep asking for "the right person" while showing up as the wrong version of yourself when you are triggered. You cannot keep demanding a perfect response while delivering imperfect behavior and calling it justified. Your life changes when your behavior becomes consistent with your demands.

That is the point of this part. The reader is not meant to feel scolded. They are meant to feel exposed—and then empowered. Because once you admit, "I have been asking for things I do not consistently practice," you stop being at the mercy of another person's evolution. You reclaim the one thing that actually transforms relationships: the standard you enforce through who you are, not through what you demand.

That is Become First in its most honest form: you become the proof of what you want to receive, and you stop calling your fear "love" just because it speaks loudly.

The Disappearing Act

You do not wake up one morning and decide to become small. You practice it—quietly, daily, almost politely—until one day you look up and realize you have been living inside a version of your life where everyone else is fully present, and you have been surviving like a supporting character in your own.

It begins as generosity. It always begins as something that flatters you. You are the one who understands, the one who adapts, the one who gives the benefit of the doubt, the one who can handle it. You make space for people who are overwhelmed, inconsistent, unfinished. You tell yourself you are doing it because you love them, because you are mature, because you are evolved. For a while, it even looks noble. It looks like strength.

Then the cost reveals itself—not through a dramatic betrayal, but through a slow erosion that is almost easy to deny. Your needs become negotiable. Your time becomes flexible. Your boundaries become soft. Your exhaustion becomes private. Your pain becomes disciplined. You do not announce the price, so nobody sees it. You keep functioning, so nobody asks. And because you keep functioning, you start getting treated like something that does not break.

That is how you become infrastructure.

The moment you become infrastructure, people stop relating to you as a person and start relating to you as a resource. This does not always happen because they are cruel; it happens because systems adapt to what is consistently available. If you always absorb the emotional weight, the room learns to stay light. If you always self-correct, the room learns it never has to correct itself. If you always soften your truth for everyone else's comfort, the room learns comfort matters more than your reality. You trained the dynamic, and the dynamic trained you back.

And the loneliness that follows has nothing to do with being alone. It is the loneliness of being useful instead of being held, admired instead of protected, relied on instead of loved. It is the loneliness of realizing that people know what you do for them but do not know what you need, not because they are blind, but because you have made the needing part of you invisible. Love cannot hold what you refuse to occupy. Love cannot care for a person who keeps showing up as a service.

The most dangerous part of shrinking is that it does not feel like shrinking when you are used to it. It feels like being reasonable. It feels like not making a big deal. It feels like choosing peace. It feels like being the bigger person. It feels like strategic patience. And because it is wrapped in virtue, it survives scrutiny. You do not call it self-erasure; you call it kindness. You do not call it fear; you call it loyalty. You do not call it avoidance; you call it emotional intelligence. But the body does not care what you call it. The body keeps records.

It records every time you say yes while something in you says no. Every time you ignore fatigue because someone else is going through a lot. Every time you swallow the sentence that would have protected you because you do not want to disturb the room. Every time you respect everyone else's limits while treating your own as an inconvenience. You can get away with that behavior for a while, because it pays you in short-term stability, but stability purchased through self-erasure is never stable. It is debt. It accumulates quietly, then it shows up as bitterness, irritation, numbness, and the strange sensation of being tired in a way that sleep cannot fix.

Most people misread that moment. They assume the problem is the other person's lack of appreciation, as if appreciation is the missing ingredient. Appreciation is not the issue. Placement is. When you repeatedly place yourself second, you normalize being second. When you repeatedly volunteer to adjust, you teach everyone else that adjustment is your job. When you repeatedly excuse people out of accountability, you train them to stay the way they are. And when you repeatedly swallow your truth to keep the atmosphere calm, you teach the atmosphere that calm matters more than you do. Eventually you start asking for respect and feel offended when it does not arrive, you start asking for tenderness and receive convenience instead, you start asking to be prioritized and get treated like an option, and the offense feels pure because the exhaustion is real. But the deeper truth is structural: an option is exactly what you practiced being.

I have lived this in scenes that were not dramatic enough to look like a crisis and were, therefore, easy to dismiss as "just life," which is precisely why they mattered. A day where I was depleted and still answered because answering felt like proof of my value. A moment where I needed space and still stayed available because availability felt safer than absence. A conversation where my truth sat on the edge of my tongue and I swallowed it because I did not want to be too much. I would walk away from those moments and tell myself I was being smart, kind, mature, and then later—in silence—I would feel the cost with a clarity that was almost physical: I had once again made my life smaller to keep the room stable, and I had called it love.

Shrinking becomes addictive because it reduces immediate risk. It reduces the chance of conflict, the chance of rejection, the chance of being misunderstood. It creates temporary safety by limiting your exposure. But that safety is not safety; it is invisibility. Invisibility has a long-term price that almost always shows up the same way: you begin living inside relationships where your presence is optional because you trained everyone, including yourself, that your presence does not require protection. You begin living inside a life where your needs are afterthoughts because you trained the room that you will handle it. You begin living in a world where your boundaries are suggestions because you trained the room that you will fold.

Then you feel unseen and you misdiagnose the problem as volume, as if intensity could produce intimacy; you assume the answer is to demand more, explain more, chase clarity harder, press for reassurance faster—when the real issue is not how loudly you ask, but how consistently you vanish. The repair is not escalation; it is occupancy. It is the decision to stop participating in any dynamic that requires your self-erasure to function, to stop treating your needs as negotiable, to stop presenting your boundaries as requests, and to remain fully present—calm, exact, and unmovable—in the space you kept abandoning.

Something always happens the moment you do that. The system reacts.

People who benefited from your disappearance will experience your presence as too much. They will call your limits selfish. They will treat your self-respect like a personality change. They will say you are different, as if different is a moral failure instead of a correction. They will try to pull you back—sometimes with guilt, sometimes with praise, sometimes with confusion, sometimes with anger—because the dynamic was stable as long as you stayed small. And you will feel the old temptation to shrink again just to restore comfort. That temptation is not weakness; it is conditioning. It is your nervous system reaching for the familiar, because the unfamiliar feels like exposure.

But comfort was never the goal. Comfort was the trap.

If your presence destabilizes a relationship, it means the relationship was stabilized by your absence. If your boundary creates conflict, it means the peace was purchased through your self-erasure. If your honesty makes someone angry, it does not automatically mean you were wrong; sometimes it means you stopped being manageable, stopped being convenient, stopped being infrastructure. Some people will adjust. Some people will punish you for changing the terms of access. Some people will disappear. None of that is tragedy. It is information. It tells you what the connection was built on.

This is where the shift becomes profound, not because you become louder, but because you become consistent. You stop abandoning your own signals.

You stop overriding fatigue as if your body is an employee. You stop volunteering your time, attention, and nervous system as collateral to keep the room calm. You stop making love into a performance where your value is measured by how little you need. You stop confusing being low-maintenance with being loved. You stop calling self-neglect "strength" simply because it looks admirable from the outside.

In this part of the book, Become First is not a phrase you say. It is a behavior you practice. It means you become first in the way you place yourself in the room, first in the way you protect your own humanity, first in the way you stop apologizing for having needs at all. It means your presence stops being a negotiation. Your boundaries stop being a request. Your truth stops being delayed until it turns into resentment. You do not become cruel. You do not become cold. You do not become a new personality. You become a whole person again.

And that wholeness changes what is possible.

The Standard That Changes the Room

There is a moment when you realize that asking is not the problem. The problem is that you have been asking from a posture that teaches people your needs are optional. You have been asking with softness that looks like permission to ignore you, with explanations that sound like negotiations, with a tone that tries to stay lovable even while you are being erased. Then you wonder why the world keeps treating your boundaries like suggestions. It is not because people are evil. It is because you have been training them— patiently, consistently—to believe you will fold.

The shift is not dramatic. It is clean.

It starts when you stop presenting your needs as a debate and start presenting them as reality. Not as a threat, not as a performance, not as a speech you rehearse to make sure nobody gets uncomfortable. Reality—the kind that does not apologize for existing, the kind that does not chase approval, the kind that does not add five paragraphs of justification as if your limits require a jury. The first time you do it, it will feel rude. It is not rude. It is unfamiliar. You have confused clarity with cruelty because you have been living in a system where everything had to be softened to be tolerated.

The most difficult part is not saying it. The most difficult part is not taking it back after you say it. Because the old you does something automatic the moment a boundary is met with resistance: you start managing. You start translating. You start smoothing the edges. You start re-explaining your limit in twelve different ways, hoping to find the one version that will make the other person comfortable enough to accept it. You start offering compromises you did not want, deadlines you cannot keep, emotional labor you do not have. And if the other person stays unhappy, you interpret their unhappiness as proof you did something wrong, instead of understanding the deeper truth: some people only feel safe when you are available to be used.

This is where the standard changes the room. Not because you become louder, but because you become consistent. The standard is what you practice without theatrics, what you enforce without punishment, what you hold even when it costs you approval. It is the moment your nervous system stops treating other people's disappointment as an emergency.

Here is what it looks like in real life.

It is late. The day has already eaten you alive—meetings, decisions, problems that did not ask permission before becoming yours. Your phone keeps lighting up with the same pattern: someone wants something now, someone needs you to "just take a quick look," someone is anxious and wants you to fix their anxiety by becoming available. You know that feeling: the pressure behind the ribs, the reflex to respond so fast you do not even feel your own exhaustion until it is too late. In the past, you would answer immediately because you believed your responsiveness was your value. You would tell yourself you are just being responsible, but the truth is you were proving you were indispensable, because being indispensable felt like a guarantee you would not be abandoned.

Then one night you do something new. You look at the message. You feel the adrenaline rise. You watch the impulse. And you choose a different behavior—not by disappearing, not by ghosting, not by punishing. By being clean. You respond once, without drama: you are not available right now; you will review it tomorrow; if it is urgent it goes through the proper channel; if it cannot wait then it is not a "quick look," it is a real request and it belongs in a real time slot. You do not over-explain. You do not apologize for being a human being with a body. You do not add a smiley face to soften your dignity. You send the sentence and you do not chase their reaction.

And the room changes, even if the room is just a screen.

Because for the first time, you are not donating your nervous system to somebody else's urgency.

Or it is closer to home. It is not business. It is intimacy, and that is where the standard matters most, because intimacy is where people attempt to negotiate access through emotion. A person you love wants reassurance in a way that quietly becomes a demand: they want the conversation now, the resolution now, the proof now, the perfect words that will calm the part of them that is scared. And you can feel the trap: you want to love them, and you also know your body is depleted. You know that if you enter this conversation right now, you will not be kind. You will be sharp, impatient, corrective. You will turn love into damage control.

In the past, you would still do it. You would sit there exhausted and force presence like a performance. You would say yes while resenting the yes. You would talk until you sounded calm while your chest was tightening, and then later you would wonder why you feel drained even by love.

Now you do something else. You do not abandon them. You do not use silence as a weapon. You do not withdraw to punish. You stay human and you stay clear. You say: I love you, and I am not available for this conversation in this state; if we talk now, I will harm the connection; I want us to do it right, and "right" requires timing. You give a time. You hold it. You do not perform guilt to soothe their discomfort. You do not offer your exhaustion as proof of devotion. And you learn something startling: the connection survives. In fact, it gets cleaner. Because love stops being measured by how much you sacrifice and starts being measured by how honest you are about what you can actually give.

That is the standard.

Or it is family—one of those conversations where the past shows up wearing the face of the present. A relative calls with a familiar tone: disappointment disguised as concern, guilt disguised as love, the old message that says, if you were a good person you would do what I want. You have lived under that tone before. You know how quickly it can shrink you, how quickly it can make you want to prove you are not selfish, how quickly it can make you hand your life over in pieces just to stop the emotional pressure.

In the past, you would negotiate. You would explain. You would defend your choices as if you needed permission to have them. You would try to win understanding, and when you did not get it, you would pay anyway. You would say yes because saying no would cost too much emotionally.

Now the standard changes. Now you do not defend your life like a criminal. You do not make your adulthood a debate. You speak plainly: you understand their feelings; your decision stands; you will not be participating in guilt as a communication method; you will not be discussing it further if the tone stays manipulative. You do not raise your voice. You do not become cruel. You do not attack. You simply remove your nervous system from the old script. That is what growth looks like when it is real: not a speech, but a boundary that does not require rage to be firm.

And here is what shocks people: the hardest ones bend to clean calm more than they bend to pleading, because pleading invites the game, and clean calm ends it. When you stop negotiating your dignity, you remove the leverage. When you stop reacting, you remove the fuel. When you stay kind without becoming available for disrespect, you become impossible to control through chaos. That is why this is not about being "nice." It is about being precise.

The reader needs to feel the mechanism: your tone is a standard, your timing is a standard, your follow-through is a standard. Your consistency is the line that changes everything.

Because what most people call "boundaries" are actually emotional speeches that end in collapse. They announce a limit and then they immediately start negotiating it. They say, "I cannot," and then they give ten reasons why they can. They say, "I need space," and then they keep texting because they are afraid space will look like rejection. They say, "Do not speak to me that way," and then they stay in the conversation long enough to be spoken to that way again, because they do not want to seem difficult.

A standard is different. A standard is quiet. A standard does not beg. A standard does not perform. A standard does not punish. A standard simply holds.

And holding is where most people fail because holding forces you to tolerate discomfort—the discomfort of someone being upset, the discomfort of not being liked in the moment, the discomfort of not fixing the mood. If you have been the one who always fixes the mood, holding will feel like danger at first. Your body will interpret it as risk. You will want to chase. You will want to smooth. You will want to undo your own limit just to restore emotional peace.

That impulse is the addiction. That impulse is the old training. The standard is you not obeying it.

This is also where people confuse "love" with availability. They think being loving means being accessible at all times, which means love becomes a subscription other people can use. But love is not access. Love is not 24/7 service. Love is not you being the emotional emergency room for everyone else. Love is not you donating your nervous system until you become numb. Love is care with structure. Love is presence with limits. Love is truth without violence.

So when you set a standard, you are not becoming cold; you are becoming real. You stop pretending you can give what you cannot give. You stop offering what you will later resent. You stop saying yes as a way to stay safe. You stop shrinking so other people can keep their comfort. You stop waiting for someone else to behave differently before you allow yourself to live differently.

And this is where the title becomes operational. You become first in your own placement. First in your own self-respect. First in the way you protect the part of you that kept disappearing. You stop asking for a kind of love you are not practicing toward yourself in real time, and you stop giving a kind of love that quietly teaches people they can place you last.

That is the standard that changes the room: not a demand for people to treat you better, but a decision to stop participating in dynamics that require you to betray yourself in order to belong. When you do that, the room either rises or it reveals itself. Either way, you win. Because you stop paying for love with your life.

The Quiet Power of Consistency

At some point, the pattern stops feeling like bad luck and starts feeling like your own handwriting. Different rooms, same dynamic: you ask, you explain, you over-give, you over-stretch, you keep the machine running, and then you stand there with the same quiet depletion—unseen, under-filled, oddly exhausted by a life you have built to look "fine." The discomfort is not only that others have failed you; it is that you keep asking for a version of support, respect, steadiness, and care that you do not consistently practice toward yourself in real time. You want the outside world to handle you with intention, while you handle yourself like an afterthought. You want people to honor your limits, while you keep presenting your limits as negotiable. You want to be prioritized, while you keep placing yourself last and then calling it maturity.

That is the turning point—not a harsh one, but a precise one. Because once the pattern becomes visible, it becomes impossible to unsee. You notice the moments that used to look innocent: the way you volunteer before anyone asks, the way you anticipate problems that are not yours, the way you correct the room before the room even knows it is wrong. You notice how often you translate for people who could learn to speak clearly, how often you absorb tension so nobody else has to feel it, how often you take responsibility for outcomes you do not control. You tell yourself you are being capable. And you are. But capability becomes a trap when it turns into a lifestyle where everyone else gets the benefit of your discipline and you get the bill.

Most people want relief without restructuring. They want the world to become softer, while they keep running the same internal program: prove your value by being useful, stay safe by being easy, stay lovable by not needing, stay in control by staying ahead. That program produces results on paper: accomplishments, reputation, reliability, "the one who always comes through." But it also produces a private cost: the slow erosion of self-care, the quiet disappearance of boundaries, the persistent sensation that life is happening around you and you are only allowed to enter it after you have earned it.

This is where the correction must be more than emotional. It has to be behavioral. A real shift does not begin with a speech; it begins with a new standard you are willing to enforce through your actions, especially in small moments. Small moments are where your life is built. Small moments are where people see what you tolerate. Small moments are where your body learns whether it is safe to rest. Small moments are where you either keep living like you are disposable, or you finally act like you are not.

This is the part that frees you: you stop confusing care with over-functioning. You stop confusing being valuable with being available. You stop confusing stability with self-erasure. You stop trying to regulate everyone else's discomfort so you can earn peace. You let people carry their own urgency. You let them feel disappointed without treating it as a crisis. You let them be adult enough to handle a no. You learn that you can be kind without being endlessly accessible, and you can be clear without being cold. You learn that the room does not need you as an emotional employee. It needs you as a person.

The paradox is that the more you respect yourself, the less you need to chase respect from others. The more you honor your limits, the less you need to beg people to honor them. The more you stop betraying yourself in real time, the less you depend on someone else's behavior to feel stable. This is not pride. It is alignment. It is the end of a negotiation you never agreed to: the negotiation where you pay for belonging by making yourself smaller.

This change will not always be applauded. Some people will adjust. Some people will test you. Some people will act confused, not because your boundary is unclear, but because your old pattern made them comfortable. That is not a reason to retreat. That is the moment your new standard proves it is real. If your presence destabilizes certain dynamics, it means those dynamics were stabilized by your absence. That information is not tragic. It is clarifying. It tells you what has been holding the relationship together, and it tells you what will be required for it to become healthier.

The most important part is this: you do not need anyone's permission to stop placing yourself last.

You do not need a dramatic exit. You do not need to burn bridges. You do not need to announce a new identity. You need one clean decision repeated over time: you will no longer ask the world to give you what you refuse to consistently give yourself—basic care, basic respect, basic protection, basic humanity. The world may still fail you sometimes. But you will stop joining the failure.

I learned this in a way that did not come through a grand lesson. It came through a small, almost embarrassing symbol that turned into a mirror I could not argue with.

I had been running on a level that looks impressive from the outside and feels unsustainable from the inside. A major event. A serious operation. A schedule that had no mercy. Travel, coordination, timing, pressure—ten exhausting days where every moving piece had to land perfectly, where every detail carried weight, where every decision had consequences. I was doing what I always do when the stakes are high: I became immaculate. Everything organized down to the most demanding detail, the kind of precision people praise as "talent" when it is really discipline under stress. Even when it was over, I was still in motion—preparing personal gifts for my collaborators, making sure everyone felt seen, making sure the machine ended gracefully, making sure the room stayed held.

And while I was doing all of that, I was talking—releasing the inner bitterness that accumulates when you carry too much: the difficulty, the demands, the communication gaps, the pressure, the expectation that you will perform without needing anything back. I was not being dramatic. I was just telling the truth in the way people do when they finally get a quiet minute to breathe.

My partner listened without interrupting, without trying to fix me, without turning my exhaustion into a debate. Then, in the middle of my sentence, he stood up. He did not announce where he was going. He did not make a point. He simply walked into the bathroom, opened the drawer, and came back holding my toothbrush.

He put it in my hand like evidence.

And he said, calmly, almost gently: "You do everything for everyone. You work harder than your own assistants. You carry the whole world. And you still have not managed to buy yourself a good toothbrush. Look at this. It is worn out. It is exhausted. It is falling apart. You take care of all of us—and you leave yourself for last."

I stared at it and felt something shift that words could not produce. Because it was true in a way that was impossible to intellectualize. I could execute at the highest level for other people. I could plan, deliver, protect, anticipate, and exceed expectations. But when it came to the smallest, simplest act of care for myself, I treated my own needs like they could wait forever. I treated my own well-being like a low priority item on a list that never ends.

That toothbrush became a symbol of the entire pattern: impressive excellence outward, quiet neglect inward. It was not shame. It was clarity. It was the end of denial. And it gave me a new standard that was not dramatic, just honest: if I can care for everyone else with precision, I can care for myself with precision too. If I can make other people feel supported, I can support myself. If I can treat other people's needs as real, I can treat my own as real. Not later. Not after I earn it. Now.

That is the liberation: you were never meant to be the infrastructure. You were meant to be a person. And the moment you stop placing yourself last, a new question rises—clean, unavoidable, and quietly powerful in its simplicity: why do you keep asking other people for what you refuse to give yourself?

CHAPTER 10

THE BURDEN YOU MUST
DROP TO RISE

The Weight You Call Responsibility

You keep calling it responsibility. That is the polite word. The respectable word. The word that makes you look mature when you are secretly exhausted. But a lot of what you carry is not responsibility. It is fear dressed as duty. It is guilt wearing the costume of loyalty. It is the old training that taught you love must be earned through effort, and that your value is measured by how much you can hold without breaking.

This is why you feel heavy even on days when nothing "big" happened. Because the weight is not coming from events. It is coming from roles. From emotional assignments you never agreed to. From invisible obligations you accepted without realizing you were signing your life away in small increments. You did not wake up one day and decide, "I will become the person who carries everyone." You became that person the way people become anything that hurts them: slowly, quietly, repeatedly, until it feels normal.

Somewhere along the line you confused being needed with being loved. You confused being useful with being valued. You confused being dependable with being safe. And once those wires crossed, you started carrying more than was yours, because you thought that was the price of belonging. That is the trap.

Not the world. Not the people. The trap is the internal logic that says, "If I do not hold it, it will fall apart, and if it falls apart, I will be blamed, and if I am blamed, I will be abandoned."

So you hold it. You hold everything. You hold moods. You hold tension. You hold silence. You hold other people's regret. You hold their inconsistency as if it is your job to translate it into stability. You hold their chaos as if your calm is the medicine that keeps the room alive. You call it being strong. You call it being the bigger person. You call it being "mature." But let us be honest: a lot of your maturity has been survival. A lot of your strength has been adaptation. And a lot of your calm has been a negotiated peace with the fear that if you stop performing stability, something will break and it will be your fault.

This is why you are tired in a way sleep cannot fix. Because this is not physical fatigue. This is identity fatigue. The exhaustion of being the person who always catches the falling glass, and then pretends the cuts were nothing. The exhaustion of always being "fine," because being fine is what keeps you wanted. The exhaustion of being the one who does not create problems, who does not need much, who does not ask for too much, who does not disrupt the room. You became excellent at not disrupting the room, and then you wondered why the room never made space for you.

Here is the harsh truth that will set you free. You are not strong. You are overloaded. And overload is not a personality trait. It is a pattern. A pattern built from repeated decisions to carry what was never yours. That pattern may have once kept you safe. It may have once made you the hero. It may have once helped you survive. But what saves you in one season can imprison you in the next. And the moment you are ready to rise, the same pattern that once protected you will become the anchor that keeps you stuck.

Most people do not understand this because they only look at the outside of your life. They see someone who "has it together." They see someone reliable. Someone capable. Someone composed. They do not see the cost. They do not see the internal pressure it takes to maintain that image. They do not see the quiet negotiations you make with yourself every day: "Just get through it. Do not react. Do not make it worse. Do not ask. Do not complain. Do not need." The world loves a person who does not need. Not because it respects them. Because it can use them without interruption.

And the reason you rarely stop it is because part of you likes the role. That sentence might sting, but stay with it. You might hate the exhaustion, but you like what the role gives you: control. Predictability. Moral authority. The right to say, "I always show up," even when you are angry that nobody shows up for you. The role protects you from the chaos you fear. It also protects you from something else: change. Because as long as you are busy carrying, you never have to face the real question. What would your life look like if you stopped?

This is the moment where people pretend they do not understand. They say, "But I cannot stop. People depend on me." No. People are used to you. There is a difference. Dependence implies necessity. Being used implies convenience. A lot of what you carry is not necessary. It is simply what others have learned they can put on you, because you will not drop it. You will not make it awkward. You will not disappoint them. You will not be the one who says, "No. This is yours." You will swallow it, solve it, and call it love. And then you will wonder why love feels like a job.

You do not rise by doing more. You rise by putting down what does not belong to you. That is why this chapter matters. Because you cannot become first while your hands are full. You cannot build a new life while your arms are wrapped around the old one. You cannot walk forward while you are dragging other people's expectations behind you like a chain.

Let me name what "burden" actually is, in the way it shows up in real life. Burden is the text you respond to instantly because you are afraid of being seen as cold. Burden is the conversation you keep having in your head long after it ended because you need to "fix" how you were perceived. Burden is the apology you make even when you were the one harmed, because conflict makes you feel unsafe. Burden is the way you keep the peace by abandoning your truth. Burden is the emotional accounting you do for people who never do emotional accounting for you.

Burden is also the role you play. The fixer. The rescuer. The rational one. The one who understands. The one who does not take things personally. The one who can handle it. The one who will not judge. The one who will not leave. The one who will not demand. The one who will not collapse. Each one of those roles sounds like a compliment until you realize they are cages. They are identities that other people benefit from. And once people benefit from a version of you, they will resist your evolution, not because they hate you, but because your evolution threatens their comfort.

That resistance is the first test of your rise. Because the moment you start putting things down, you will be called selfish by people who are used to you being selfless. You will be called changed by people who preferred you unchanged. You will be accused of not caring by people who equated your over-functioning with love. This is why many people stay stuck. Not because they cannot rise. Because they cannot tolerate being misunderstood while they rise.

But you do not need everyone to understand you. You need you to stop misunderstanding yourself. You need to recognize the difference between love and obligation. Between care and control. Between loyalty and fear. Between being good and being used. Because right now, a part of your life is built on emotional debts you never agreed to pay. Debts that were assigned to you through guilt, through expectation, through family roles, through relationship dynamics, through the quiet social contract that says, "If you are capable, you must carry more."

That contract is not a law. It is a habit. And habits can be broken the same way they were built: through repeated decisions.

This is where your old identity will fight back. Because the moment you consider dropping the burden, your nervous system will panic. Not because the burden is good for you, but because it is familiar. Familiar pain feels safer than unfamiliar freedom. That is why you will feel guilty. That is why you will feel anxious. That is why you will start generating reasons why you "cannot" change right now. Your body will interpret release as danger, because it has learned that your value is tied to your performance. So when you stop performing, it feels like death. Not literal death. Identity death. The death of the version of you who earned love by being useful.

And that is exactly the version that must end if you want to rise.

Here is the turning point. You are not here to manage your life better. You are here to reclaim it. You are not here to become a slightly improved version of the same exhausted person. You are here to stop living as a container for other people's needs. You are here to stop being the emotional employee in relationships where you are supposed to be equal. You are here to stop carrying what keeps you small.

Because "rise" is not an emotion. Rise is a consequence. It is what happens when your hands are empty enough to reach for your own life. It is what happens when you stop paying emotional debts that were never yours, and you finally have energy left for the one person you have been postponing: you.

So, before we talk about how to drop it, we need to get brutally honest about what you are actually carrying. Not the story. Not the justification. Not the identity. The weight. The real inventory. The roles, the debts, the expectations, the invisible promises you have been keeping out of fear.

You do not need a dramatic exit. You do not need a speech. You do not need to become cruel. You need to become clear. Because the moment you see the pattern for what it is—roles, debts, expectations, and invisible promises—you stop calling it responsibility and you start calling it what it really is: a contract. And once you see the contract, you can finally decide whether you keep paying it.

The Contracts You Didn't Know You Signed

There are contracts in your life you never consciously agreed to. You did not sit at a table and sign them. No one slid a paper across the room and said, "Here. This is your role." But you signed anyway—through repetition. Through silence. Through the way you kept showing up without questioning why you were always the one doing it.

That is how most burdens are created. Not through one dramatic decision, but through a thousand small ones. You answer because you always answer. You fix it because you always fix it. You apologize because you are trained to keep the peace. You over-explain because you are afraid of being misunderstood. You soften your no because you cannot tolerate being seen as "cold." And every time you do, you reinforce a contract that says: *I will carry what is not mine, and I will call it love.*

This is why you cannot "manage your stress" out of this. You cannot meditate your way out of a contract. You cannot self-care your way out of a role you keep signing up for. This is not about rest. This is about ownership. It is about what belongs to you, and what never did. It is about what you agreed to carry because you believed your worth depended on it.

Let us name the contracts. Not the poetic version. The real ones.

Contract One: "I will be the emotional adult."

This is the contract you sign when you grew up around volatility. When moods were unpredictable. When love had conditions. When chaos could erupt without warning. You learned that stability was not something you could rely on. It was something you had to produce.

So you became the calm one. The mediator. The translator. The one who could sense the temperature of the room and adjust your personality accordingly. You learned to read faces like weather forecasts. You learned to speak carefully. You learned to move strategically. You learned to avoid triggers. You learned to make yourself small when tension was high and useful when tension was rising.

That skill may have saved you once. It may have prevented explosions. It may have earned you approval. But it also trained you to live with one foot outside yourself, always monitoring the environment. And when you live that way for long enough, you stop asking, "What do I feel?" and you start asking, "What do they need me to be?"

That is how self-abandonment becomes a lifestyle. You do not call it abandonment. You call it maturity. You call it being reasonable. You call it "not making it worse." But the truth is, you have been managing other people's emotions, so you do not have to face the anxiety of letting them manage their own.

Contract Two: "If I do not fix it, I am not safe."

This is the contract that turns you into a fixer. A rescuer. A problem-solver who cannot relax until everything is stable. You think you are being helpful. But a lot of fixing is not kindness. It is control. And control is not power. It is fear trying to feel powerful.

You fix because it gives you predictability. Because unresolved tension makes your nervous system scream. Because disorder reminds you of what you lived through. Because you associate uncertainty with danger. So you solve. You arrange. You correct. You manage. You clean up. You take over. You do what needs to be done before anyone asks, because being asked would mean you failed. And failing feels like being punished. So, you become perfect at preventing problems.

Then you resent everyone for depending on you.

This is what people do not want to admit. Sometimes the burden is not only put on you. Sometimes you pick it up because you cannot tolerate the discomfort of letting someone else struggle. Sometimes you carry it because the moment you do not, you will feel powerless. And that feeling is unbearable.

So you call it responsibility. But it is not. It is a coping mechanism you have been mistaking for character.

Contract Three: "I must earn love by being useful."

This is one of the most expensive contracts you will ever sign. Because it turns relationships into transactions. Not on the surface. On the inside. It makes you feel like you cannot just be loved. You have to justify your place. You have to prove your value. You have to show your usefulness.

So you over-give. You anticipate needs. You show up early. You stay late. You carry emotional weight. You provide stability. You become the person others can rely on, because you are terrified of being the person others can leave.

And the moment you stop being useful, you panic. Not because you are weak. Because you are trained. The training says: *If I am not needed, I am disposable.* The training says: *If I do not contribute, I do not deserve.* The training says: *Love is conditional, so I must remain valuable.*

This is why you struggle to receive. Because receiving feels passive. And passive does not feel safe to someone who had to earn everything. It feels like waiting. It feels like depending. It feels like placing your worth in someone else's hands. So you stay in the giving role, even when you are empty. Even when you are bitter. Even when your body is begging you to stop.

You do not need more love from others. You need to stop building your worth on usefulness.

Contract Four: "Their disappointment is my responsibility."

This contract is subtle. It hides behind empathy. Behind kindness. Behind being considerate. But in truth, it is people-pleasing with a halo.

You feel responsible for how others feel about your choices. You feel responsible for their reactions. You feel responsible for their comfort. You feel responsible for their narrative about you. So you over-explain. You soften boundaries. You prepare speeches. You rehearse conversations. You try to say the truth in a way that will not upset them, which means you do not fully say the truth.

And when they are disappointed, you interpret it as a moral failure. You interpret it as "I did something wrong." Not "They do not like it." Not "They are adjusting." Not "They are entitled." You interpret it as *I harmed them*, and then you rush to repair it.

This is how you become easy to manipulate. Not because you are naive. Because your conscience has been weaponized against you. People learn that your guilt is the easiest handle to grab. They do not need to force you. They only need to imply you are selfish. And your internal alarm will do the rest.

Here is the correction: their disappointment is not your responsibility. Your integrity is. Their feelings are theirs. Your boundaries are yours. Your life is yours. You are not here to manage other people's reactions to your growth.

Contract Five: "I owe loyalty even when it costs me."

This is the contract that keeps you stuck in relationships, family dynamics, friendships, even careers that drain you. Because you confuse loyalty with self-sacrifice. You confuse history with obligation. You confuse "they were there once" with "I must stay forever."

So you keep paying for a past version of someone. You keep investing in a story. You keep honoring old agreements you never consciously made. You stay because you feel you owe them, even if they do not treat you with basic respect now. You stay because leaving would make you the villain in their story. You stay because you cannot tolerate being seen as the one who "abandoned" them, even when you have been abandoning yourself for years.

Loyalty is not a virtue when it is one-sided. Loyalty is not integrity when it requires self-erasure. Loyalty is not love when it demands you betray your own life.

This is where many people get angry. They say, "But I am not the type of person who leaves." That sounds noble. It is also how people build prisons out of personality.

You do not win by being the type of person who never leaves. You win by being the type of person who never leaves yourself.

Contract Six: "If I set a boundary, I will lose love."

This is the contract behind all the others. This is the root. The fear that clarity will cost you connection. That standards will cost you closeness. That self-respect will cost you belonging.

So you negotiate with yourself instead. You tell yourself, "It is not that bad." You tell yourself, "They mean well." You tell yourself, "This is just how they are." You tell yourself, "I do not want to be difficult." You tell yourself, "I can handle it." You tell yourself, "It is fine."

And then it is not fine. It becomes resentment. It becomes emotional distance. It becomes passive aggression. It becomes fatigue. It becomes a slow internal death. Not dramatic. Not visible. But real.

The reason you fear boundaries is because boundaries expose truth. They reveal who is only comfortable with you when you are convenient. They reveal who benefits from your lack of standards. They reveal who calls your growth "selfish." And that revelation is painful. But it is also liberation.

Because it is better to know what you are standing on than to keep building your life on people who collapse when you finally stand up.

Now, here is where we turn the knife in the right direction. Not to punish you. To free you.

If you recognize yourself in these contracts, do not shame yourself. Shame keeps you stuck. Shame makes you hide. Shame makes you perform change instead of making it. The point is not to judge your past. The point is to understand how you got here so you can stop repeating it.

You did not sign these contracts because you were weak. You signed them because you were trying to survive. Because you were trying to belong. Because you were trying to avoid pain. Because you were trying to be good in a world that taught you goodness meant sacrifice.

But you are not in that season anymore. You are not the child in the chaos. You are not the person who needs to earn a seat by carrying extra weight. You are not the emotional employee of other people's lives.

You are the owner.

And ownership begins with one brutal distinction: what is yours, and what is not.

Because once you see that clearly, you will understand something that changes everything. A lot of what you have been carrying is not love. It is fear. It is obligation. It is old identity. It is a contract you kept honoring because you did not know you were allowed to renegotiate it.

In the next part, we do exactly that. We stop honoring the contracts that keep you small. We put down the emotional debts you never signed. We drop the roles that made you valuable but not free. And we do it without speeches, without drama, without over-explaining.

Not angrily. Cleanly.

Because your rise does not require more effort. It requires less weight. And the moment you start putting it down, you will feel it—first as discomfort, then as relief, and then as something you may not have felt in a long time.

Space.

And when you finally have space, you can do the one thing you have been postponing for years.

You can reach for your own life.

But this is exactly where Become First begins to separate from every other idea you have ever tried. Become First is not a mood. It is not a quote. It is not a motivational moment. It is an internal transfer of ownership. It is the point where you finally stop confusing fear with duty, guilt with loyalty, and endurance with love. Ownership requires one brutal distinction: what is yours and what is not. Once you see that clearly, you cannot unsee it. And when you cannot unsee it, you cannot keep carrying what was never yours without feeling the cost in your body, your relationships, and your self-respect.

This is the line between your old life and your next one: what is yours, and what is not. Once you see that clearly, you stop negotiating with guilt. You stop calling fear "loyalty." You stop calling self-erasure "being good." And that is when the real move happens—not in theory, but in behavior. You put it down.

The Drop

The moment you decide to put something down, your nervous system will argue with you. Not because the burden is good for you, but because it is familiar. Familiar pain can feel safer than unfamiliar freedom. That is why people say they want change and then stay in the same role for years. It is not laziness. It is conditioning. It is the internal alarm that whispers, "If I stop doing this, I will lose love. If I stop carrying this, I will be rejected. If I stop being useful, I will be disposable." Become First requires you to hear that alarm and still choose yourself anyway.

That is the difference between dropping a burden and merely taking a break. A break is temporary relief so you can go back to the same identity. The Drop is identity surgery. It is the moment you stop confusing your function with your worth. Most people do not realize this, so they try to "set boundaries" with speeches. They try to explain themselves into respect. They try to negotiate their way out of a role. But roles do not end because you explained them. Roles end when you stop performing them.

This is where you need to be brutally honest: you have been over-carrying for so long that your life has adapted around it. People expect it. Systems rely on it. Relationships are built on it. Some people will not be angry because you changed; they will be angry because they lost access. They will call it selfish, because selfish is the easiest word to throw at someone who stops being convenient. And if you are not careful, you will interpret their reaction as proof that you were wrong. You will feel guilt and you will run back to the old role to restore peace. That is how the prison stays intact. Become First means you stop using other people's comfort as your compass.

So how do you drop it without becoming cold, cruel, or dramatic? You do it with clarity and consistency. You do it like a person who finally understands: "I do not need to punish anyone. I just need to stop carrying what is not mine." The Drop has three moves. Not three slogans. Three real moves that change how you live.

First: identify what you are actually carrying. Not the story. Not the justification. The weight. Ask yourself, "What am I currently responsible for that I did not choose, that does not belong to me, or that is not being reciprocated?" You will notice something immediately: the burden is rarely one big thing. It is a collection of small, repeated behaviors. The instant replies. The emotional babysitting. The constant translating. The fixing. The rescuing. The smoothing. The being available. The being "understanding." The being the one who never makes it hard for anyone. That list is your map. Become First begins when you stop romanticizing the burden and start auditing it.

Second: name the contract behind it. Because the burden is not the burden. The contract is. The contract might be, "If I do not fix it, I am not safe." Or, "If I disappoint them, I will lose love." Or, "If I stop, everything will fall apart." Or, "If I say no, I will be punished." Do not rush this step. If you only drop behaviors but keep the contract, you will pick the burden back up the moment stress hits. Your nervous system will run to the old role like a drug. When you name the contract, you pull it into the light. And once it is in the light, it cannot run your life quietly anymore.

Third: return what is not yours. Not with a fight. Not with a long explanation. With a decision. This is where people panic because they think returning means confrontation. It does not. Most returns are behavioral, not theatrical. Returning can look like not responding immediately. It can look like letting someone solve their own problem. It can look like staying silent when you normally jump in to regulate the room. It can look like saying, "I cannot take that on," and ending the sentence there. No apology tour. No biography. No courtroom defense. Become First does not require you to be harsh; it requires you to be clear.

Here is the rule: the longer your explanation, the more you signal that your boundary is negotiable. Explanations invite debate. Clarity ends it. If you need to justify your no, it means you do not fully believe you are allowed to have it. That is why your first boundaries will feel unnatural. You will feel rude. You will feel selfish. You will feel like you are doing something wrong. But you are not doing something wrong. You are doing something new. You are training your identity to stop reaching for the old role every time discomfort appears.

Now let us talk about the part nobody wants to admit: you are going to lose something when you drop the burden. Not always people. Sometimes you lose your position. Your moral high ground. Your identity as the one who "always shows up." You lose the story that kept you feeling superior while you were secretly resentful. You lose the excuse of being too busy to face your own life. You lose the addictive feeling of being needed. And yes, you may lose access to some relationships that were only stable as long as you were self-abandoning. That sounds scary until you realize what you gain: energy, clarity, self-respect, and the first real sense of ownership you have felt in years. Become First is expensive in one currency and priceless in another.

A drop list is not journaling. It is proof. It is three concrete lines that expose the contracts you have been living under and the role you have been performing without even realizing it. One role you stop performing. One emotional debt you stop paying. One expectation you stop carrying. Keep it specific, not poetic—because vagueness is how people hide from change while still calling it growth.

For the role, name it plainly: you are done being the fixer. You are done being the one who automatically solves, regulates, rescues, and makes the room stable. For the debt, name what has been draining you for years: you are done paying guilt for saying no, done purchasing peace with self-betrayal, done treating other people's disappointment like it is your moral emergency. For the expectation, call out the pattern that turned you into a convenience instead of a person: you are done being available on demand, done responding as if access to you is a right instead of a privilege.

Then you add one sentence under each—not a promise, not a motivational statement, not a speech you rehearse for someone else. Evidence. A first behavioral move that proves the standard is real. With the fixer role, the evidence is that you stop offering solutions unless you are asked. With the guilt debt, the evidence is that you say no once and you do not explain yourself into permission. With availability, the evidence is that you respond on your timeline, not theirs. Nothing dramatic. Nothing theatrical. Just a clean refusal to return to the old contract.

That is where the shift actually happens. Not in insight. Not in agreement. In behavior. In the small decisions that feel uncomfortable precisely because they are new. This is where people stop consuming self-help like entertainment and start living self-leadership like a standard. This is where Become First stops being a concept you admire and becomes a posture you maintain— quietly, consistently, and without needing anyone else to approve it.

Here is what nobody tells you: most people do not fail at change because they lack willpower. They fail because they cannot tolerate the social and emotional consequences of being different. They can do the diet. They can do the gym. They can do the morning routine. But they cannot tolerate disappointment. They cannot tolerate being misunderstood. They cannot tolerate someone else's discomfort without rushing to fix it. They cannot tolerate the silence that follows a boundary. They cannot tolerate not being needed.

So they retreat. They go back. They pick the burden up again. Not because it belongs to them, but because it restores the old balance. It makes the room calm. It makes the relationship predictable. It makes the family dynamic familiar. It makes the employer satisfied. It makes the friend comfortable. It makes the partner stop sulking. It makes the guilt quiet down. And that is the trap: the burden comes back disguised as peace. The burden comes back disguised as "being a good person." The burden comes back disguised as "I do not want drama." And because you have been trained to value peace at any cost, you buy it with your own life.

Become First is the moment you stop buying peace that way.

This is where you need precision. Not motivation. Precision. Because what you are doing is not simply "setting boundaries." You are changing the financial system of your identity. You are no longer paying emotional debts that were never yours. You are no longer funding other people's comfort with your own exhaustion. You are no longer investing in relationships that require you to disappear for them to feel secure. That is not a small shift. That is a structural shift. And structural shifts always trigger resistance.

Resistance will not always look like conflict. Sometimes it looks like confusion. Sometimes it looks like, "Are you okay?" Sometimes it looks like, "You have been distant." Sometimes it looks like, "You changed." Sometimes it looks like someone suddenly acting fragile so you will resume the role of caretaker. Sometimes it looks like someone becoming irritated, not because you did something cruel, but because you did not do what you always do. People do not only react to what you do. They react to what they can no longer expect from you.

This is why your new baseline cannot depend on their reactions. If your boundary holds only when they approve it, then it is not a boundary. It is a request. If your standard is only real when it is celebrated, then it is not a standard. It is a performance. Become First is not about being applauded for choosing yourself. It is about choosing yourself when nobody claps. Especially when nobody claps. Especially when choosing yourself makes you temporarily less convenient, less predictable, less easy to use.

You do not need to become cold to become free. You need to become clear. Coldness is avoidance. Clarity is ownership. Coldness says, "I do not care." Clarity says, "I care, but I will not carry what is not mine." That distinction matters, because you are not here to punish people. You are here to stop punishing yourself. You are here to stop living as a container for everyone else's needs while your own needs stay unpaid like an abandoned invoice.

The most dangerous burden is the one that hides inside your identity. The role you take pride in. The role you defend. The role you protect with, "That is just who I am." That phrase has destroyed more lives than any enemy. "That is just who I am" is what people say when they are terrified of who they could become. It is what people say when they have built their value on suffering and do not know how to be valuable without it.

You might not say it out loud. But you live it. You live it when you rush to fix. You live it when you absorb tension. You live it when you apologize to end discomfort. You live it when you say yes while your body says no. You live it when you keep paying for being accepted by being easy. And the longer you live it, the more your nervous system associates self-respect with danger. That is why the guilt feels so loud. That is why the anxiety spikes when you do something as simple as not responding immediately. That is why you rehearse messages before sending them. That is why you feel the urge to "clarify" your boundary into something soft and harmless.

But clarity is not supposed to be harmless. It is supposed to be honest.

There will be moments where you feel the old reflex rise like a wave. The reflex to manage. The reflex to rescue. The reflex to smooth. The reflex to explain. The reflex to prove you are still "good." And here is where you make the decision that changes your life: you let the wave rise, and you do not obey it. You let someone be disappointed without turning their disappointment into your assignment. You let someone handle their own emotions without becoming the emotional babysitter. You let someone sit with consequences without rushing in to save them from what they earned. You let silence exist without filling it with self-justification. You do not do this because you are mean. You do this because you are done being trained.

This is what real strength looks like. Not carrying more. Holding your line.

Holding your line will feel unnatural at first. That is how you know it is real. When you have lived your life as the one who over-functions, under-asks, and over-gives, a normal boundary will feel extreme. A normal standard will feel selfish. A normal no will feel like betrayal. That does not mean you are doing it wrong. It means you are doing something that your old identity cannot understand yet.

Your old identity will argue with you using morality. It will say, "But what if they need me?" It will say, "But what if I hurt them?" It will say, "But what if I am being unfair?" It will say, "But what if I am overreacting?" It will say, "But what if I regret it?" And because you are not a cruel person, because you actually care, you will feel that argument deeply. That is why this is difficult. Not because you lack character. Because you have character. You have conscience. You have empathy. And your empathy has been used as a leash.

Become First is the moment you unclip it.

Do not misunderstand this. You will still love people. You will still help people. You will still show up. But you will no longer show up in a way that empties you. You will no longer help in ways that make others weaker. You will no longer give in ways that teach people they can take without consequence. You will no longer be the one who pays for every imbalance with your own life. Love without standards is not love. It is submission with nice words.

And you are done submitting.

Here is the clean truth about burdens: they do not disappear because you become aware. They disappear because you stop rehearsing the same behaviors that keep them alive. That means your life will have to tolerate a period of adjustment. A period where the room feels slightly unstable because you are no longer holding it together. A period where some people test you. A period where someone tries to trigger your guilt because it used to work. A period where your own mind tries to scare you back into the role that made you acceptable.

Expect it. Not with paranoia. With maturity. If you know the pattern will try to return, you will not be surprised when it knocks. And when it knocks, you will have an answer that does not require an essay.

The answer is not a speech. The answer is a standard.

A standard is quiet. It is not dramatic. It does not need a press release. A standard is what you do when nobody is watching and when you do not get permission. A standard is the internal posture that says, "I do not carry what is not mine." A standard is the decision to stop explaining yourself into safety. A standard is the refusal to buy comfort with self-betrayal. A standard is the ability to let someone misunderstand you without rushing to correct it, because you are no longer building your life on being understood by people who benefit from you being small.

You will notice something as you hold your line: the people who love you will adjust. They might not like it at first, but they will adjust, because real love adapts to truth. The people who use you will resist. They will push. They will guilt. They will question. They will label you. They will tell themselves stories about why you changed, because it is easier to label you than to face what your boundary reveals about them.

Let them have their stories. You do not need to be the hero in someone else's narrative. You need to be the owner of your own life.

Because here is the most important point: a clean life requires clean hands. Not morally clean. Practically clean. Hands that are not constantly busy holding other people's emotions, solving their chaos, managing their expectations, paying their debts, and protecting them from reality. When your hands are full of other people, you cannot hold your health. You cannot hold your goals. You cannot hold your marriage with presence. You cannot hold your future with focus. You cannot hold your own mind in a steady place. You cannot Become First while your entire existence is built around being last.

This is why the burden is not just tiring. It is identity-threatening. Because the moment you stop carrying, you will face the question you have been postponing: what do you do with the energy you get back? What do you build when you are no longer busy maintaining other people's comfort? That question scares people more than the burden itself, because it removes the excuse. It removes the story. It removes the "I cannot" that has protected you from the risk of becoming who you actually are.

That is why some people unconsciously prefer the burden. It gives them a reason to stay in the same place while pretending they are doing something noble. It gives them a socially acceptable reason to postpone their own life. It gives them a role that earns praise. It gives them an identity that feels valuable. It gives them a way to avoid the terrifying responsibility of freedom.

But freedom is not terrifying because it is dangerous. It is terrifying because it is honest. Freedom forces you to see what you have tolerated. Freedom forces you to see what you enabled. Freedom forces you to see where you participated. Freedom forces you to stop blaming others for what you kept choosing. And that is exactly why accountability is freedom, and why Become First is not a slogan. It is a turning point.

So let the guilt rise. Let the discomfort rise. Let the temptation to fix rise. Let the urge to explain rise. Let it all rise, and do not obey it. Not because you are above it, but because you are done living under it. You do not need to win every argument in someone else's head. You do not need to be liked in rooms that only like you when you are convenient. You do not need to be the one who holds everything together at the cost of your own collapse.

You need one thing: the discipline to stop picking it back up.

And discipline is not punishment. Discipline is devotion. It is devotion to the life you say you want. It is devotion to the person you say you are becoming. It is devotion to the standard that says, "My life is mine." That standard will be tested. It will be tested in small moments that look harmless. A message. A request. A subtle guilt trip. A crisis that is not yours. A tone that used to trigger you. A silence you used to fill. That is where your real transformation lives: not in big declarations, but in the small decisions where you either return to the old contract or you choose yourself.

Become First means you choose yourself.

Not loudly. Not for attention. Not to prove anything. Quietly. Consistently. So consistently that the burden has nowhere to hook into you anymore. So consistently that the old role feels foreign. So consistently that people stop expecting you to carry what is not yours. So consistently that your life finally has space for the things that matter: your health, your peace, your goals, your relationships, your future. Not because you learned a new concept, but because you made a new decision and refused to negotiate with it.

That is the drop. Not a moment. A line you stop crossing.

You will be tempted to make this dramatic. To announce the drop. To post it. To explain it. To make sure everybody knows what you are doing and why you are doing it. That temptation comes from the same place as the burden:

the need to be understood in order to feel allowed. But you are not here to be allowed. You are here to decide.

Real dropping is quiet. It is not a performance. It is not a negotiation. It is not a therapy session in public. It is a private standard you keep when nobody is applauding you and nobody is validating you. Most people talk themselves out of change, because they think change must be defended. They think a boundary needs a courtroom. They think self-respect needs a press release. It does not. It needs repetition.

And repetition is where your life splits. Because the burden does not return as the exact same burden. It returns as "just this one time." It returns as "this is different." It returns as "they really need me." It returns as "I will deal with myself later." It returns as "it is not worth the conflict." It returns as "I do not want to look cold." It returns as "I do not want to be the bad guy." The burden is patient. It waits for your tired days. Your lonely days. Your stressed days. Your sentimental days. Your guilt days. It waits for the moment you forget that every time you pick it back up, you pay with your future.

The way you win is not by being stronger than the burden. It is by being loyal to the standard. Because standards do not depend on feelings. Standards do not change when the weather changes. Standards do not collapse because someone is disappointed. Standards do not melt because someone is emotional. A standard is what remains when the old reflex shows up and you do not obey it.

That is why the drop becomes the rise. Not because you dropped one thing. Because you became the kind of person who does not pick it up again.

You will learn something brutal as you do this: some people will only respect you when you stop trying to be respected. They respected the version of you they could predict. They respected the version of you they could use. They respected the version of you that kept paying. When you stop paying, they call it disrespect. When you stop explaining, they call it attitude. When you stop rescuing, they call it cold. When you stop being easy, they call it selfish. But those labels are not your identity. They are their withdrawal.

And you do not negotiate with someone else's withdrawal.

Here is the line that changes everything: you are not responsible for other people's feelings about your self-respect. You are responsible for your self-respect. That is it. Every time you confuse those two responsibilities, you pick the burden up again. Every time you remember the difference, your life gets lighter.

That lightness will feel strange at first. You might even feel empty. Not because you lost something valuable, but because you lost constant noise. You lost constant urgency. You lost constant emotional management. You lost constant over-functioning. Your system will reach for chaos the way an addict reaches for a fix. That does not mean you are broken. It means you were trained.

Do not let your training write your future.

If you have lived as the one who carries, then carrying feels like love. Carrying feels like loyalty. Carrying feels like being a good person. But carrying is not love when it erases you. Carrying is not loyalty when it is one-sided. Carrying is not goodness when it teaches people they can take without consequence. Sometimes the most loving thing you can do is stop participating in the dynamic that keeps everybody small.

Because the truth is, your life has been delayed by what you kept tolerating. Not only from them. From you. The compromises you made with your own standards. The excuses you kept repeating. The contracts you kept signing with your silence. The burdens you kept claiming as "just life." And you can call it generosity, you can call it patience, you can call it being the strong one—

but if it costs you your health, your peace, your truth, your body, your time, your future, then it is not strength. It is a slow leak.

Become First is how you stop leaking.

It is not a mood. It is not a motivational day. It is not a quote you save and forget. It is a permanent decision about what you carry and what you refuse to carry. It is a commitment to stop being the landfill of everyone else's unresolved emotions and unfinished responsibilities. It is the internal posture that says, without drama and without apology, "I do not carry what is not mine."

And the moment you live by that posture, a different life becomes possible. Not because the world suddenly becomes fair. Not because people suddenly become mature. Not because everything becomes easy. But because your hands finally become free. Free to build. Free to heal. Free to choose. Free to become a person who does not need permission to exist at full volume.

That is what rising actually is. Not climbing while exhausted. Not hustling while resentful. Not proving while depleted. Rising is what happens when you stop dragging what was never yours and finally walk forward with your own life in your hands.

So put it down. Not once. Not for a week. Put it down in the only way that matters: by becoming the kind of person who does not pick it back up.

That is the burden you drop to rise. And that is the point where you stop being available for your old life—and start becoming available for the one you actually want.

CHAPTER 11

WHEN GROWTH FEELS
LIKE BETRAYAL

The Guilt That Arrives with Growth

Growth does not always feel like relief. Sometimes it feels like a crime. You do one clean thing—one boundary, one honest sentence, one refusal to over-function—and the room goes quiet in a way that makes your nervous system flinch. Not because you were aggressive, not because you were cruel, but because you did something you are not "supposed" to do in the old version of your life: you stopped adjusting yourself to keep everyone else comfortable. That is the first shock. The second shock is how quickly your body interprets that choice as danger.

Most people think betrayal looks like an act. It does not. Betrayal, in real life, usually feels like a sensation. A tightness in the chest after you say no. A panic in the stomach when you do not answer immediately. A pressure behind the eyes when you let someone be disappointed without rushing to repair it. And the mind does what it always does when the body feels unsafe: it starts building a story. It tries to explain your growth as wrongdoing because wrongdoing is familiar. Wrongdoing gives you a script. Wrongdoing gives you a punishment you already understand. Freedom does not. Freedom is open space, and open space is terrifying to a person who learned that safety comes from being useful.

This is why guilt shows up right on time when you finally start moving. You have been trained for years—maybe decades—to associate "being good" with being accommodating, being loyal, being easy, being available, being the one who does not create problems. You learned that the fastest way to keep connection is to minimize yourself. You learned that the fastest way to prevent conflict is to over-give. You learned that the fastest way to avoid abandonment is to become indispensable. So when you stop doing those things, the old training screams. It does not scream with words. It screams with guilt.

Guilt is powerful because it feels moral. It feels like truth. It feels like conscience. And yes, sometimes guilt is conscience. Sometimes guilt is the part of you that knows you crossed a line and you should repair it. But the guilt that arrives with growth is a different species. It is not the guilt of harm; it is the guilt of disobedience. It is the guilt you feel when you stop fulfilling a role that other people have come to expect from you. It is the guilt you feel when you stop paying emotional debts that were never yours. It is the guilt of becoming unfamiliar to the people who were most comfortable when you stayed predictable.

The beginning of Become First is rarely glamorous. It is not applause. It is not a sudden glow. It is a private moment where you choose a standard and then you feel sick about it. That sickness is not proof you are wrong. It is proof you are rewiring. You are breaking the old internal agreement that said: "I will trade my peace for approval." You are stepping out of a version of yourself that was built to survive, not to live.

Growth does not threaten people because you became "better." It threatens them because the old arrangement stops working. Every relationship has an unwritten agreement—who carries, who gets forgiven, who gets accommodated, who gets the benefit of your silence. One person regulates the room. One person absorbs the chaos. One person translates tension into "fine." And nobody calls it a system until you stop playing your part. The moment you shift, it is not theory to them. It is loss of access. That is why your change gets met with pressure, confusion, guilt, or the classic line: "You changed." You did. That is the point. Become First is not you becoming cold—it is you refusing to keep financing a dynamic that only works when you shrink.

When you are the one who has been holding that system together, you start to believe that your over-functioning is love. You start to believe that your patience is maturity. You start to believe that your self-erasure is loyalty. And then you wonder why love feels like fatigue. You wonder why closeness feels like obligation. You wonder why your body is tired in a way sleep cannot fix. You wonder why you keep fantasizing about disappearing for a week—not to punish anyone, not to prove anything, but simply to have one day where nobody expects you to be the emotional infrastructure of the room.

Then you do something small and clean. You do not fix. You do not rush. You do not explain. You do not over-apologize. You do not absorb the tension. You do not volunteer your nervous system as a public service. And suddenly someone reacts as if you attacked them. They say they "do not recognize you." They say it with that tone that is half accusation, half mourning, as if the old version of you died and you did not ask permission before you buried him.

And I know that tone. I have heard it in different mouths, in different years, in different rooms—same script. There were years where I thought I was "moving," but if I am honest, I was often just changing sets. New streets, new faces, new voices, different costumes and haircuts, different ages, different skin—same movie, new cast. And the most unsettling part is not that it happened. It is that I could feel the loop forming before the dialogue even arrived, like my nervous system recognized the storyline faster than my mind wanted to admit it.

It always began the same way: I met someone who carried need like a scent. Not the clean kind of need that asks and respects the answer. The kind that leaks. The kind that makes a room tilt. The kind that quietly says, if you do not step in, something collapses. And because I have always had a reflex for collapse, I stepped in. I slowed down. I listened longer than I planned. I made space. I became shelter without calling it shelter. I wrapped my arms around people and tried to hold them together until they could hold themselves.

I did not only give advice. I gave structure. I gave introductions. I gave strategy. I gave my credibility. I gave my calendar. I gave nights that were supposed to be mine. I gave mornings I needed for my own recovery. I gave patience and emotional regulation like it was a public resource. And yes—I gave money. Not as a power move. Not as a transaction. As a hand reaching into the water to pull someone up when they were sinking. I watched people stabilize. I watched them stand. I watched them breathe again. And every time, a part of me mistook that moment for proof that this was love.

Then the shift happened. It was never loud. It was almost elegant. The "thank you" became shorter. The requests became more casual. The dependency learned to smile. "Can you just…" "It is nothing…" "I only need five minutes…" "Quick question…" The favors were small on paper but heavy in the body, because they were not really favors anymore. They were expectations wearing soft clothing. The giving stopped being something I chose and became something the room counted on.

And this is the part most people do not understand until they live it: the more you give without cost, the more the world starts acting like cost does not exist. Your time becomes invisible. Your energy becomes infinite. Your attention becomes a faucet that is supposed to run. You are no longer a person to them; you are a function. A service. An emotional infrastructure—quietly stabilizing their chaos so they do not have to grow up inside it.

The loop always reached the same scene: the moment I realized I was not "helping someone evolve," I was training someone to stay the same while I paid the difference. I was pouring and pouring and pouring, and nothing was changing—not because they were monsters, but because my constant rescue had made change optional. My generosity had become a postponement plan. I kept buying time for them with my life.

So one day, without a speech, without drama, without a grand exit, I hit the wall. The wall is not rage. The wall is depletion. The wall is the body saying: there is nothing left. Not time. Not money. Not strength. Not nervous system capacity. Not the ability to keep carrying consequences that do not belong to me. And something in me finally said what I had avoided saying for too long: I cannot keep building other people while I am slowly dismantling myself.

That is when I did the thing that always looks cruel to the people who benefit from your softness: I stopped. I did not stop to punish anyone. I stopped because I realized that what remained of me had to be gathered, protected, and reassembled into a life that was not built around emergencies. I turned inward. I began collecting my pieces like a man cleaning up after a war he did not declare.

And that is when the room turned on the character it had been feeding off of. Not with honesty. With narrative. Suddenly I was cold. Distant. Selfish. Suddenly I had "changed." Suddenly I "did not recognize people anymore." The same hands that took from me without shame started pointing at me with moral language. The same mouths that accepted my sacrifices started calling me "hard" the moment I stopped bleeding in front of them.

It is a specific kind of rage you meet when you withdraw from being useful: people do not argue the facts; they attack your identity. They do not say, "I miss the help." They say, "I miss the old you." They do not say, "This is inconvenient." They say, "You became a different person." Because if they can make your boundary sound like a character flaw, they do not have to face what your boundary reveals: that the old arrangement depended on you being endlessly available, endlessly forgiving, endlessly giving.

And that is the cinematic part of it—the part that makes you feel like a spectator watching the same movie on repeat. You can almost see the camera angle before it happens. The moment you stop, the script flips and you become the villain in a story you funded. Different protagonists, same betrayal scene. Different faces, same accusation. Different era, same sentence: after everything I did for you… as if "everything" was not exactly what you were finally trying to stop doing.

I can live with losing money. I have lost money more than once. I do not care. I am a worthy man, and I will make the money again. And I do. Every time.

What breaks me is not the money. What breaks me is the time.

Because money returns. Time does not. And nothing hurts like realizing you paid for someone else's comfort with hours of your one life.

That is the moment the room rewrites your self-respect as cruelty—because your "no" ends their comfort.

And that is when growth feels like betrayal: when other people treat your self-respect as a personal loss, and you feel the old panic rise as if you committed a crime. For a moment, you believe their version. You start searching your memory for evidence that you were too harsh. You replay the conversation. You draft alternate lines in your head. You bargain with yourself: maybe keep the boundary, but softer; maybe keep the standard, but with an apology; maybe keep your dignity, but still make them feel okay. That is the old role returning. That is the old contract trying to reattach.

This is where most people fail. Not because they cannot grow, but because they cannot tolerate the emotional backlash of growing. They can tolerate hard work. They can tolerate discipline. They can tolerate pushing through a goal. But they cannot tolerate being misunderstood. They cannot tolerate someone else's discomfort without making it their responsibility. They cannot tolerate the quiet threat of rejection. And because they are not cruel people, because they actually care, they interpret discomfort as harm and run back to the old behavior to restore peace.

But peace is not always peace. Sometimes peace is compliance. Sometimes peace is you surrendering your truth so the room stays calm. Sometimes peace is you paying again so nobody has to feel the consequences of their own behavior. Sometimes peace is you becoming smaller so someone else does not have to adjust. That is not peace. That is a hostage negotiation where you keep offering yourself as the ransom.

Become First begins when you stop doing that. Not loudly. Not for drama. Cleanly. Quietly. And because it is quiet, it is easy to doubt. Loud change looks brave. Quiet change looks suspicious—especially to the old you who used performance as proof.

If you have spent years earning your place, receiving will feel dangerous. Being cared for will feel awkward. Letting someone else carry will feel wrong. And the moment you stop carrying, your mind will accuse you of selfishness because selfishness is the simplest label for "I am no longer available for the old arrangement." You will feel guilt, not because you harmed someone, but because you stopped being convenient.

This is why evolving creates guilt, especially around people who benefited from your old self. People do not always realize they benefited. Some benefited consciously. Some benefited unconsciously. Some benefited because they were entitled. Some benefited because they were simply used to you doing what you do. But benefit is benefit, and human beings resist losing benefits. When you stop over-functioning, you remove a comfort they built their life around. When you stop absorbing tension, you force the room to feel what it has been avoiding. When you stop being the translator, you force people to speak for themselves. When you stop being the fixer, you allow consequences to exist. And consequences make people angry at the person who stopped hiding them.

So they call your growth betrayal. They frame your boundary as abandonment. They speak as if you owe them the old version of you because that version was "nice." But nice is not always love. Nice is sometimes fear, with manners. Nice is sometimes guilt, wearing perfume. Nice is sometimes a lifetime of training that taught you that being accepted requires you to be easy to manage.

This is where the real work happens: you start distinguishing between love and access. Love can be uncomfortable and still remain love. Love can be challenged and still remain love. Love can adjust. Love can renegotiate. Love can say, "I do not like this," without punishing you for it. Access cannot. Access panics when it is reduced. Access demands the old pattern to return. Access uses guilt as a weapon because guilt is the fastest way to put you back in your role.

If you want to Become First, you have to learn to sit inside that pressure without folding. Because the pressure will come. It will come as silence. It will come as passive aggression. It will come as "Are you okay?" that does not mean care but means, "Return to the role." It will come as "I miss the old you," which often means, "I miss the version of you I could predict and use." It will come as a sudden crisis that appears right after you set a boundary, because people sense the shift and unconsciously test whether you still respond on command.

And your nervous system will beg you to fix it. Not because fixing is right, but because fixing is familiar. Familiar pain can feel safer than unfamiliar freedom. So, your body will generate urgency where there is none. Your mind will create scenarios. Your mouth will prepare explanations. Your empathy will go into overtime. You will want to show them that you still care. You will want to prove you are not selfish. You will want to re-establish your goodness.

That is the trap. Because when you start proving your goodness, you return to the old job: emotional employee. You clock in. You justify. You soothe. You translate. You repair. You pay. You keep the environment stable at your own expense. You call it maturity. You call it love. And then you hate yourself later for doing it again.

You do not need to become hard to survive this. Hardness is armor. Armor keeps you safe, but it also keeps you closed. What you need is clarity—the kind that stays present and still refuses to bargain. Clarity does not punish. It does not vanish. It simply stops paying for peace with self-betrayal. It lets someone be uncomfortable without turning their discomfort into your emergency. It holds a "no" without attaching a biography to it. It allows misunderstanding without running back to the old behavior to restore your image. That is Become First: not coldness, not cruelty—just the decision to stop abandoning yourself to keep access.

Growth feels like betrayal because your old identity was built on belonging at any cost. If your family system taught you that love is conditional, then conditions become your reflex. If your relationships rewarded you for over-giving, then over-giving becomes your identity. If your friendships were stable only when you were the "strong one," then strength becomes your cage. And when you try to leave the cage, your body feels like it is leaving the tribe. That is ancient wiring. Human beings fear social exile more than they fear exhaustion. That is why so many people choose the burden. The burden keeps them included.

But inclusion is not intimacy. Being needed is not being loved. Being tolerated is not being seen. And Become First is the moment you stop confusing those things because your life depends on it. Your health depends on it. Your peace depends on it. Your relationships depend on it, even if the relationships do not know that yet.

Now, here is the truth that lands like a slap when you finally see it: you did not betray anyone. You stopped betraying yourself. That does not mean you became perfect. It does not mean you will never misstep. It does not mean you will not hurt people sometimes. It means you stopped participating in a dynamic where your value was tied to your self-erasure.

If someone can only love you when you are convenient, that is not love. If someone can only stay close when you are over-functioning, that is not closeness. If someone needs you to be small so they can feel safe, that is not safety. That is dependency disguised as loyalty.

And this is the part that will test you: some people will not respond to your growth with maturity. They will respond with labeling. They will say you changed like it is an insult. They will speak about the old you like it was the "real you." They will treat your boundary as an offense because it forces them to face a truth they were comfortable avoiding. They will try to pull you back into the old agreement using guilt because guilt worked before.

Your job is not to win the argument in their head. Your job is to hold the line in your life. This is the moment where Become First stops being inspirational and starts being operational. It becomes a behavior, a posture, a baseline. You do not abandon people. You simply stop abandoning yourself to keep them comfortable.

There is grief here, and it is real. You grieve the version of you that survived by being easy. You grieve the years you spent paying for belonging. You grieve the time you lost. You grieve the relationships that were built more on access than on love. You grieve the illusion that if you just gave enough, sacrificed enough, explained enough, and carried enough, you would finally be safe.

But grief is not regression. Grief is the cost of telling the truth. And the truth is that your growth will change the dynamics around you whether you announce it or not. The question is not whether the system will react. It will. The question is whether you will interpret that reaction as proof you are wrong, or as evidence that the old arrangement depended on you staying the same.

Because that is what this part is really doing. It is separating two things that your life has been mixing together for too long: love and obligation. Care and control. Loyalty and fear. Goodness and self-erasure. When those wires are untangled, guilt becomes something you can survive without obeying. You can feel it, but you do not treat it as a command.

And that is the first real threshold. Not confidence. Not empowerment. The threshold is this: you can tolerate being temporarily disliked while you become permanently free. You can tolerate someone else's disappointment while you maintain your integrity. You can tolerate the nervous system panic without returning to the old role to sedate it. That tolerance is not coldness. It is maturity.

You are going to be tested the moment you change. Not with big confrontations—small ones. A sudden crisis that is not yours. A disappointed tone meant to pull you back into the old role. A "joke" that is really a label. A guilt question disguised as concern. "Are you okay?" meaning "Are you still controllable?" "You changed," meaning "You stopped making this easy for me." This is how a system tries to restore the old version of you: not by arguing with your growth, but by hooking your conscience. And this is where most people fold—not because they do not know the truth, but because they cannot tolerate the pressure of holding it. Become First means you do. Quietly. Cleanly. You let the hook pass, you keep your standard, and you do not buy peace with self-betrayal again. And then the resistance shows itself—not as a fight, but as a pattern.

The Resistance Pattern

You will notice it in the air before you notice it in your mind. The moment you stop doing what you always did, something subtle shifts: the room loses a service it never admitted it was receiving. You stop absorbing tension. You stop translating moods. You stop rescuing people from the consequences of their own behavior. You stop smoothing every edge so nobody has to feel the truth. And because the old system was stabilized by your unpaid labor, your refusal will not be read as neutrality. It will be read as disruption.

That is why resistance rarely arrives as a clear confrontation. It arrives as atmosphere. A colder tone. A delayed reply. A sudden distance that makes you question yourself. Not because you did something immoral, but because you removed a convenience. Most people do not fight your logic; they test your nervous system. They wait for the moment your body starts bargaining on their behalf, because they know the old version of you was easiest to summon through discomfort, not debate.

This is the pattern: you set one clean boundary, and then the system checks if it can still access you through old channels. The request returns in a softer form. The same expectation comes back dressed as a "small" favor. The guilt arrives disguised as concern. The message sounds polite, but it is weighted. "Just checking on you." "You have been distant." "Are we okay?" The words are not the point. The reflex they trigger is the point. If you were trained to keep harmony, you will feel your body move toward repair before you even decide you want to repair. You will want to fix the air. You will want to explain your tone. You will want to restore warmth. That is not love. That is conditioning.

Then comes the identity hook. Labels show up because labels are faster than truth. "You changed." "You are selfish." "You are cold." Those words are designed to make you defend yourself. Defense is how people pull you back into the old role: once you are defending, you are explaining; once you are explaining, you are negotiating; once you are negotiating, your boundary is no longer a boundary—it is a discussion. The system does not need to win the argument. It only needs you to treat your self-respect like something that requires approval.

And this is the distinction that saves you: some people do not miss you. They miss the function you served. They miss the version of you that made life easier for them, the version that carried what they refused to carry, the version that stayed available, so they never had to tolerate inconvenience, the version that managed emotional mess quietly, so nobody had to mature. When you stop performing that function, they experience it as loss. They call it betrayal because they confuse closeness with access. They confuse history with entitlement. They confuse your past generosity with a permanent contract.

The resistance will also show up as timing. It will arrive when you are tired, when you are sentimental, when you are already stretched, because that is when the old identity becomes tempting again. You will hear yourself thinking, "Maybe I was too much." "Maybe I should clarify." "Maybe I can meet them halfway." Halfway is where standards die politely. Halfway is where you keep telling yourself you evolved while still playing the same role with improved vocabulary. Halfway is not balance. Halfway is relapse with manners.

So the question is not whether resistance appears. It will. The question is whether you treat it as evidence that you are wrong, or evidence that the old arrangement depended on you staying the same. A boundary does not become real the first time you say it. It becomes real the first time you hold it after the atmosphere changes. It becomes real when you stop negotiating with reactions. It becomes real when you let someone be disappointed without turning their disappointment into your emergency.

This is where clarity becomes your discipline. Not long explanations. Not emotional essays. Not the performance of being "reasonable." Clarity that is short enough to survive repetition. "I cannot do that." "That does not work for me." "I am not available." "You will have to handle that." The old you will call this cold. It is not cold. It is clean. Clean means you stop paying for connection with self-betrayal.

You are not trying to punish anyone. You are refusing to be trained by withdrawal. You are refusing to chase warmth that only appears when you surrender. You are refusing to live in a system where your value is measured by how quickly you erase yourself. That is what breaks the pattern: not one brave conversation, but consistency. The refusal to return. The willingness to let the room adjust to the new physics without you rushing in to stabilize it.

And when you do that long enough, the resistance loses its leverage. The hooks stop working because you stop feeding them. The labels lose their power because you stop treating them as verdicts. The guilt rises, peaks, passes, and you stay aligned anyway. That is when growth stops feeling like betrayal and starts feeling like ownership. Quiet ownership. The kind that does not need to be announced. The kind that shows up in the most adult sentence you will ever learn to say and mean: no.

Withdrawal — When the Old You Tries to Reclaim You

Nobody prepares you for how physical this becomes. You think you are making a decision, but what you are actually doing is interrupting a nervous-system program that has kept you alive in other people's rooms for years. You stop over-functioning and the body does not applaud; it alarms. The chest tightens like you just committed a social crime. The stomach starts negotiating before your mind even forms a thought. Sleep gets weird, appetite gets weird, focus gets weird, because your system is not used to peace that is not purchased through performance. The old version of you was not a personality; it was a survival strategy, and survival strategies do not retire politely.

This is why so many people mistake withdrawal for a sign they are wrong. They set one clean boundary, and then they experience the internal backlash: urgency, guilt, intrusive rehearsals, mental courtroom defenses, that compulsive need to "just clarify." They call it empathy, but it is not empathy— it is fear with good manners. It is the reflex that says: restore the atmosphere before the atmosphere becomes punishment. If you grew up learning that tension leads to consequences, then a cold tone will feel like danger even when no one is actually threatening you. Your body will interpret mild disappointment as exile, and exile is ancient terror. The mind will then do what it has always done to keep you safe: it will tempt you to return to the role.

And the role always returns dressed as something noble. It does not announce itself as self-erasure. It shows up as responsibility. It shows up as being "the bigger person." It shows up as, "I just do not want conflict." It shows up as, "Let me handle it so it does not get worse." It shows up as, "They are going through something." It shows up as compassion that quietly converts into labor. That is the trap: you learned to package your self-abandonment as character. You learned to call it loyalty. You learned to call it maturity. You learned to call it love. So, when you finally stop, the mind accuses you of becoming someone you despise, because your identity has been built around being the one who absorbs. Withdrawal is the moment your nervous system tries to keep you loyal to an old identity by making the new one feel immoral.

This is also where the world tests whether your change is real. Not in big speeches, not in dramatic confrontations, but in tiny, perfectly timed hooks that target your reflexes. A message arrives when you are tired, when you are already stretched, when you are sentimental. A "quick question." A "small favor." A "five minutes." A problem that is not yours but appears at your door like it is. The request is never really the request; it is the leash. It is the system checking if it can still summon you with mild pressure, with a disappointed tone, with the hint of withdrawal. If you respond, the system learns the new boundary is just a mood. If you explain, the system learns your clarity is negotiable. If you soften until you surrender, the system learns it only has to wait you out. This is why the third repetition is the real test: the boundary is not proven by the first no; it is proven by the moment you can keep it while your body is screaming to rescue the atmosphere.

The hardest part is that you will be tempted to repair not because you want to, but because you want to stop the internal discomfort. You will mistake urgency for truth. You will think, "If I do not fix this, I am cruel," when what you really mean is, "If I do not fix this, I will have to tolerate the feeling of being misread." The old you spent years paying to avoid that feeling. You paid with time, with money, with health, with attention, with life force, because being misunderstood was unbearable in a nervous system trained to equate misunderstanding with punishment. So you built a strategy: be so helpful that nobody can accuse you. Be so available that nobody can abandon you. Be so reasonable that nobody can label you. That strategy worked, in the short term. But it also turned you into a permanent employee in other people's emotional economy, clocking in every time the room got uncomfortable, calling it love, while your body kept the receipts.

So, the question becomes brutal and simple: are you willing to feel the withdrawal without obeying it? Are you willing to let someone be disappointed without collapsing into a service role? Are you willing to let a tone be cold and still keep your standard? Are you willing to let the air in the room thicken without rushing to thin it with explanations? Because if you cannot tolerate that, you will keep returning to the same arrangement in new outfits. Different faces, different settings, different ages, same system. The system is not "the other person." The system is the deal: you provide stability, they provide belonging. You provide patience, they provide permission. You provide sacrifice, they provide closeness. And the moment you stop providing, they call you "changed" as if change is betrayal, because the old contract was written in invisible ink: your peace for their comfort.

This is where Become First stops being a concept and becomes a discipline. Discipline is not intensity; it is repetition. It is the ability to stay clean when your old self tries to negotiate a return. It is the refusal to turn your boundary into a debate, to turn your no into a biography, to turn your dignity into a document you must defend. You start learning a new language—short, clear, adult—and you accept the cost: some people will not like it. The old you would rush to fix that; the new you will learn to let it be. Not because you are hard, but because you are done confusing discomfort with danger. You are done mistaking withdrawal symptoms for moral instruction. You are done paying to keep everyone calm while you bleed quietly.

And there is a moment, usually private, where you realize the real addiction was not being needed—it was being "safe" through usefulness. Usefulness gave you leverage. Usefulness gave you identity. Usefulness gave you a story where you were good even when you were exhausted. That is why the first stage of freedom feels like loss: you are not just removing a behavior; you are dismantling the scaffolding that held your identity together. Of course it shakes. Of course it hurts. Of course your mind tries to pull you back with guilt, because guilt is the fastest path back to the old role. But if you hold the line long enough, something changes that you cannot fake: the body starts believing you. The nervous system starts learning that disappointment is survivable. The mind starts losing the need to explain. The hook passes without you grabbing it. The urge rises, peaks, and leaves, and you remain standing.

That is the threshold right before release: the moment you realize you can feel all of it—guilt, anxiety, loneliness, the desire to repair—and still not return to self-betrayal. You do not need their approval to stay aligned. You do not need warmth to validate your boundary. You do not need to be understood to be clean. And when that becomes true inside your body, not just in your mind, the dynamic outside you has no choice but to reveal itself.

Some people adjust because love can renegotiate. Some people tighten the leash because access cannot. Either way, the story turns honest. Not in words—in consequences. You see who can meet you, and who only knew how to take you. And that is when the body stops negotiating. The nervous system stops bargaining. You feel the truth like weight.

Because there is a moment—quiet, final—when you realize you cannot climb your own mountain with four grown adults on your back. Not because you are cruel. Because gravity is real.

The Summit You Owe Your Life

The fog clears and you finally see what is real. Not what you hoped was real. Not what you paid to keep real. Not what you performed into existence with patience, money, excuses, and emotional labor. You see the arrangement as it is: who adjusts when you speak plainly, who only "loves" you when you are useful, who becomes generous the moment you stop being generous, who calls your self-respect cruelty because it ends their comfort. And that clarity is not gentle. It does not arrive like an affirmation. It arrives like altitude. It arrives like oxygen. It arrives like a body that has been quietly keeping receipts for years and finally hands you the bill.

This is the part nobody romanticizes, because it is not flattering. It does not make you look like a saint. It makes you look like a man who waited too long to admit a brutal truth: the heroic version of you is not always noble. Sometimes the heroic version of you is an addiction. Sometimes it is the cleanest costume for a survival strategy that kept you safe in other people's rooms. You learned early that being needed protected you. Being useful made you untouchable. Being "the one who carries" gave you belonging, and belonging felt like love. So you became the infrastructure. You became the calendar, the crisis hotline, the strategist, the shelter, the lender, the spine. You became the person who could not fall apart because everybody else was already doing it for you.

And then you woke up one day and realized you were not climbing your mountain anymore. You were running a rescue mission halfway up somebody else's. You were doing five steps forward and getting pulled three steps back, not by fate, not by circumstances, not by "bad timing," but by your own reflex to carry what was never yours. The loop was not bad luck. The loop was a contract. The contract said: you will trade your peace for connection, and you will call it love, so you do not have to face what it really is.

The mountain is the perfect place to tell the truth, because the mountain does not respond to excuses. The mountain does not care about your intentions. The mountain does not care how kind you are, how loyal you are, how compassionate you are, how many times you saved somebody who did not save themselves. The mountain cares about weight. It cares about oxygen. It cares about distance. It cares about physics. And physics is the one language your nervous system cannot manipulate with guilt.

You start the climb the way everyone starts a climb: with hunger, with vision, with that private certainty that there is something up there meant for you. The summit is not just success. It is the view you have been missing your whole life because you have been busy managing other people's weather. It is a moment of stillness where you can finally hear your own mind without translating it into something more palatable for the room. It is the reward your body has been begging you for: a life that does not feel like a constant negotiation with other people's needs.

And on the way up, you meet the familiar scene. Someone's rope snaps. Someone is hanging. Someone is stuck near the foothills, exhausted, panicked, convinced they cannot continue. They look at you like you are the answer because you have been the answer before. You have the strength, the strategy, the composure, the resources. And your old identity wakes up like a trained dog hearing its name. You step in. You do not even call it sacrifice. You call it being human. You call it being a good person. You call it loyalty. You call it love.

At first it feels manageable. One person on your back. A temporary pause. A little money. A little time. A few introductions. You tell yourself you will catch up. You tell yourself the summit is patient. You tell yourself you have a big heart and that is your gift. You keep climbing.

Then the weight multiplies. The first person you carry becomes a precedent. The second person sees you can carry and asks to be carried. The third person does not even ask anymore, because your giving has already taught them that "give" is your default setting. The fourth person arrives in a nicer costume, speaks in softer language, but the script is identical: "Just five minutes." "Quick question." "Can you just…" "I only need…" They package their dependency in politeness so you can call it harmless. But your body knows. Your body always knows. Your body feels the truth before your mind admits it.

This is where the climb turns from cinematic to terrifying, because now the slope is steeper and you are not only carrying weight; you are carrying consequences. You are carrying the consequences they refused to carry. You are carrying the consequences they postponed with charm, with excuses, with self-pity, with "bad luck," with endless stories about why today is not the day they can stand on their own. You are carrying the consequences of their choices while they keep the luxury of believing they are victims of the world.

And then it happens: you are halfway up, and the math stops working. You go five steps forward, and the weight pulls you three back. You fight again, you claw again, you push again, and you gain two steps, and then you lose four. You start spending your energy just to not fall, and you tell yourself that is normal, that life is hard, that this is what love looks like. But deep inside, there is a second voice, a colder voice, a voice you have been avoiding because it scares you. It says: you are not climbing anymore. You are maintaining a system. You are stabilizing other people's refusal to grow.

This is the moment growth stops being inspirational and becomes a decision that feels brutal. Not because you want to hurt anyone. Because you finally see the real stakes. If you keep carrying them, you do not reach the summit. You do not reach it with them. You do not reach it without them. You simply do not reach it. And worse, you risk something that your old identity never accounted for: you all fall. Not as a metaphor. As a life.

That is the first real form of adulthood: accepting that your empathy does not override physics. Accepting that your loyalty does not cancel reality. Accepting that your heart cannot carry what your body cannot. Accepting that a man can be compassionate and still be responsible, and that sometimes responsibility looks like letting the consequences exist without you acting as the shock absorber.

So you reach the wall. The wall is not rage. The wall is depletion. The wall is the moment your nervous system finally refuses to be a public service. The wall is your body saying, with no poetry and no drama: there is nothing left. Not time. Not strength. Not money. Not attention. Not capacity. Not the kind of patience that used to make you feel like a good man. The wall is not emotional. It is mechanical. It is the engine running dry.

And in that moment, you hear yourself say the sentence you have been avoiding for years, because it sounds cruel in a world addicted to access: I cannot do this anymore.

Not "I do not love you." Not "I am leaving." Not "You are a bad person." Just the truth. I cannot do this anymore.

This is where the old you panics, because the old you believes that stopping equals abandonment. The old you believes you must keep carrying to remain "good." The old you believes that if someone falls, it will be your fault, and your conscience will never forgive you. That is the hook. That is the guilt. That is the ancient wiring that equates tension with danger and disappointment with exile.

But here is the truth that breaks the spell: setting someone down is not the same as throwing them away. Setting someone down is refusing to die with them.

There is a difference between cruelty and clarity. Cruelty is leaving someone to suffer because you enjoy power. Clarity is leaving a dynamic because staying inside it is destroying you, and destroying you will not save anyone. Clarity is the moment you realize you are not responsible for outcomes you did not create. Clarity is the moment you stop confusing compassion with self-erasure.

And the mountain demands clarity, because the mountain does not accept your guilt as currency. The mountain does not care how guilty you feel. The mountain only asks: can you carry this and still live?

So, you do the thing that feels like betrayal to people who benefited from your softness: you set the weight down.

Not with speeches. Not with essays. Not with a courtroom defense of your character. You set it down cleanly, because you learned the hard way that the longer you explain, the more you negotiate, and negotiation is how your boundaries become jokes. You say less. You mean more. You do not turn your dignity into a debate.

And then the cinematic part happens, the part you have seen in different rooms with different casts, the part that makes you feel like a spectator watching the same film on repeat: the script flips. The moment you stop carrying, you become the villain in a story you funded. The same hands that took without shame pick up moral language. The same mouths that accepted your sacrifices start calling you "hard" the moment you stop bleeding. The same people who were comfortable with your exhaustion suddenly become philosophers about loyalty.

They do not say, "I understand you are depleted." They say, "You changed." They do not say, "I can stand now." They say, "You are selfish." They do not say, "I relied on you too much." They say, "After everything I have been through…" They do not say, "I miss your help." They say, "I miss the old you."

Because if they can rewrite your boundary as cruelty, they do not have to face what your boundary reveals: that the old arrangement depended on you being endlessly available, endlessly forgiving, endlessly paying.

This is where you learn something that will change your entire life if you let it: some people do not miss you. They miss the function you served. They miss the emotional infrastructure. They miss the man who made consequences disappear. They miss the version of you who kept the air warm by sacrificing his own oxygen.

And your nervous system will want to fix it. It will want to restore warmth. It will want to explain your tone. It will want to prove you are not a monster. It will want to apologize for having limits. This is the most dangerous moment, because it feels like morality, but it is actually conditioning. It is fear with manners. It is the reflex that says: if I do not repair the atmosphere, I will be punished. It is the child in you trying to stay safe in a room that once made safety conditional.

So you stand there, in the cold air of your own growth, and you make a new decision. You let them be uncomfortable without turning their discomfort into your emergency. You let them be disappointed without buying back approval with self-betrayal. You let your name be questioned without returning to your role. You accept that misunderstanding is survivable. You accept that being temporarily disliked is not death. You accept that the price of integrity is sometimes a colder room.

This is where the real strength shows. Not the strength of carrying. The strength of not carrying.

Because carrying is easy for you. You were trained for it. You have done it your whole life. It is your default skill. It makes you feel powerful. It makes you feel necessary. It makes you feel safe.

Not carrying is the hard thing. Not carrying is the moment you stop using usefulness as your armor. Not carrying is the moment you stop building security on being needed. Not carrying is the moment you stop confusing indispensable with loved.

And when you stop carrying, something else becomes visible: time.

Time is the only currency you never get back. Money can be rebuilt. You already proved that. You can lose it, you can rebuild it, you can create it again because you have a mind that generates value. You can start over financially and still win, because your worth is not the number in your account. Your worth is your ability to create.

But time does not return. Time does not negotiate. Time does not care about your intentions. Time does not refund you because you were kind. Time is the one thing that tells the truth without emotion. It simply passes.

And that is why the deepest wound is not the money you gave. It is the years. The hours. The seasons of your life you spent stabilizing other people while your own summit stayed distant. The moments you could have been building your health, your peace, your marriage, your craft, your legacy, your life, but you were busy keeping someone else comfortable so you could continue being "good."

So, you say the sentence you have said to everyone, the sentence that sounds like pride but is actually grief and clarity at once: I can live with losing money. I have lost money more than once. I do not care. I am a worthy man, and I will make the money again. And I do. Every time.

And then you say the part that is not performance, the part that is raw, the part that lands like a blade: what breaks me is not the money. What breaks me is the time.

Because money returns. Time does not. And nothing hurts like realizing you paid for someone else's comfort with hours of your one life.

This is the moment the room rewrites your self-respect as cruelty—because your "no" ends their comfort. This is the moment growth feels like betrayal, not because you harmed anyone, but because other people treat your boundary like a personal loss. They act as if you stole something from them, when the only thing you reclaimed was yourself.

And now the last test arrives: not the world's reaction, but your own internal bargaining. Your mind will open a courtroom inside your head and put you on trial. It will replay the conversations. It will draft better lines. It will imagine how you could have said it "softer." It will offer you a deal: keep the boundary, but with an apology. Keep the standard, but with guilt. Keep your dignity but still make them feel okay. That is the old contract trying to reattach itself to your spine.

This is where most people fold. Not because they are weak, but because they cannot tolerate the emotional backlash of being clean. They can tolerate hard work, discipline, pain, ambition, risk. They cannot tolerate being misread. They cannot tolerate someone else's disappointment without making it their responsibility. They cannot tolerate the sensation of the room getting colder without rushing to pay for warmth.

Relapse does not look like failure. It looks like a polite return. You do not go back to love—you go back to the job. You step into the old posture, you soften the standard, you call it 'keeping the peace,' and for a few hours it even feels like relief. But it is not peace; it is you restoring the old agreement so the room can stay comfortable. You hand your truth back in exchange for quiet. You erase the edge so nobody else has to adjust. You buy calm the same way you always did: by paying upfront, so consequences never have to arrive. And that is why the pull is so dangerous—it does not come as temptation, it comes as responsibility dressed in good manners. Pressure returns the way it always returns: not as truth, as timing. It waits until you are tired, sentimental, stretched thin—until your guard is low and your old reflex is loud. Then it shows up as something 'small.' A quick question that is never quick. A small favor that is never small. A crisis that is not yours, delivered to your door like it is. The request is rarely the request. It is a leash. It is the old arrangement checking whether your boundary is a standard or a mood.

At altitude you learn a rule the hard way: you do not waste oxygen negotiating. You do not write essays for people committed to misunderstanding you. You do not chase warmth that only appears when you surrender. You stop volunteering your nervous system as a public service. The language gets short enough to survive repetition, clean enough to leave no handles: "I cannot." "I am not available." "That does not work for me." "You will have to handle that." "No."

And at first, that "no" detonates inside your own body like you committed a crime, because you trained your nervous system to equate boundaries with danger. The chest tightens. The mind runs courtroom arguments at full speed. Empathy flares like an alarm. You feel the pull to repair the air, soften the tone, explain, apologize, restore warmth—because somewhere in you, a cold room still means punishment.

Holding the line teaches you something no philosophy ever could: the sensation peaks, and it passes. You stay standing. Nothing collapses because you refused to self-betray. Disappointment is survivable. Misunderstanding is survivable. A colder room is survivable. Loneliness is survivable. The world does not end because you stopped being convenient.

That is where relief starts—not applause, not validation, not a performance of strength, but alignment. Your nervous system begins to believe you. Your body stops bracing for consequences that never arrive. Your mind stops rehearsing explanations. You stop scanning faces and messages like it is your job to stabilize the room. You stop living like a thermostat. You become a man with temperature of his own.

Stopping the carry does not make you less loving. It makes you precise. Rescue separates from love. Need separates from intimacy. Loyalty separates from self-erasure. History separates from entitlement. Some people adjust because real love can renegotiate; real love can dislike your boundary and still respect it, can feel inconvenience without punishing you, can stay close without demanding you shrink. Some people cannot adjust because access cannot renegotiate; access panics when it is reduced, uses guilt as a weapon, calls your self-respect cruelty because your "no" ends their comfort. That is not love dying. That is a contract being exposed.

And once the contract is exposed, the fog clears. Guessing stops. Performing stops. Financing the same dynamic with improved vocabulary stops. The humiliating truth lands clean and the liberation stays: you were not trapped by other people as much as you were trapped by the deal you kept making with yourself—carry them so they do not leave, over-give so you do not get disliked, pay for peace with self-betrayal because conflict terrifies you.

The deal breaks the only way real things break: not in one dramatic scene, but in quiet repetition. A hundred moments where your body begs you to return and you refuse. A hundred times guilt rises and you do not obey it. A hundred hooks float by and you let them pass. Standards become real when they hold under atmosphere.

That is Become First: unbuyable. Unbuyable by guilt. Unbuyable by withdrawal. Unbuyable by praise that only arrives when you surrender. Unbuyable by roles that keep you useful and small. You are not a function. You are a man. And when you finally live like that, the mountain stops feeling like punishment and starts feeling like truth—carrying only what is yours, walking forward without apology, and giving yourself the one thing you cannot replace.

Time.

CHAPTER 12

YOUR OLD LIFE NO LONGER FITS

The Room Doesn't Recognize You

It starts as something you cannot defend in a conversation, because it is not an argument. It is a sensation. You walk into a room you have walked into a hundred times and your body reacts like it has never been there before. The lighting is the same, the voices are the same, the jokes land in the same places, but your chest tightens anyway. Your stomach goes slightly hollow, not from fear, from recognition. Your nervous system reads the air faster than your mind can translate it.

You try to reason with yourself the way you used to. You tell yourself to be normal. You tell yourself not to make it a thing. You tell yourself you are being dramatic, because that is the oldest trick the old life uses: it makes your truth sound like an attitude. You take a breath and put your face on, because you were trained—by childhood, by relationships, by survival—to treat discomfort as a problem to solve, not a message to respect. You smile at the right moments, you nod at the right cues, you behave like the person they recognize, and you can feel the muscle strain in your jaw as if you are holding up a ceiling.

It is not that something is wrong with the room. It is that something is different in you, and the room can feel it before it can name it. You did not announce a new version of yourself, you did not make a speech, you did not redesign your personality in front of anyone. You made one small internal change that was invisible from the outside: you stopped volunteering your nervous system as a payment method. You stopped translating other people's discomfort into your responsibility. You stopped doing the quick mental math of how to keep the peace at your own expense.

The old life hates that kind of change because it cannot negotiate with it. It cannot argue you out of it because you are not arguing. You are simply not offering yourself in the same way anymore. You are not delivering the old performance on time. You are not filling the emotional silence with your explanations. You are not making yourself smaller so the room can stay comfortable. And suddenly the same people who have always "liked you" begin to act as if you are becoming difficult, when the only thing you did was stop being easy.

The camera moves closer here, because this is the moment most people miss. They think growth is a loud transformation, visible to everyone, celebrated, applauded, obvious. They expect progress to feel clean. They expect it to feel like a new outfit that fits perfectly. But the truth is that growth often feels like being slightly out of place everywhere you used to belong. It feels like your skin doesn't sit right on your body for a while. It feels like you are standing inside your own life with a different posture and no one has updated the script.

That is why "not fitting" is so confusing. Your mind wants to label it as failure because failure is familiar. Failure at least gives you a task: fix yourself, adjust, try harder, apologize, get back in alignment. Your old life loves that interpretation because it keeps you chasing approval like a dog chasing a moving car. But elevation is different. Elevation does not ask you to try harder at being who you used to be. Elevation asks you to stop trying to fit where your nervous system cannot breathe.

Look closely at what is actually happening. It is never just "I do not vibe with this anymore." It is much more specific. You are listening to a conversation you used to participate in, and you can feel your throat tighten, because your body knows the price of pretending to agree. You are sitting at a dinner table where you used to swallow your opinions for dessert, and the old habit rises in you like reflux. You are watching someone take a casual swipe at your boundaries—a small joke, a light comment, a harmless suggestion—and you feel your stomach flare because you know how those "small" moments add up when you never correct them. You are being offered a familiar role again and again, and the offer is dressed as love.

This is the part nobody wants to admit: many relationships do not actually run on love. They run on access. They run on predictable patterns. They run on who you are willing to become so the other person does not have to adjust. In the old life, you were rewarded for being flexible in a way that looked like kindness but functioned like compliance. You were praised for being "understanding" when what you were really doing was abandoning your own needs quietly, so the room would not have to deal with them.

Peace is not always peace. Sometimes peace is just you surrendering your truth so nobody else has to adjust. Sometimes peace is you paying again so consequences never arrive. Sometimes peace is a hostage negotiation where you keep offering yourself as ransom and calling it maturity, because you are too exhausted to name it honestly.

The first sign that your old life no longer fits is that your body stops cooperating with the lies. You can still say the polite words, but you cannot swallow them the same way. You can still show up, but you cannot float above yourself like you used to. The distance between what you feel and what you pretend becomes too wide, and your nervous system starts sending invoices. You leave gatherings and feel drained for no "reason." You go home and your shoulders ache as if you carried furniture. You wake up with a tight chest and you cannot explain why. The body keeps receipts, and at some point, it stops accepting "it is fine" as payment.

People will tell you that you are overreacting, because that is what people say when your reaction threatens their comfort. They will call you sensitive, because sensitivity is the easiest insult when they do not want to look at their behavior. They will say you are making everything about you, because that is what they say when you start making your life about you. They will say you have changed, as if change is a betrayal, as if the only acceptable form of love is the kind that preserves the old contract.

But here is what you need to understand, and you need to understand it with your spine, not with your ideas: your old life does not let go quietly. It does not fade out like a song ending. It pulls. It tests. It provokes. It will give you moments that feel like nostalgia so you confuse familiarity with safety. It will put you back in front of old triggers and see if you reach for the old coping mechanisms. It will offer you approval again, but with conditions. It will make kindness contingent on your return to the role.

That is why one small change within you shifts everything around you. Because once you stop feeding the dynamic, the dynamic gets hungry. And hungry dynamics do not politely ask for their food. They become louder. They become more manipulative. They become more emotional. They become more "hurt." They weaponize misunderstanding. They play innocent. They act confused. They act like victims of your boundaries. They do everything except meet you at your new level, because meeting you at your new level would require them to change too.

This is where the pressure comes. Not as a direct threat, most of the time. Pressure comes as subtle cues. A look. A tone. A delay in response. A withdrawal of warmth. A sudden coldness where there used to be easy access. Pressure comes as you noticing you are being "punished" for not performing your old self. Pressure comes as that familiar anxiety in your belly when you realize: they are waiting for you to fold. They are waiting for you to explain. They are waiting for you to return to being manageable.

The old you would have folded quickly, not because you were weak, but because you were trained. You were trained to read moods like weather reports and adjust. You were trained to treat tension as an emergency. You were trained to believe love meant never making anyone uncomfortable. You were trained to believe your needs were negotiable if someone else's emotions were loud enough. And in that training, you became excellent at preventing conflict, which means you became excellent at preventing consequences.

Now you are changing. Not in some dramatic, cinematic way that looks impressive on social media. In a quiet, internal way that nobody claps for. You are changing by tolerating the discomfort of not fixing the room. You are changing by letting other people feel what they feel without running to manage it. You are changing by letting silence exist without filling it with your performance. That one change is enough to rewrite the entire social physics around you.

Because the room is not just a room. It is a system. Every family is a system. Every friendship group is a system. Every workplace is a system. Every relationship is a system. Systems do not like disruption. Systems are designed to maintain themselves. They punish deviations. They reward compliance. They label the person who changes as the problem, because that is easier than admitting the system benefits from their old behavior.

So you start to feel it. You are treated differently. You are spoken to with slightly less patience. Your boundaries are questioned more. Your absence is resented more. Your no is negotiated more. Your clarity is interpreted as cruelty. Your standards are framed as arrogance. Your self-respect is painted as selfishness. The room begins to tell a story about you, not because the story is true, but because the story keeps you in the old position.

If you take this personally, it will break you. If you take this as information, it will free you.

The moment you feel "I do not fit," you will be tempted to do what you have always done: adapt. Bend. Smooth it over. Prove you are still the same. Make a joke. Offer extra warmth. Over-explain. Reassure. Apologize for the inconvenience of your growth. That temptation is not random. It is the old contract pulling you back into place.

So the real question is not whether you fit. The real question is: what have you been fitting into?

Some people have been fitting into roles their entire lives. They are the calm one. The responsible one. The forgiving one. The one who never needs anything. The one who always understands. The one who takes the high road. The one who makes everyone feel safe. The one who absorbs impact so other people can stay soft. They call it being mature. They call it being strong. They call it being loving. And then they wonder why they feel empty, why their body is inflamed, why their sleep is light, why they cannot relax in their own home.

You cannot relax when your nervous system has been trained to stay on duty. You cannot feel safe when safety is conditional. You cannot feel loved when love is offered as access, then withdrawn as punishment. You cannot thrive in a life where your peace depends on your compliance.

This is where the book becomes practical without becoming a poster. Because the shift you need is not a new philosophy. It is a new tolerance. You need to build tolerance for the first wave of discomfort that comes when you stop fitting.

That wave is real. It feels like withdrawal because it is withdrawal. You are withdrawing from a substance: approval. You are withdrawing from a pattern: being needed. You are withdrawing from an identity: the one who fixes it.

When you withdraw from those patterns, your body will crave them, not because they are good for you, but because they are familiar. Familiarity is not safety. Familiarity is repetition.

So you will crave the old relief: the moment when everyone smiles again because you made it easy. The moment when tension dissolves because you offered yourself. The moment when you feel "back in place" because you sacrificed your own truth for the group's comfort. That relief is not peace. It is sedation.

Real peace feels different. Real peace feels like the quiet after you stop arguing with your body. Real peace feels like your shoulders dropping, because you are no longer performing. Real peace feels like sleeping deeply, because you did not betray yourself during the day. Real peace is not the room being calm. Real peace is you being intact.

Watch what happens when you do not fit. The system will try to make you responsible for the tension. It will look for a way to blame your boundaries rather than their entitlement. It will try to frame your growth as a personal attack. It will accuse you of thinking you are better. It will say you are cold. It will say you are distant. It will say you have changed, as if change is a crime.

This is the crossroads. This is where most people go back. Not because they want to, but because they cannot tolerate being misunderstood by the people they love. They cannot tolerate the story that is being told about them. They cannot tolerate the idea that someone is disappointed. They cannot tolerate that the room is not pleased. And in that intolerance, they give up their own next level to maintain an old peace that was never truly peace.

But the call toward your next level does not come with comfort. It comes with clarity. It comes with a new internal standard that you cannot unsee. It comes with the realization that you have been living in a shape that does not match your soul anymore. It comes with the moment your body says, quietly but firmly: not this.

You do not need to demonize your old life to outgrow it. You do not need to hate the people you used to love. You do not need to rewrite history and pretend nothing good happened there. That is not strength. That is coping. Growth is more honest. Growth can say: this gave me something once, and now it costs me too much.

Because that is what changes. The math changes. The same behavior that once felt like kindness now feels like self-erasure. The same tolerance that once felt like loyalty now feels like cowardice. The same silence that once felt like peace now feels like complicity. The same availability that once felt like love now feels like being used.

Your old life no longer fits because you have matured past the point where you can lie to yourself without consequence.

And once you see that, you cannot unsee it.

You will begin to notice the micro-moments where you used to betray yourself. You will notice how quickly you would say yes to avoid someone's disappointment. You will notice how often you would laugh at things that hurt you. You will notice how often you would minimize your own needs so you would not be labeled demanding. You will notice how often you would explain yourself like you were on trial, as if your boundaries needed a jury.

Those moments were your old life's currency. You paid with your truth. You paid with your energy. You paid with your body. You paid with your time. You paid with your future. And you did it so consistently that it became invisible to you. That is why the first real change feels like stepping out of a costume you forgot you were wearing. You suddenly feel exposed, not because you are unsafe, but because you are no longer hidden from yourself.

Now the room reacts. The room always reacts. The room has a memory of you that is convenient. The room has a version of you it knows how to handle.

The room has a role for you that keeps the system stable. And when you stop playing it, the system experiences it as chaos.

Your job is not to re-stabilize the system by shrinking. Your job is to stabilize yourself by staying honest.

That does not mean you become cruel. It means you become clear. It means you stop confusing softness with surrender. It means you stop confusing politeness with self-abandonment. It means you stop confusing love with access.

Because love that requires your self-betrayal is not love. It is a transaction where you are the product.

So, you stand there in that familiar room, and you feel the tightness in your chest, and you do something radical. You do nothing. You do not rush to fix. You do not rush to smooth. You do not rush to apologize for existing differently. You stay in your body. You let the discomfort move through you. You let the room be what it is without making yourself responsible for it.

And in that moment, you begin to understand the truth most people never learn until they are exhausted: you were not fitting because you were meant to stay small. You were fitting because you were afraid of what would happen if you stopped.

Now you are stopping.

Enough.

The First Test Costs Something

There is a moment that comes after the realization, after the sentence you finally admit to yourself: *this does not fit me anymore.* The mind thinks the hard part is over once you can name it. But naming it is not the shift. Naming it is the beginning of the pressure. The real shift happens when the old life tests whether you meant what you saw. It does not test your insight. It tests your behavior. It tests whether you will keep paying the old price the moment discomfort shows up, the moment someone's mood changes, the moment warmth gets withdrawn, the moment you are offered "peace" in exchange for your silence.

This is why people stay stuck even after they become "aware." Awareness is easy compared to consequence. Awareness can live in your head without disturbing anything. Consequence is where the old agreement is forced into daylight. Consequence is where you learn what the relationship was actually built on. Not love. Not loyalty. Not history. The deal. The deal that said, without saying it: you stay small, I stay comfortable. You stay available, I do not have to grow. You swallow the tension, I get to avoid responsibility. You keep the air pleasant, and we call it connection.

When you outgrow the deal, you do not need to announce it. You do not need to "have a talk." Most of the time, the deal is broken by something embarrassingly simple. You do not answer immediately. You do not show up when you are exhausted. You do not laugh at the same disrespect. You do not soothe someone who keeps creating the same crisis. You do not say yes out of reflex. You do one ordinary thing differently and suddenly the room turns strange. Your phone feels heavier. Your chest tightens. Your stomach does that familiar drop. Not because you are in danger, but because your nervous system remembers the old rule: keep the room calm or pay.

That is the first test. And it rarely looks like a dramatic confrontation. It looks like an invitation that assumes you will come. It looks like a "quick call" that is never quick. It looks like a message that sounds casual but carries weight: *Are we okay? You have been distant.* It looks like concern that is not really concern; it is a probe. A probe to see if you will return to your role. A probe to see if you will shrink back into the version of you that made everything easy for everyone else.

If you have been the steady one, the reliable one, the understanding one, you were not just a person in your old life. You were an infrastructure. People built their habits around your availability. They built their emotional timing around your willingness to absorb. They built their comfort around your flexibility. When you stop, even slightly, they experience it as instability. And humans react to instability in predictable ways. Some become honest. Some become manipulative. Some become cold. Some become sentimental. The method varies, but the goal is the same: restore the old arrangement.

Here is how it happens in real life.

A friend calls you after weeks of silence. In the past, you would have been grateful for the call, because you were trained to treat scraps as proof of love. You would have jumped in, asked questions, carried the conversation, offered energy, offered reassurance, offered your attention like a donation. You would have ignored the quiet resentment in your body because you did not want to seem "needy." You would have pretended the imbalance did not matter, because pretending felt like maturity. But now you feel something new: a calm awareness. Not anger. Not drama. Just accuracy. You notice that your friend only calls when they need something. You notice that your life does not exist in their world unless it is convenient. You notice that you have been providing access without reciprocity and calling it loyalty.

So you do something small. You do not punish them. You do not attack them. You simply do not rush to make it okay. You say, cleanly, "I cannot talk long today." Or you say, "I am not available for that." Or you ask one honest question you avoided for years: "Do you only reach out when you are in crisis?" The words are not the point. The shift is the point. The shift is you refusing to shrink to keep the connection.

This is where the contract reveals itself. Because a person who values you will not make you pay for clarity. They might feel exposed. They might feel uncomfortable. They might even be surprised. But they will stay present. They will adjust. They will not retaliate. A person who values the function you served, not you, will respond differently. They will get offended fast. They will go cold. They will act like you are attacking them. They will say you are "keeping score." They will reframe your honesty as negativity. They will turn the conversation into a trial where you must prove your boundary is justified.

And the old you would have stepped into that trial immediately. You would have started defending. You would have started explaining. You would have started listing examples, trying to sound reasonable enough to be respected. You would have started shrinking your truth, so they could swallow it without choking. You would have done all that, because you confused being understood with being safe.

But this is the moment you must remember the first law of your life: you do not wait for someone else to become accountable before you act with self-respect. Waiting is how you keep the deal alive. Waiting is how you keep paying the monthly fee. Waiting is the polite version of surrender. You do not wait for the room to approve your growth. You become first. Not first as in superior. First as in you stop coming last.

So you do not argue. You do not recruit them into understanding. You do not give a speech about friendship and loyalty. You simply hold the line. You let their discomfort exist without treating it as an emergency. You let them be disappointed without rushing to buy your way back into warmth. You notice how your body begs you to repair the mood, and you do not obey it. That is the work. That is the shift. That is the part that changes your life more than any insight ever will.

Then comes the second test, and it is usually family.

Family pressure has a unique flavor because it is older than your adult logic. Family pressure does not argue like a stranger. It speaks like a memory. It speaks in tone. It speaks in obligation. It speaks in the language of "after everything we have done," as if love is a debt collector. It speaks with disappointment disguised as concern. It speaks with the unspoken message you have heard your whole life: a good person sacrifices. A good child adjusts. A loving one endures. If you do not endure, you are selfish.

If you were trained inside that environment, you know what happens in your body the moment that tone appears. Your throat tightens. Your chest gets heavy. Your mind starts scanning for the fastest way to restore peace. Your nervous system does not want the argument. It wants relief. And relief used to come through one thing: compliance. You would say yes. You would explain. You would promise. You would smooth. You would carry the emotional weight so nobody else had to feel uncomfortable.

Now your life asks you a harder question: is the peace you are trying to restore actually peace, or is it just the absence of conflict bought with your self-erasure? Because those two things are not the same. Peace that requires you to disappear is not peace. It is compliance wearing perfume.

So you choose a different sentence. Not a dramatic sentence. A sentence your body can live with. "I understand how you feel. I am not doing that." Or: "I hear you. My decision stands." Or the simplest one, the one that feels like a crime to your old identity: "No." You do not add ten reasons. You do not decorate it with guilt. You do not apologize for existing. You speak as an adult, not as a defendant.

And here is what will happen if you actually do it. Someone will push harder.

They will raise their voice. They will accuse you of changing. They will bring up your past to regain leverage. They will try to make you feel like you are abandoning the family, the tradition, the role you have always played. They will imply that you are ungrateful. They might even cry, because tears have been currency in many families for generations. None of this means they are evil. It means the old system is losing a convenience: your willingness to shrink. The system does not know how to stay stable without your surrender, so it escalates.

And you will feel the old reflex: fix it. Explain more. Prove you are still good. Offer something. Give them a softer version of the truth so they stop reacting. But that is exactly how people spend their lives trapped in family dynamics that never evolve. They keep giving their adulthood away in pieces, and they call it love.

This is where you remember the second law: stop shrinking to support others. Support is not self-erasure. Love is not you being the shock absorber for everyone's immaturity. Kindness is not you disappearing, so other people do not have to adjust. You can be respectful without being controlled. You can be loving without being available for manipulation. You can honor your family without betraying yourself.

So you hold your tone. You do not become cruel. You do not attack. You do not threaten. You simply do not move. That stillness will feel unnatural at first, because you were trained to believe that stillness equals abandonment. But it is not abandonment. It is leadership. It is you becoming first in your own life, not waiting for permission to be whole.

Then comes a third test, and it is the one most people never want to look at, because it exposes something uncomfortable: sometimes the old life is not only something you endured. Sometimes it is something you benefited from. Not in a healthy way, but in a familiar way. Your role gave you identity. Your over-giving gave you control. Your constant availability gave you a sense of being needed. Your willingness to carry gave you moral superiority. Your ability to "handle more than others" became your armor.

That is why the first real boundary can feel like withdrawal. You are not only removing your energy from others. You are removing your own sedative. You are no longer soothing your anxiety with usefulness. You are no longer soothing your fear with service. You are no longer soothing your loneliness by being indispensable.

When that sedative is gone, you feel the raw thing underneath: emptiness, uncertainty, the silence you avoided. And this is where people relapse. Not because the old life was good, but because the old life was loud. Loudness can feel like purpose when you have forgotten how to be at peace. Chaos can feel like intimacy when you have not experienced calm connection. Being needed can feel like love when you have not learned how to be chosen.

So your old life will offer you a deal. It will offer you access again. It will offer you warmth again. It will offer you the familiar dopamine of being pulled back in. It will come in the form of a message you have received a hundred times: *I miss you. I need you. Can we talk?* It will come with nostalgia, with compliments, with the reminder of history. It will sound like reconciliation. But you have to look for the hidden clause: will the access return without respect, or will the relationship rise to meet your standard?

This is where most people confuse love with access. They think if someone wants access to them, it means they are valued. But access is not a human right. It is earned. And it is maintained by behavior. When you finally understand that, you stop being impressed by someone "coming back." People come back for many reasons. Some come back because they love you. Some come back because they miss the convenience. Some come back because the consequences finally touched them. Some come back because their other sources dried up. The question is not whether they return. The question is whether the contract changes.

So you test it. Not with games. With reality.

You do not offer the full version of yourself immediately. You do not rush to prove you are still warm. You do not hand over your nervous system like a peace offering. You watch behavior. You watch consistency. You watch whether accountability appears without you having to beg for it. You watch whether respect shows up when you are not performing. You watch whether they can handle your "no" without punishment.

This is the point where people accuse you of being cold. But cold is not the word. The word is *sober*. You are no longer drunk on potential. You are no longer drunk on history. You are no longer drunk on the fantasy that if you love hard enough, it will transform someone who refuses to transform themselves. You are no longer gambling with your self-respect.

Sober love is different. Sober love has structure. Sober love does not need you to abandon yourself to prove loyalty. Sober love can tolerate boundaries. Sober love does not punish you for being real. And when you start living from that place, something becomes obvious: a lot of what you called love in your old life was actually fear trying to manage abandonment.

That is why the first test costs something. Because if you do this correctly, you will lose access. You will lose invitations. You will lose easy closeness. You will lose the instant relief that came from smoothing the mood. You will lose the identity of being "the one who always shows up." And if that identity has been your entire sense of worth, losing it can feel like death.

But here is the truth that changes everything: it is not death. It is detox.

Your body will protest at first. Your nervous system will tell you that you are doing something wrong because it cannot tell the difference between unfamiliar and unsafe. It will create guilt. It will create doubt. It will create a desire to "just clear the air." It will tempt you to send the message that always brings you back into the role: *I did not mean it like that. I hope you are not upset.* That message is not peace. That message is the leash.

When you do not send it, you will feel exposed. The silence will feel loud. You will feel like you are floating without an anchor. You will feel the urge to rebuild the old stability even if that stability was built on your self-erasure.

This is the exact moment where you either change your life or keep repeating it.

Because patterns do not break when you understand them. Patterns break when you stop feeding them.

In practice, this looks like something very unglamorous: you let the discomfort sit in your body without converting it into action. You let the tightness in your chest be there without running to fix the mood. You let the anxiety exist without confusing it for a sign that you should go back. You let someone be unhappy with you. You let someone misinterpret you. You let someone withdraw. You let them do what they do while you remain aligned with what you know.

That alignment is what creates the new you. Not the version of you who talks about boundaries. The version of you who holds them without rage. The version of you who does not need to punish to be firm. The version of you who can stay kind without being accessible to disrespect. The version of you who does not collapse the moment the room gets cold.

And then the sorting begins.

Some people adjust. It may take them time, but they adjust. They ask better questions. They show up differently. They stop using guilt as communication. They learn to respect your timing. They learn that you are not a service they can activate whenever they feel like it. Those relationships get cleaner. They get quieter. They get stronger, because they are no longer maintained by your self-sacrifice.

Some people do not adjust. They get louder. They get sharper. They get more sarcastic. They start telling others that you changed. They try to recruit the room against you. They do this because they cannot control you directly anymore, so they try to control the narrative. If you are still addicted to being seen as good, that will destroy you. You will chase your reputation, explain yourself, manage perceptions, and accidentally return to the role through a different door.

But if you are ready for your next level, you will recognize this for what it is: proof that the relationship was never about mutual respect. It was about access.

And some people simply fade. No fight. No closure. No big ending. They just disappear when the deal stops being profitable. That one hurts in a particular way because you cannot argue with it. You cannot "fix it." You cannot negotiate with absence. You are forced to face the clean truth: the relationship existed because you kept it alive through effort. When your effort stopped, it died.

You will grieve that. You should. Grief is not weakness. Grief is the honest cost of becoming real.

But do not let grief trick you into rewriting the contract as love. Do not let grief make you romanticize what was actually draining you. Do not let grief make you go back to prove you were still worthy of being kept. Worthiness is not what you earn by being used gently. Worthiness is what you remember when you stop volunteering for emotional poverty.

This is where the chapter becomes practical, not inspirational. Because the reader does not need another concept. The reader needs a mechanism they can recognize in their own life. The mechanism is simple: when you stop shrinking, the old system will test you. The test will come through discomfort. Your body will beg you to repair. Your mind will invent reasons to soften. Your identity will tell you to go back to keep peace. Your job is to hold.

Holding is not passive. Holding is an active refusal to betray yourself. Holding is discipline in emotional form. Holding is the quiet proof that you meant what you said. Holding is you not waiting for the room to change before you change your behavior. Holding is you not shrinking to support people who refuse to support the version of you that is becoming whole.

And once you hold long enough, something changes in a way that surprises you. Your nervous system starts trusting you.

It does not happen because everything becomes easy. It happens because you stop abandoning yourself the moment tension rises. Your body learns a new rule: I will not sacrifice my dignity to restore comfort. I will not buy peace with self-betrayal. I will not trade my self-respect for access. I will not wait for someone else to become safe before I act like my life matters.

That new rule creates a quiet strength that cannot be faked. It changes the way you speak. It changes the way you listen. It changes the way you respond. You stop sounding like someone asking for permission to exist. You start sounding like someone who knows they are not available for certain dynamics anymore. Not because you are angry. Because you are done.

Done is not bitter. Done is clean.

And in that cleanliness, you finally get something you have been craving more than love, more than validation, more than closure: internal congruence. Your words match your actions. Your standards are not just ideas; they are laws in your life. Your boundaries are not speeches; they are behavior. Your nervous system is no longer living in contradiction, begging you to be honest while your mouth keeps pretending.

That is what it means when your old life no longer fits. It is not a statement of superiority. It is a statement of alignment. You cannot keep living in rooms that require you to shrink without eventually resenting everyone inside them, including yourself. You cannot keep waiting for people to become accountable while your own life keeps passing. You cannot keep supporting everyone else with your self-erasure and call it love.

The first time you choose differently, it will feel like loss. The tenth time, it will feel like power. Not loud power. Quiet power. The kind of power that shows up as a relaxed jaw. As a slower heartbeat. As a phone that no longer controls your mood. As a life that is no longer managed around someone else's unpredictability.

This is the cost of growth. You pay it up front, once, with courage. Or you pay it monthly, forever, with your peace.

Hold.

Your Standards Start Choosing for You

After the first test, something changes that is both subtle and irreversible: you stop treating your standards like preferences. You stop treating them like moods. You stop treating them like ideas you admire on good days and abandon on hard ones. They become law, not because you are trying to be rigid, but because you finally understand what your old life was built on. It was built on you being flexible in ways that slowly destroyed you. It was built on you negotiating your own needs until you forgot they were needs at all.

This is where the reader usually gets scared, not because the truth is harsh, but because the consequences become real. When your standards become law, certain doors stop opening. Certain people stop calling. Certain invitations dry up. Certain "easy" connections fade. And at first, that looks like loss. It looks like you are being punished for becoming healthier. It looks like you did the inner work and got rewarded with silence. But that silence is not a punishment. It is the sound of you no longer being available for dynamics that survived only because you fed them.

Your old life will try to interpret this phase as proof that your change was a mistake. It will whisper, "See? If you were more understanding, this wouldn't be happening." It will tell you that you are creating distance. It will tell you that you are overthinking. It will suggest a compromise that is never a compromise, only a return. It will say, "Just this once," because "just this once" is how people stay stuck for ten more years.

The truth is simpler and more sobering: when you stop shrinking, the world has to renegotiate its relationship with you. Some people renegotiate with respect. Some renegotiate with manipulation. Some refuse to renegotiate at all. That sorting is not a side effect. It is the mechanism. It is how your life is upgraded without you having to fight anyone.

This is also where you begin to feel your body differently. The first phase of change is loud in the nervous system. It feels like withdrawal. It feels like you are resisting a reflex that has kept you alive. The second phase is quieter but deeper. You start noticing how much of your day used to be spent in low-grade tension, just waiting for the next demand, the next mood shift, the next moment where you would need to manage the air. You start noticing how often you were bracing without realizing you were bracing. You start noticing that your "normal" was a subtle form of stress.

When you stop feeding the old pattern, your body does not instantly become calm, but it becomes more honest. Your chest does not tighten as quickly. Your stomach does not drop as often. Your jaw unclenches sooner. You begin to recognize tension as information instead of as a command. You do not have to act on every emotional alarm the way you used to. You begin to separate discomfort from obligation. That separation is the beginning of actual freedom.

This is where the reader must understand the real enemy in this phase: the urge to make the discomfort mean something about your worth. When the room gets cold, you will be tempted to interpret it as rejection. When someone withdraws, you will be tempted to interpret it as proof you are unlovable. When a relationship shifts, you will be tempted to interpret it as proof you are hard to deal with. But those interpretations are not truth. They are programming. They are the old life's language trying to force you to translate your growth as failure.

That is why the next test is not always external. Often the next test is internal. It shows up as self-doubt disguised as reasonableness. It shows up as the voice that says, "Maybe I should just explain better." It shows up as the impulse to send the follow-up message that repairs the mood. It shows up as the fantasy that if you just phrase it correctly, the person who benefits from misunderstanding you will suddenly decide to understand you. That fantasy is not optimism. It is negotiation with a system that has already shown you what it values.

Once your standards start choosing for you, you stop debating obvious things. You stop entering conversations that are actually traps. You stop explaining to people who are committed to twisting your words. You stop trying to win fairness from people who are invested in control. You stop calling it communication when it is really interrogation. You stop calling it misunderstanding when it is really refusal. You stop calling it love when it is really access.

That does not make you cold. It makes you clean.

Clean does not mean harsh. Clean means you do not add extra suffering to a situation by pretending it is something it is not. Clean means you do not keep participating in a dynamic and then act surprised when it keeps being the same dynamic. Clean means you stop waiting for someone else to become accountable before you allow yourself to live as if you matter. That is not self-help. That is self-respect put into motion.

The reader will recognize this moment because it happens in a way that feels almost boring. It is not a big fight. It is not a dramatic ending. It is the moment you are invited back into a familiar pattern and you simply do not go. It is the moment someone tries the old guilt and you do not bite. It is the moment a person uses silence as pressure and you do not chase. It is the moment someone frames your boundary as cruelty and you do not defend. You feel the discomfort in your body, you notice the old reflex to repair, and then you choose a different action. That is the moment your life begins to reorganize around your integrity.

A lot of people think integrity is moral. In practice, integrity is neurological. It is what happens when your nervous system finally believes you will not abandon yourself for approval. That belief changes everything. It changes how you walk into rooms. It changes how you answer messages. It changes how you handle tension. It changes how you love, because you stop loving from fear. You stop loving as a strategy to prevent abandonment. You start loving as a choice you can sustain without losing yourself.

This is where the contrast becomes undeniable: love that respects you feels calm. Access that uses you feels addictive. Love that respects you can handle your honesty. Access that uses you needs you to stay confused. Love that respects you does not require you to prove your worth through suffering. Access that uses you calls your suffering "loyalty." Love that respects you does not punish your boundaries. Access that uses you treats boundaries like betrayal.

Once you see that, the old life becomes hard to tolerate, not because you are "above it," but because you can finally read it clearly. You can feel the transaction in the air. You can feel when warmth is conditional. You can feel when closeness is offered as a reward for compliance. You can feel when someone's kindness is actually a negotiation tactic. And when you can feel it, you cannot unknow it. This is why your old life no longer fits. You have developed a new sensitivity, not the fragile kind, the accurate kind.

In this phase, you will also notice something that can shake the reader if they are not ready: some people will improve only when you stop protecting them from consequences. Not because they suddenly become good people. Because the structure changes. When you stop doing the emotional labor, they either step up or they lose you. When you stop absorbing the chaos, they either clean up or they face the mess. When you stop smoothing the air, they either learn to communicate or they live in tension. That is when the truth becomes undeniable: your old kindness was often a way of keeping other people comfortable at the cost of their growth.

That is a hard pill, because many readers have made an identity out of being the "good" one. The forgiving one. The patient one. The one who does not make waves. They built a self-image around endurance and called it virtue. But if your virtue requires your self-erasure, it is not virtue. It is fear with good branding. And fear, no matter how beautifully it is packaged, will always keep you in the same room.

This is where you must bring the reader back to the two laws in lived form, not as slogans. The first law is that the life you want does not arrive while you wait for other people to change. Waiting is not neutral. Waiting is participation. Waiting is the decision to keep the old agreement active. When the reader says, "I will do it when they stop," what they are really saying is, "I will keep paying until I am empty enough." The second law is that shrinking to support others is not love, and it is not sustainable. It is simply a delayed collapse. It buys temporary peace and creates long-term resentment. Those laws are not philosophy. They are survival.

Once the reader truly absorbs that, a new kind of question appears in their mind. It is not, "How do I make them understand?" It is, "Why am I still trying to be understood by people who benefit from misunderstanding me?" That question is not dramatic. It is deadly accurate. And accuracy is what changes a pattern.

Patterns survive on fog. Fog is where you doubt yourself. Fog is where you keep hoping. Fog is where you keep interpreting someone's inconsistency as depth. Fog is where you keep accepting crumbs because you are afraid of emptiness. Your next level requires clarity. Clarity is not always comforting, but it is always clean.

The most common way people sabotage this phase is by confusing loneliness with regression. When some relationships fade, there is a gap. That gap can feel like loneliness, and loneliness can feel like proof you made a mistake. So people return to the old life for relief. They go back "just to check in." They go back "just to keep the peace." They go back "because life is short." But what they are really doing is using the old pattern as a sedative for the discomfort of transition.

Transition is supposed to feel uncomfortable. It is the space between identities. It is the space where you are not yet surrounded by people who match your standard, but you are no longer willing to tolerate the old deal. If the reader cannot tolerate that space, they will keep repeating the same pattern forever. They will choose familiar pain over unfamiliar peace. They will choose predictable disappointment over honest solitude. They will choose access over love. And then they will wonder why their life never changes.

The work in this phase is simple and brutal: you stay. You do not run back to the old room to prove you still belong. You do not try to rebuild the old connection by shrinking. You stay in the gap long enough for your life to reorganize around your new standard. That takes discipline, not motivation. Motivation comes and goes. Discipline is you choosing your future even when your nervous system is begging you for familiar relief.

The reader will also need to understand that the gap is not empty. It only feels empty because you are no longer drowning it in noise. The gap is where your self-respect becomes real. The gap is where you rediscover your preferences, because you are no longer living as a response to other people's needs. The gap is where your energy returns. The gap is where your life becomes yours again. People underestimate how much of their identity has been a reaction.

When the reaction stops, you feel blank at first. That blankness is not who you are. It is what remains when you stop performing.

Then you start to rebuild, and rebuilding is not a big vision board moment. It is a series of small, accurate decisions. You choose conversations that do not require you to brace. You choose relationships where your honesty is not punished. You choose work that does not thrive on your overextension. You choose routines that stabilize your body. You choose environments that do not trigger the old coping patterns. These choices are not glamorous, but they change your nervous system's baseline. And when your baseline changes, your standards stop being effort. They become natural.

This is also where the reader starts to see the difference between being "nice" and being kind. Nice is automatic. Nice is the reflex to smooth. Nice is the instinct to say yes. Nice is the performance of harmony. Kindness is different. Kindness can say no. Kindness can disappoint someone without collapsing. Kindness can tell the truth without humiliating. Kindness can hold a boundary without rage. Kindness respects both people. Nice often respects only the loudest emotions in the room.

The old life trained you to worship loud emotions. Whoever was loud got priority. Whoever was upset got control. Whoever withdrew got leverage. Whoever threatened the peace got accommodated. That training makes you excellent at managing chaos, and terrible at building a stable life. Your next level is where you stop worshipping loudness. You stop giving power to moods. You stop making your life a response to someone else's emotional weather. You become your own standard even when the room is stormy.

When you practice this long enough, you begin to notice something unexpected: the people who are capable of real connection start getting closer. Not everyone, but the right ones. Real people do not require you to be small. Real people do not interpret your boundaries as attacks. Real people might not always agree with you, but they do not retaliate against your integrity.

They might feel challenged, but they do not weaponize their discomfort. They can handle a relationship where respect is not optional.

Those people are not attracted to your performance. They are attracted to your congruence. Congruence is what creates trust. Trust is not built by you being endlessly accommodating. Trust is built by you being consistent. Your yes means yes. Your no means no. Your boundaries do not shift based on guilt. Your availability is not purchased through pressure. That consistency makes you safe in a way that your old flexibility never could.

This is where the reader must hear the hard truth without sugar: if your connection with someone collapses the moment you stop over-giving, then the connection was built on your over-giving. If your relationship becomes cold the moment you stop being convenient, then convenience was the foundation. If someone's affection disappears when you stop complying, then affection was the reward for compliance, not love. That is not a moral judgment. It is math. And math does not care about your nostalgia.

Nostalgia is one of the biggest traps in this phase. Nostalgia makes the past look cleaner than it was. Nostalgia edits out the tension you carried, the sleep you lost, the anxiety you normalized, the self-respect you negotiated away. Nostalgia makes you remember the laughs but forget the cost. And that is why people go back. Not because it was good, but because it feels like an identity.

Your new life will not feel like an identity at first. It will feel like a choice you keep making. That is why the reader needs repetition in behavior, not repetition in concepts. The concept is already clear: the old life no longer fits. The behavior is what builds the new fit. The behavior is you refusing the old contract in real time. The behavior is you tolerating the gap. The behavior is you letting consequences exist. The behavior is you not waiting and not shrinking, even when your old instincts scream.

This is where you start to become dangerous to your old life, not because you attack, but because you are no longer available. People who rely on your confusion cannot control you when you are clear. People who rely on your guilt cannot move you when you stop negotiating your worth. People who rely on your fear cannot keep you when you refuse to be managed. That is what real growth looks like: not louder, not more dramatic, not more "spiritual," just less controllable.

And as that becomes true, you begin to recognize the call toward your next level in a way that is unmistakable. The call is not a voice. It is not a sign. It is the moment your body feels relief when you choose the new standard, even if you lose something. It is the moment your sleep gets deeper after a hard no. It is the moment your chest feels lighter after you stop chasing someone's warmth. It is the moment you realize you are not as anxious when you are not participating in the old dynamic. Your body begins to reward your integrity. That reward becomes addictive in the right way. It becomes the new relief.

Relief is the currency of this chapter. In the old life, relief came from compliance. You caved, the mood got better, the room warmed up, and your nervous system learned: surrender equals safety. In the new life, relief comes from congruence. You hold your boundary, the room might stay cold, but you go home intact. Your nervous system learns a new rule: integrity equals safety. That rule changes everything.

This is how the chapter moves. Not with theory. With the turning of the internal algorithm. Your old algorithm was: keep access, avoid conflict, stay liked, stay safe. Your new algorithm becomes: keep integrity, accept discomfort, stay real, stay free. The reader can feel that shift in their own life if they are honest. They know exactly where they sell themselves for peace. They know exactly where they overexplain. They know exactly where they wait. They know exactly where they shrink. They do not need another inspirational paragraph. They need permission to stop the pattern and tolerate the first cost.

Because the first cost is always the same: you lose the old type of comfort. You lose the comfort of being convenient. You lose the comfort of being needed. You lose the comfort of controlling the mood. You lose the comfort of predictability. You lose the comfort of the role. You lose the comfort of being "the good one." That loss can feel like identity death. But the truth is simpler: you are not dying. You are exiting a contract that was never designed to let you become whole.

And when you exit it, the air changes.

You might not feel euphoric. You might not feel "healed." You might feel quiet. You might feel tender. You might feel the ache of what you wished it could have been. But under that, something steadier begins to form. A calm that does not depend on anyone else behaving. A peace that is not compliance. A self-respect that is not a concept. It is your life.

That is what the reader needs to understand before the chapter can move into its final turn: when your standards start choosing for you, you stop living like a person who can be negotiated out of their own reality. You stop being a negotiable human. You become a fixed point. Not stubborn. Not rigid. Just real.

And once you become real, the old life does not fit because it cannot hold you without breaking its own rules.

The Fit Is a Standard

At some point, you stop asking the room for feedback. You stop scanning faces, stop adjusting your truth mid-sentence, stop measuring your worth by how softly you can land. You learn the most expensive lesson: when you outsource your sense of fit, you spend your life editing yourself for people who never planned to meet you fully. The old life trained you to treat discomfort like an alarm that meant "fix this." Fix the mood, fix the silence, fix the misunderstanding, fix the tension you did not create. You became efficient at restoring peace, and nobody told you what you were really restoring: the old contract.

The new life is not built on restoration. It is built on alignment, and alignment is quieter than you expect. It does not arrive as a victory speech; it arrives as your body no longer arguing with your decisions. It arrives as your chest staying open after you say no, even if the room goes cold. It arrives as sleep that does not require you to re-litigate conversations in your head like a lawyer trying to prove you are still good. It arrives as your phone lighting up and your nervous system not bracing, because you are no longer trained to expect a demand disguised as connection. This is the real proof: your body stops punishing you for choosing yourself.

Your old life will still try to call you back, and it will not come with honesty. It will come with nostalgia, sentiment, urgency, and the language of history. It will say "we have been through so much" as if shared history is a license for present-day disrespect, and it will say "you are different now" as if growth is something you did *to them*. It will say "life is short" as if the answer is to spend it returning to the same pattern that made you smaller. You will feel the pull because you are human, and because familiarity can masquerade as safety when your nervous system is tired. But the pull no longer decides, not when you can finally separate love from access and peace from compliance without needing to hate anyone to do it.

This is the part where your standards stop being inspirational and start being operational. You stop treating boundaries like a debate you must win, and you stop treating your clarity like something that needs a jury. You do not keep showing up where your honesty is punished, and you do not keep explaining yourself to people who benefit from misunderstanding you. You do not keep paying for connection with the currency of your self-abandonment, then calling it maturity because you are embarrassed to admit you were afraid. You can still be kind, still be tender, still care deeply, but you stop confusing tenderness with surrender. You stop donating your peace so other people never have to adjust.

This is where the fit becomes a standard, and a standard becomes a filter. Not a filter that judges people, a filter that protects you from repeating your own pattern. The question stops being "How do I make them understand?" and becomes "What does my life look like when I stop negotiating my dignity?" That question changes your behavior in real time. You answer fewer late calls that always turn into emotional labor, you accept fewer invitations that require you to brace, you stop giving instant access to people who only show up when it is convenient. You stop doing the thing you always did—over-explaining, over-giving, over-performing—just to buy warmth back. You let the room have its feelings without turning your body into a payment plan.

There is a cost to this, and it should be named without drama. Some relationships do not survive when you stop feeding them, because they were built on your flexibility, not on mutual respect. Some people fade without closure, and you are forced to face the clean math: it lasted because you carried it. That grief is real, and it is not a sign you were wrong. It is the honest cost of becoming accurate. Accuracy does not always feel good in the beginning, but it stops you from wasting years in fog, trying to earn a kind of love that only exists when you are convenient. You stop romanticizing crumbs, and you stop calling inconsistency "depth" so you can keep hoping.

Then, almost without you noticing, the relief changes shape. In the old life, relief came from surrender; you caved, the mood improved, and your nervous system learned that compliance equals safety. In the new life, relief comes from congruence; you hold your boundary, the room might stay cold, but you go home intact. That is a different kind of safety, and it is the kind your body respects. You begin to trust yourself, not as an idea, but as a lived experience. You begin to believe, in your nervous system, that you will not abandon yourself the moment tension rises. That belief is quiet power, and it is not motivational; it is structural.

This is how your old life stops fitting. Not because you become perfect, and not because the world suddenly becomes kind. It stops fitting because you stop making yourself small enough to fit inside it. You stop shrinking to support others, and you stop waiting for other people to become accountable before you act with self-respect. You stop negotiating with patterns that have already proven what they value, and you stop participating in dynamics that survive only when you betray yourself. The fit becomes a standard, and the standard becomes your life.

When the dust settles, the chapter does not end with fireworks. It ends with something more valuable: a clean, internal decision that holds even when nobody claps. You do not need to announce your next level to anyone; you only need to live like your own peace matters. The moment you do that consistently, you do not "find yourself." You stop losing yourself. And that is when the old life, finally, has nowhere left to hook into you.

CHAPTER 13

HEALING THAT SHOWS UP

The Body Remembers

People talk about healing like it is a thought you accept and then your life cooperates. Like you wake up one day and you are simply lighter. Like clarity flips a switch and your habits fall into place out of gratitude. But your body is not impressed by your insights. Your body is impressed by what you repeat. It responds to what you stop doing when nobody is watching, and what you choose at the exact moment your system wants the old relief. A mind can change its vocabulary overnight; the body changes its posture slowly. A mind can promise a new life and still reach for the same sedatives in the next hour. The body does not forget how you survived. It does not forget how you stayed functional inside environments that were not safe for your truth. It does not forget what you trained yourself to do to get through a day without feeling the full weight of reality. It remembers the shortcuts: the quick dopamine, the late-night scrolling, the extra snack, the extra drink, the extra conversation you did not want but agreed to because saying no felt like risk. It remembers the way you learned to keep yourself numb enough to keep performing.

This is why "self-improvement" fails for so many people who are intelligent, self-aware, and tired. They try to change their lives with motivation while their physiology is still living under old rules. They build new habits on top of a body that is still bracing. They talk themselves into discipline while the system is still convinced that discomfort equals danger. So they win for a week, then collapse, and they call it willpower. It is not willpower. It is misdiagnosis. It is you trying to act like a calm person with a body that is still on duty, still scanning, still anticipating impact, still treating ordinary life like something you have to survive.

Your habits are not just habits. They are agreements. They are rituals of self-relationship. They reveal what you believe you deserve when you are not in a heroic mood, and what you think you must do to earn peace. Some people do not binge because they love food; they binge because the body is trying to sedate a feeling it does not trust. Some people do not overwork because they are ambitious; they overwork because stillness feels unsafe. Some people do not chase people because they are romantic; they chase because silence triggers withdrawal, and the body mistakes withdrawal for abandonment. That is what the body remembers: the old pattern that once protected you, even if it now destroys you.

Healing that shows up does not begin with better affirmations. It begins with the moment you stop confusing relief with recovery. Relief is immediate. Recovery is honest. Relief is what you reach for to make your inside stop screaming. Recovery is what happens when you teach your system a new rule: you are safe even when you do not soothe yourself with the old sedative. This is where the two laws stop being motivational and become physiological. You do not wait for the world to change before you act like your life matters. You do not shrink to support other people while your own body carries the bill. Those are not moral statements in a vacuum. They have consequences you can feel. They decide whether you live in constant low-grade emergency or in a baseline quiet enough to breathe.

Look at what most people call "stress." It is not only the workload, the schedule, the bills. It is the internal contradiction: your body sensing one thing and your behavior doing another. It is your chest tightening while you keep smiling. It is your gut warning you while you keep saying yes. It is your system sending a red signal while you negotiate your boundary into a polite apology so the room stays comfortable. That gap between what you feel and what you do becomes inflammation in the soul. It becomes jaw tension. It becomes shallow breathing. It becomes sleep that never goes deep. It becomes waking up tired even when you slept. It becomes that constant feeling that you are behind, even when you are "doing fine," because your body is living in a future where you will have to abandon yourself again.

Your body keeps receipts. Not as punishment. As proof. Proof that you cannot keep living out of alignment and call it normal. Proof that you cannot keep buying peace with self-betrayal and expect your body to relax. Proof that your system was never designed to be your employee. It is your partner. And eventually it refuses to cooperate with the lie, because the body can play along only for so long before it starts sending invoices you cannot ignore.

Most people try to outrun those invoices the way they have always outrun themselves. They call it "being busy." They call it "handling things." They call it "staying strong." But the body does not care what you call it. The body cares what it costs. It cares what happens to your breathing when you swallow your truth. It cares what happens to your digestion when you keep saying yes with a nervous system that is screaming no. It cares what happens to your heart rate when you keep living in anticipation—anticipation of conflict, of disappointment, of someone's mood, of the next demand you already know you will accept and then resent.

And this is where people get humbled, because the body is brutally fair. It does not punish you for one bad day. It holds you accountable for the pattern. The pattern of living slightly outside yourself. The pattern of performing calm while your system is bracing. The pattern of making other people comfortable at the expense of your own baseline. You can do that for a while and still function. That is the trap. Functioning becomes the proof you use to deny the cost. You say, "I'm fine," because you are still producing. Meanwhile your shoulders live near your ears. Your jaw stays tight even when you are smiling.

Your breath stays shallow even when you are resting. You stop noticing because it becomes normal.

A dysregulated body can look successful. It can look disciplined. It can look "high-functioning." But high-functioning is not healing. High-functioning is often just you being efficient at abandoning yourself. It is you staying useful enough to avoid being questioned. It is you staying productive enough to avoid sitting still long enough to feel what you have been carrying. And the body keeps tracking all of it. Not only the big betrayals. The small ones. The daily ones. The ones you dismiss because they seem harmless: one more late night, one more meal eaten standing up, one more conversation where you swallow your truth to keep the atmosphere polite, one more "I'll deal with it later," when later is always your life.

That is why the body eventually forces the conversation you kept postponing. It does it quietly at first. A tension you cannot stretch out. A sleep that does not restore you. A hunger that is not hunger. A fatigue that coffee cannot fix. A brain that cannot settle. You think you need a new plan. Often what you need is a new honesty: you cannot keep living one life on the outside while your body lives another one on the inside.

And when you finally stop arguing with the signals, you realize the truth is not abstract. The truth is physical. It is measurable. It shows up in the places you cannot fake. It shows up where your nervous system tells the truth before your mouth does.

This is why healing starts showing up in places people do not romanticize. It shows up in sleep first, because sleep is where the body tells the truth about safety. People say they cannot sleep because they think too much. Most of the time they cannot sleep because their system does not believe their life is stable. It does not believe their boundaries will hold. It does not believe tomorrow will be predictable. It expects tomorrow to bring another demand, another mood, another situation where you abandon yourself to keep peace. So it stays alert. One eye open. Rest becomes something you almost reach but never land, because your body learned that rest is what happens right before impact.

When you start healing for real, you do not just sleep longer. You sleep deeper. Your body stops scanning the dark for a threat that is actually an email, a text, a disappointment, a conflict you are anticipating because you have been trained to manage other people's emotions. You start waking up without that immediate punch in the chest and that instant list of problems arriving before your feet hit the floor. You may still have responsibilities. You may still have a hard life. But your body is no longer treating existence like an emergency. That is not motivation. That is repair. That is your system beginning to trust you.

Healing also shows up in appetite, and people get uncomfortable here, because they want food to be a simple equation. Calories in, calories out, discipline, cheat days. But appetite is not only hunger. Appetite is also regulation. When your system is overwhelmed, it looks for a lever. Sometimes that lever is sugar because sugar is fast relief. Sometimes it is volume because fullness sedates. Sometimes it is restriction because control is a substitute for safety. When you start healing, you begin to notice the difference between hunger and anxiety dressed as hunger. You begin to notice that the craving is not always for food. Sometimes it is for quiet. Sometimes it is for comfort. Sometimes it is for the feeling of being held—something you have been trying to manufacture with texture and taste because you did not know how to give yourself safety any other way.

If this makes you feel judged, you are missing the point. There is no judgment here. There is clarity. When you understand the function, you stop hating yourself for the symptom. You stop calling yourself weak when your body is trying to survive. You stop shaming yourself for coping. You stop confusing coping with healing. Coping kept you alive. Healing gives you your life back, which is a very different thing.

The body remembers the years you lived as a reaction. The years you lived on standby. The years you lived waiting for the next message, the next shift, the next demand, the next emotional storm. And while you were waiting, you were also shrinking. Shrinking your needs, shrinking your truth, shrinking your rest, shrinking your joy. Shrinking to keep the room calm, to keep the relationship stable, to keep the job safe, to keep the family pleased. You learned that when you take up space, someone gets uncomfortable, and discomfort felt dangerous, so you became skilled at disappearing without leaving.

A body that lived that way does not instantly trust a new philosophy. It trusts repetition. It trusts evidence. Healing that shows up is the evidence you give your body through behavior. It is the quiet proof that you will not sacrifice yourself to restore comfort. It is the proof that you can tolerate tension without turning it into self-betrayal. It is the proof that you can feel a craving, a panic, an impulse to smooth, and not obey it.

Most people think the first sign of healing is peace. Often the first sign is discomfort in a new way. Because once you stop sedating yourself, you feel everything you have been avoiding. You feel the loneliness you covered with noise. You feel the anger you swallowed to stay "mature." You feel the grief you postponed with productivity. You feel the exhaustion you overrode with adrenaline. When those feelings rise, your old system will label them as failure. It will tell you, you are getting worse. You are not getting worse. You are getting honest. You are becoming present in your own body again, and presence can feel like pain when you have been numb for a long time.

Early healing can feel like withdrawal. Withdrawal from chaos. Withdrawal from approval. Withdrawal from the sedative of being needed. Withdrawal from the quick relief of giving in. Withdrawal from the false safety of compliance. Your body will crave the old patterns, not because they were good, but because they were predictable. And predictability is what the system mistakes for safety when it has not experienced stable love.

So the question becomes brutally practical: when you feel that familiar tension, what do you do? When your chest tightens, do you reach for the phone to repair something? When your stomach drops, do you reach for food to soften it? When your mind races, do you reach for scrolling to numb it? When the day feels heavy, do you reach for a person who gives you access but not respect, because their attention feels like air? Those are the moments that reveal what your body remembers. Those are also the moments where you teach it something new.

There is a reason people do great in the morning and fall apart at night. The morning has structure; the night has memory. At night the world quiets down, and the noise you used as cover disappears. The system presents you with unpaid bills: the feelings you did not process, the loneliness you kept busy, the resentment you swallowed. The body asks for something to take the edge off. That is where patterns live—not in your inspirational moments, but in your private ones; in your tired ones; in your bored ones, because boredom is where the mind wants stimulation and the body wants regulation.

Healing that shows up is what you do in those moments. Not a flawless day, not a perfect routine, not a new identity you perform. It is small decisions that signal self-respect to your system. You go to bed when you are tired instead of when you are finally numb. You eat in a way that does not punish you for being human. You move your body as care, not as apology. You build a day that does not require you to abandon yourself just to be productive.

People misunderstand self-respect because they confuse it with self-control. Self-control is often fear in a suit: managing yourself like a problem. Self-respect is different. It is treating your body like it matters. It is refusing to negotiate your well-being for someone else's comfort. It is choosing stability even when chaos feels exciting. It is choosing consistency even when inconsistency feels romantic. It is choosing rest even when rest triggers guilt because you were trained to equate exhaustion with worth.

Your body remembers how you learned worth. Maybe it was praise for being helpful. Maybe approval for being easy. Maybe safety earned through silence. Maybe love delivered as a reward for compliance. Whatever the origin, the body remembers the rule. The rule becomes habit. Habit becomes personality. Personality becomes destiny if you never interrupt it. That is the relationship between habit and identity without therapy language: the habit is a contract you sign with yourself every day. I matter or I do not. I am safe or I must earn safety. I deserve care or I must perform for it. I deserve rest or rest is laziness. I deserve nourishment or nourishment is a reward.

When someone says, "I just need to be more disciplined," they are usually standing in front of a deeper truth: they do not trust themselves. They do not trust their needs will be honored. They do not trust their boundaries will hold. So they live in reaction. Reaction creates instability. Instability creates craving. Craving creates shame. The loop repeats. Discipline is not the solution when the system is destabilized. Stabilization is. And stabilization begins with self-respect.

Self-respect looks like structure that protects you from old impulses—not punishment, protection. It looks like a bedtime treated as a boundary, not a suggestion. It looks like feeding your body before it becomes desperate, so desperation does not decide your night. It looks like movement that discharges tension, so your mind does not have to carry it. It looks like quiet built into your day, so you do not need to sedate yourself at night. It looks like refusing constant stimulation, because constant stimulation is a form of self-abandonment that gets praised as productivity.

Some readers will resist this because they are addicted to intensity. Intensity can feel like being alive when calm feels unfamiliar. Drama can feel like intimacy when steady connection feels boring. Overworking can feel like purpose when purpose is missing. The body learns to run on adrenaline, and adrenaline becomes home. Then when you try to live calmly, you feel restless, like something is wrong. That feeling is not proof calm is wrong. It is proof you are detoxing from chaos.

This is where the two laws return as consequences, not slogans. If you keep waiting for life to calm down before you treat your body with respect, you will wait forever. Life shifts. Life asks. Life demands. Life surprises. If you wait for the perfect week to sleep well, eat well, move well, and protect your peace, you are choosing the old agreement: my well-being comes last. You do not need perfect conditions. You need the decision that you stop coming last.

If you keep shrinking to support others, your body eventually rebels—through fatigue, weight, anxiety, insomnia, tension that never leaves. Not to punish you. To force you into honesty. Because your body can only be used as a payment method for so long before it refuses the transaction. And for many people, the hardest part is accepting that self-respect will feel selfish at first. Not because it is selfish, but because you were trained to confuse self-respect with abandonment. You learned that caring for yourself meant someone else would suffer. You learned your needs were an inconvenience. So, when you start honoring yourself, guilt appears.

Guilt is not always a moral compass. Sometimes guilt is withdrawal. Sometimes guilt is the system begging you to return to the old role because the old role was familiar. If you do not understand that, you will interpret guilt as a sign you are wrong. You will retreat, soften, negotiate, and call it compassion. But compassion that requires your collapse is not compassion. It is fear trying to stay socially acceptable. Real compassion includes you. It includes your sleep, your health, your right to be stable.

The body remembers the times you did not include yourself: the nights you pushed through exhaustion because you did not want to disappoint, the meals you skipped because you were busy being useful, the workouts used as punishment because you hated what stress did to you, the mornings you woke up already behind because you went to bed too late numbing something you did not want to feel. It remembers. And once you start healing, it remembers the first time you chose differently. The first time you say no and your stomach does not collapse afterward, even if the other person is upset. The first time you go to bed without scrolling yourself into sedation. The first time you eat like a person who deserves stability. The first time you walk to return to your body, not to burn calories. Those are not small wins. Those are new contracts.

Belief changes you, but not belief as inspiration. Belief as evidence. Evidence built through repetition. That is how healing shows up: a quieter baseline, less urgency, fewer reactions, a body no longer sending invoices for the ways you betray yourself. Your body is not your enemy. It is your witness. And when you stop bargaining with your health, your body stops fighting you. It starts trusting you. Trust is what makes a life sustainable.

Withdrawal From Chaos

The moment you stop sedating your life, you start feeling the life you have been sedating. People do not like that sentence because it ruins the fantasy that healing is a glow and a clean new version of yourself with better routines and less appetite for destruction. The truth is the first thing you feel is the edge. The edge you used to take off with food, noise, endless scrolling, work, sex, shopping, drama, late-night conversations you did not want but could not resist, because silence felt like abandonment. You remove the sedative and the system finally speaks in its own language: tension, restlessness, cravings, irritability, insomnia, and that internal shaking that has nothing to do with weakness and everything to do with detox.

Withdrawal does not always look dramatic. Most of the time it looks like pacing your house without knowing why. Opening the fridge and staring at it, not hungry, just searching for a sensation that changes your internal weather. Picking up your phone to check something that does not matter, then checking again, because the act itself became regulation. Wanting to text someone you know is bad for you, not because you miss them, but because your body remembers the spike their attention used to create. You mistake relief for healing when you have lived too long in a body that only relaxes after impact.

This is where people sabotage themselves without realizing it. They start doing the right things and panic when it feels worse. They eat cleaner and feel moodier. They go to bed earlier and feel more anxious. They stop drinking and feel more emotional. They begin moving and feel exposed. They interpret this as proof the new habits are not working. The truth is the new habits are removing the cover. The cover was never healing. The cover was coping— something designed to keep pain manageable, not to make it disappear.

If you want healing that shows up, you have to respect this phase because this is where the body rewrites its definition of safety. For a lot of people, safety has been confused with stimulation. Chaos was not just what happened around you; it became what you used to feel alive. It became the rhythm your system learned to expect. When that rhythm is gone, your body does not instantly say thank you. It says, where is the noise. It says, what is the next hit. It says something is missing, and it tries to fill the missing with whatever used to work fastest.

The brain is not moral. It is efficient. It remembers what provided relief at the lowest cost in the shortest time. That is why people with high self-awareness still fall into old loops. They can name their pattern perfectly and still be pulled by it at midnight when the day finally goes quiet. Insight is not the master key. Regulation is. Regulation is what makes insight usable. Without regulation, insight becomes another tool for self-judgment: you watch yourself repeat, you call yourself pathetic, shame spikes, stress spikes, craving spikes, and you repeat again. The loop does not end because you learned new words. The loop ends when your body learns a new baseline.

You have to understand what chaos did for you. Chaos gave you a job. It gave you something to manage. It kept you focused outward so you did not have to feel inward. It made you needed, and being needed can feel like love when you have not learned how to be held. Chaos also gave you an identity: the one who handles things, the one who keeps it together, the one who shows up. That identity is flattering, but it is exhausting. It makes rest feel like betrayal. It makes stillness feel like danger. It makes a quiet day feel empty, and emptiness triggers the urge to fill.

So, the withdrawal you experience is not only from a substance. It is withdrawal from an identity. Withdrawal from being the fixer. Withdrawal from being the one who absorbs the impact. Withdrawal from living in anticipation. When you stop anticipating, you feel strange. When you stop bracing, you feel exposed. When you stop managing everyone's emotions, guilt shows up. That guilt is not always truth. Often it is your system searching for the old assignment, so it can feel useful again.

This is why healing cannot be a vibe. It has to be a practice. A practice that understands discomfort is not automatically a problem. Some discomfort is the cost of leaving an old room. Some discomfort is your body learning a new language. Some discomfort is recalibration after years of being trained to respond to chaos as normal. You are not failing when you feel restless. You are detoxing from urgency. You are detoxing from the belief that you must always be "on." You are detoxing from the reflex to fix the room.

Most people quit here, not because they cannot change, but because they do not recognize the shape of early change. They expect immediate calm and get internal noise. They expect instant motivation and get irritability. They expect discipline to feel empowering, and instead they feel grief. And it is grief. Grief for the years spent self-medicating. Grief for the health traded for temporary relief. Grief for realizing you were not lazy—you were overloaded. You were not undisciplined—you were dysregulated.

Dysregulation creates predictable behaviors: procrastination that is not about time management but about avoiding internal discomfort, overeating that is not about hunger but about sedation, insomnia that is not about lack of tiredness but about lack of safety, overworking that is not about ambition but about control. It creates a life where you are always catching up because you never feel stable enough to move forward cleanly.

When you start healing, your body tests you. Not because it is cruel, but because it is loyal to what it knows. It tests you at the exact times you used to reach for the old sedative: late night, after conflict, after rejection, after a long day, after a quiet day. When your phone is silent and your mind starts inventing stories. When you are alone and you remember how loud your head can get when the world is not distracting you. Those are the moments you will crave the old chaos, not because you love it, but because it was predictable.

This is where self-respect becomes visible—not as an idea you admire, but as a choice you make while your body is begging you to betray it. Self-respect looks like eating before you are desperate, because desperation makes decisions for you. It looks like going to bed before you are numb, because numbness is not rest. It looks like turning off the stimulation even when it feels like your only company, because constant input is not connection. It looks like moving your body, even gently, not to punish it, but to discharge tension so your system can settle without needing a hit.

At first you might not feel better immediately. You might feel worse because you are no longer escaping. That is why you stop evaluating healing by how you feel in the first hour and start evaluating it by what it builds in the first month. The first hour is protest. The first month is retraining. If you quit during protest, you stay owned by your old relief.

Old relief is seductive because it is instant. Sugar changes your mood in minutes. Scrolling changes your state in seconds. A message to the wrong person changes your heart rate immediately. Work turns anxiety into control.

These feel like solutions because they change your state, but changing your state is not the same as changing your life. Your life changes when you choose things that make your state more stable over time, even if they are uncomfortable in the moment.

This is what people miss about discipline. Discipline is not punishment. Discipline is delayed relief. It is choosing a discomfort that leads to peace instead of choosing a comfort that leads to chaos. Most people choose the comfort because they are tired, but what they are really tired of is living in instability. Stability gives energy. Chaos drains it. When you build stability, you build energy—not in one day, but reliably, if you stop interrupting the process every time your body complains.

Your body complains because it is loyal to your past. Your past kept you alive. Even when your past is unhealthy, it is familiar, and familiarity is the currency your nervous system uses to buy safety. That is why you can crave what hurts you. People think craving is desire. Often craving is conditioning: the body reaching for a known lever. You cannot shame conditioning out of yourself. You replace it with a new pattern repeated enough times that the body starts trusting it.

Trust is the real metric. Do you trust yourself to keep your word to your body? To stop negotiating your sleep for another hour of noise? To stop using food as anesthesia? To stop using work as emotional avoidance? To stay present when you are uncomfortable? If you do not, you will keep living in negotiation, and negotiation keeps you unstable.

Negotiation sounds reasonable. It sounds mature. It sounds like balance. In practice, it is often your old life finding a loophole: just tonight, you deserve it, you have been good, you will start tomorrow. That voice is not evil. It is simply the part of you that wants relief now and does not believe you can tolerate discomfort. Healing is you proving that voice wrong without fighting it. You do not need to hate it. You just need to stop obeying it.

For many people, the phone is the cleanest example. The phone is not the problem. What it became is: a portable sedative, a portable distraction, a portable way to avoid being alone with your own body. You pick it up without thinking, open it without choosing, scroll without seeing, and then wonder why you are exhausted. Because your system never gets quiet. It never drops into processing. It is constantly being fed stimuli, and stimuli keeps it activated. You become addicted to activation, and then calm feels boring, which is how you know you have been living in overstimulation for too long.

Withdrawal from overstimulation feels like boredom at first. That "boredom" is discomfort. It is your system asking for its hit. When you do not give it the hit, it presents you with restlessness, itchiness, impatience. That is not weakness. That is recalibration. You are not losing your mind. You are regaining it.

Food works the same way. The body does not only want calories. It wants comfort, rhythm, predictability. If your emotional life has been unpredictable, your body looks for predictability chemically. That is why cravings show up at night. Not because you are broken, but because the day is done and your system wants a soft landing. If you start feeding your body with steadier inputs, cravings change. Before they change, they spike. Your system negotiates. Your job is not to negotiate back.

Then there is self-talk, which is where many people truly lose. They do not fail because they eat the thing or skip the walk. They fail because of what they tell themselves after. Hopeless. Always ruin everything. Cannot stick to anything. That language is not honesty. It is sabotage. If you label one slip as proof you are broken, you will return to the old pattern, because shame makes stability feel impossible. Stability is built by returning to baseline without drama. Punishment is another form of chaos. It keeps you in intensity. Healing requires a cleaner relationship with yourself.

Clean does not mean soft. Clean means you do not lie. If you are sedating, you name it. If you are avoiding, you name it. If you are using stimulation to numb your life, you name it. Naming is not condemnation. Naming is clarity. Clarity creates choice. Condemnation creates collapse, and collapse returns you to the old room because the old room gives you a familiar identity: the one who fails, the one who tries but cannot, the one who is "just like this." That identity is comfort disguised as defeat.

A lot of what you have called your personality is a coping style. The constant urgency, the constant multitasking, the constant need to be engaged. That is not always who you are. Sometimes it is what you had to be to survive your life. When you remove the need, the identity begins to dissolve, and dissolving can feel like emptiness. People panic when they feel empty, because empty feels like nothing. But empty is often space—the space where your real preferences can finally appear. If you never allow emptiness, you never meet yourself.

You cannot hack your way out of self-abandonment. You cannot supplement your way out of a nervous system that does not feel safe. You cannot cold plunge your way into peace, if your daily life is built on low-grade betrayal. The body is too honest for that. It will take your hacks and still hand you the invoice. Withdrawal from chaos is not a phase you endure and then forget. It is a rite of passage: your system learning it does not have to live on spikes. It can live on stability.

Stability is not glamorous. It is powerful. It is the foundation of everything you say you want: better health, better sleep, less weight, more focus, more peace, better relationships. Without stability, every improvement becomes temporary, because pressure will always return you to what you know.

Pressure will hit. That is not pessimism. That is life. And when pressure hits, the question is not whether the urge arrives—it will. The question is whether you treat the urge like a command or like information. A command says: feed me now, scroll now, text now, escape now. Information says: I am activated; I need regulation; I need safety. Your old life treated urges as commands. Healing treats urges as information.

Information changes your response. If you are activated, you do not need a binge. You need breath that is not shallow. Shoulders down. Jaw unclenched. Tension discharged instead of stuffed. Water. Real food. Screen off. Bedtime honored. None of this is romantic. That is the point. It is not a performance. It is care.

Care is what self-respect looks like in real time. Not what you post, but what you choose on a Tuesday night when nobody is applauding. What you choose after you slip, when you could spiral into shame or return to baseline with maturity. What you choose when you are bored and want stimulation, and you sit in the boredom long enough for your system to calm down without being fed. That is not suffering. That is retraining.

Retraining takes repetition, and repetition takes patience. Patience means tolerating imperfection without collapsing into identity stories. You do not need a perfect streak. You need a consistent return. Every time you return, you teach your body a new rule: we do not run from discomfort anymore. We do not sedate immediately. We do not abandon ourselves for relief. We stay. We regulate. We choose stability.

That rule will feel foreign at first. It might even feel like deprivation. But you are not depriving yourself of pleasure. You are depriving yourself of quick relief that steals your future. You are refusing the comfort that costs you health, sleep, self-respect, and peace. There is nothing noble about suffering. There is something clean about refusing a trade that keeps you sick.

Eventually the shift arrives quietly. The craving does not last as long. The urge arrives and leaves. The restlessness becomes manageable. The quiet becomes spacious instead of threatening. You get tired in a normal way at night, not wired and exhausted at the same time. You wake up and feel your body as a place you live, not a problem you manage. These shifts are subtle, which is why people miss them, but they are the first signs of stability becoming baseline.

When stability becomes baseline, everything becomes easier—not because you become "better," but because your body stops fighting you. The fight was never laziness. The fight was a system that did not trust a calm life. Once it starts trusting, it stops demanding the old hit. It stops needing chaos to feel alive. It stops confusing intensity with connection. It stops confusing stimulation with safety.

Healing that shows up is not an aesthetic. It is physiological trust earned through repeated proof: proof you do not wait for a perfect week to treat your body with respect, proof you do not shrink your well-being so your schedule can look impressive, proof you do not negotiate your sleep, food, movement, and peace into extinction to keep an old identity alive. Your body remembers that proof through a calmer chest, a quieter gut, a steadier appetite, deeper sleep, and a mind that does not need constant stimulation to tolerate itself. Once your body trusts you, you stop needing chaos as a sedative, because you no longer feel like you are in danger when life gets quiet.

Standards That Protect Your Heart

If healing is real, it changes what you tolerate. Not what you understand. Not what you can explain. Not what you can forgive in theory. It changes what you allow to touch you repeatedly without consequence. People can read ten books on regulation and still hand their peace to the first person who speaks in a certain tone. They can learn every concept and still fold when warmth is withdrawn. That is not stupidity. That is conditioning: the body learned a rule long before the mind had language. Connection equals survival, and survival requires adaptation.

Standards are where that old rule gets challenged in real time. A standard is not a demand you make on other people. It is a boundary you keep with yourself, especially when you are lonely, tempted, tired, or nostalgic. It is the line you do not cross even when access is being offered again. It is the decision you keep even when your body wants the hit and your mind tries to negotiate the price down to something you can swallow. That is why standards feel brutal at first. Your nervous system reads the removal of familiar access as danger—even when that access has been poisoning you slowly. Healing does not begin when you learn new language. It begins when your behavior becomes evidence your body can trust.

Most people do not break patterns because they cannot see them. They see them. They break patterns when they finally refuse the price. And the price is never only emotional. It is physical and cumulative: the stomach drop every time the phone lights up, the jaw tension that becomes your default face, the sleep that never goes deep because you are always anticipating the next shift. It is appetite that is not hunger but regulation. It is that low-grade bracing you carry as "normal." Your body was not being dramatic. It was being accurate. It kept registering the same truth: you were calling it love while your system was preparing for impact.

A lot of relationships survive because one person keeps paying. They pay with explanations, extra softness, time they do not have, generosity that looks noble but functions like fear. They translate disrespect into stress, inconsistency into "they have a lot going on," contempt into "they are overwhelmed," because naming reality might cost them access. Sometimes what you are protecting is not the relationship. You are protecting your access to being chosen, even if the choosing is inconsistent, because inconsistency still feels like being alive when steadiness feels unfamiliar. Standards remove the loopholes that let you keep calling the same dynamic "complicated," so you do not have to call it what it is.

Standards show up in unglamorous moments. Someone disappears and returns with a smile, expecting the slate to be clean because time passed. Someone speaks to you with contempt, then calls you sensitive when you react. Someone crosses a boundary, then offers affection as if affection erases behavior. Someone drip-feeds warmth and withdraws it like leverage, and your body tightens before your mind admits what is happening. In the old contract you worked harder, softened faster, overexplained your pain so the other person would not feel accused, made your truth polite. In the new contract you stop negotiating obvious things—not because you have no feelings, but because your feelings are no longer allowed to bankrupt you.

People confuse standards with aggression, because they assume boundaries harden you. Boundaries do not harden you. They make you honest, and honesty prevents bitterness. Standards stop you from smiling while resenting people quietly. They stop you from becoming passive-aggressive, because you never said what was real. A standard does not remove tenderness. It protects it from being used against you. It keeps your softness from becoming a weapon someone else learns to swing. It also keeps you from turning love into a performance where you prove you can tolerate more than you should.

Intermittent reward is one of the most underestimated addictions in adult relationships. Some people confuse anxiety with attraction, waiting with devotion, intensity with intimacy, because their body learned unpredictability as chemistry. That is why they feel restless with someone stable and obsessed with someone inconsistent. Standards interrupt that cycle with clarity. They stop treating access as proof of love and start treating consistency as the minimum requirement for safety.

There is a second addiction hiding under intermittent reward, and it is quieter: the addiction to explanation. People think they need the other person to understand. They think if they phrase it better, softer, smarter, the outcome will finally change. They stay in conversations that are not conversations; they are negotiations with reality. They keep offering context like it is currency, hoping clarity will purchase respect. But respect cannot be purchased with better sentences. Standards are what happens when you stop trying to win understanding from someone who benefits from misunderstanding you.

A standard is also what you do when you are alone. That is the part nobody warns you about. When you raise standards, you do not only lose the wrong person; you lose the familiar rhythm. You lose the ping of the phone, the spike of attention, the drama that made your nervous system feel engaged. You lose the false intimacy of constant processing, the late-night loops, the "are we okay" conversations that kept you tethered even when you were not being treated well. At first, that absence feels like withdrawal. Your body mistakes the quiet for rejection because it was trained to equate intensity with closeness. And this is where most people fold—not because they miss love, but because they cannot tolerate the silence that reveals what they were calling love.

Your nervous system will try to bargain. It will tell you that you are being too strict, too cold, too proud. It will whisper that maybe you overreacted, that maybe it is not that serious, that maybe you should be "the bigger person." It will dress old self-abandonment in the language of maturity. But maturity is not reopening a door that cost you your health. Maturity is being able to sit in the discomfort of loneliness without turning it into a reunion with what broke you. Healing becomes visible when you can tolerate the temporary emptiness without filling it with familiar pain.

This is also where guilt becomes a weapon, and not always from the other person. Sometimes guilt is self-generated, because you were trained to treat access as something you owe. You were trained that love means availability. That if someone wants you, you must answer. That if someone is upset, you must fix it. That if someone withdraws warmth, you must chase it back. Standards interrupt that training. Standards say: my nervous system is not public property. My sleep is not negotiable. My dignity is not something you earn and lose based on your mood. And if that makes someone call you difficult, then difficult is simply the name they give to a person they can no longer control.

A lot of people do not realize how much of their "good heart" has been fear. They were not soft because they were noble. They were soft because they were trying to prevent consequences. They learned that consequences create conflict, and conflict felt dangerous, so they became experts at smoothing. They learned to forgive quickly, to explain endlessly, to lower the bar quietly, to accept "almost" because "almost" kept access. But your body knew the truth the whole time. Your body tightened around certain names. Your stomach dropped before certain conversations. Your breath got shallow when a certain tone arrived. That was not anxiety for no reason. That was your system reading pattern.

A standard uses that information without apologizing for it. It does not require courtroom-level proof. It does not require a confession. It does not require a public trial. It requires one thing: repetition. If a behavior repeats, you treat it as truth. You do not keep giving "benefit of the doubt" to someone who keeps cashing it like a paycheck. You do not keep offering access to a person who turns access into entitlement. The standard is simple and clean: patterns matter more than promises. Consistency matters more than chemistry. Repair matters more than words.

Standards also make you confront something painful: some people were in your life because you were easy to consume. Not because you were loved. They enjoyed your softness, your patience, your generosity, your willingness to take blame to keep peace. They enjoyed you when you were low-maintenance, when you did not ask for clarity, when you did not name the cost. Then you raise your standard and suddenly you are "too much." You did not become too much. You became expensive. Not in money. In accountability. In consequences. In self-respect. And what cannot afford you will try to discount you.

This is why you do not announce standards like a speech. You live them like a contract. You stop giving immediate access to someone who has not earned emotional safety. You stop teaching people that your forgiveness is automatic. You stop responding to hot-and-cold with warmth. You stop treating mixed signals as a puzzle you must solve. You stop explaining what should be obvious to a grown adult who understands perfectly well what they are doing. A standard is often one sentence, delivered once, and then behavior that does not waver. Not because you are playing games. Because your nervous system has already spent enough years being gamed.

And, yes, this will cost you. That is the part people do not romanticize. Raising standards can cost you friends, family closeness, familiar dynamics, social convenience, even certain opportunities. It can cost you the version of yourself who was praised for being agreeable. It can cost you the dopamine of being needed. It can cost you the fantasy that if you just love harder, life will reward you with respect. But what it gives you back is not abstract. It gives you your baseline. It gives you your sleep. It gives you your appetite back. It gives you your focus. It gives you the feeling of being at home in your own body, because you are no longer living in contradiction.

The deepest standard is this: you stop making your peace dependent on someone else's mood. You stop renting your emotional stability to people who pay in inconsistency. You stop giving people the power to reset your nervous system with a text. And when you do that, something subtle changes. Your body starts believing you. Not your affirmations—your actions. It starts believing that when you feel that old pull, you will not betray yourself to end the discomfort. It starts believing that you can survive someone being disappointed in you. It starts believing that love does not require panic. That is healing that shows up. That is a heart protected by standards, not hardened by them.

This is where the distinction becomes clean: repair versus reset. Repair looks like ownership without you having to beg for it, changed behavior that stays changed after the mood passes, respect that does not disappear when you say no. Reset looks like tears, words, affection, gifts—and then the same behavior returning as if nothing happened. Time is not an apology. Warmth is not accountability. A standard is what you do when someone returns without repair, expecting you to provide the forgetting that keeps their pattern convenient.

When you raise standards, the first thing that happens is not that better people arrive. The first thing that happens is the old people test you. They test whether your "no" is negotiable, whether your clarity is performative, whether you will return to the role once the room gets cold. They test with silence, guilt, nostalgia, sudden affection, or a crisis that conveniently requires you. Sometimes it is not even conscious manipulation. It is simply what worked before, because your old flexibility trained them that consequences do not exist. The hardest part is realizing your biggest enemy is not their behavior; it is your reflex to repair tension by betraying yourself.

Standards become visible in how you move, not in what you announce. You stop answering at certain hours. You stop accepting last-minute chaos. You stop granting immediate access to people who have not earned trust. You stop feeding circular conversations where the goal is control, not understanding. You do not do this to punish. You do it to protect your nervous system from being used as a payment method. Over time, your body begins to trust your standards the way it used to fear your flexibility, and that trust changes your sleep, appetite, baseline, and the way you experience love.

Some connections crack when you stop being the glue, and the grief is real. It can feel like you lost something, but often you lost an illusion: that love can exist without mutual effort. This is also where you stop romanticizing potential, because potential is one of the most expensive drugs people take. They fall in love with who someone could be, then tolerate who they are, while waiting for the future to pay them back. Standards bring you back to the present with one question you cannot decorate: is this nourishing now, or only promising to be later?

A life with standards is not a life without pain. It is a life where pain is not repeated as a lifestyle. You will still be disappointed. You will still lose people. You will still feel lonely sometimes. But you will not build your worth on endurance. You will not keep paying for closeness with anxiety. You will not keep shrinking to keep access. Healing becomes relationally visible when the trigger no longer controls your behavior—when you feel the pull and still choose dignity, when you stop living like you are negotiable. That strength is not loud. It is quiet and final, because it is built on evidence: you watched what it costs you to keep paying, and you decided you are done.

If a person wants to be in your life, they will meet you at your standard. They will not require you to shrink. They will not punish you for clarity. They will not demand access as proof of love. They will bring accountability without you having to beg for it. And if they cannot, you do not make them your project. You do not wait. You do not shrink. You keep your word to yourself.

Stand.

CHAPTER 14

I DON'T WAIT FOR ANYONE. I GO FIRST.

Becoming First in your Body: Discipline as Self-respect in Motion

Most people think "going first" is an attitude. They treat it like confidence, like charisma, like a mood you either have or you do not have. But the truth is simpler and πιο αμείλικτη: going first is a physical decision. It is a decision your body either believes or it does not. Your mind can swear you are ready for a new life, and your mouth can say all the correct sentences, and still your body will reveal the truth with what it repeats. That is why discipline belongs here. Not as punishment. Not as obsession. Not as a performance for the mirror or the world. Discipline is the most practical form of self-respect you can practice in real time, because it is the moment you stop negotiating with the part of you that always wants the old relief.

If you want to know what you truly believe about yourself, do not listen to your affirmations. Watch your defaults. Watch what happens at night when you are tired and nobody is watching. Watch what happens when you feel a little lonely, a little restless, a little bored, a little anxious. Watch what you reach for, and how quickly you reach for it. People do not break discipline because they lack information. They break discipline because their nervous system is trained to worship immediate relief. They have lived too long confusing comfort with care and convenience with kindness. The body is not immoral; it is efficient. It remembers what took the edge off. It remembers the shortcut. It remembers the sedative. And when pressure shows up, it does what it knows.

That is why "discipline" is the wrong word for many people, because they hear it and imagine military behavior, denial, coldness, a joyless life. But real discipline is not denial. It is direction. It is you acting like you matter while your older wiring begs you to postpone yourself again. It is you refusing to treat your body as a tool you exploit until it breaks. It is you treating your energy as capital, your sleep as a boundary, your health as non-negotiable, and your future as something you protect now, not something you apologize for later.

Becoming First in your body is not about being perfect. It is about being honest about consequences. Your body already told you the truth in Chapter 13: it keeps receipts. Not to punish you, but to document reality. Reality is that every time you abandon yourself for short-term relief, you pay for it in sleep, mood, cravings, inflammation, anxiety, brain fog, and a quiet resentment you carry, because you keep living in contradiction. Most people think their problem is discipline. Often the problem is that their daily life is designed to drain them, and then they blame themselves for trying to survive it the only way they know. A person who is chronically depleted will always crave the fastest comfort. That is not weakness. That is physiology. But physiology does not absolve you of responsibility. It simply tells you where to start: stabilize first.

This is where "I go first" becomes a lifestyle rule, not a slogan. You stop building your day as if your body is optional. You stop treating sleep like something you earn after you exhaust yourself. You stop treating food like an emotional regulator you use when you cannot tolerate your own internal weather. You stop treating movement like punishment for existing in a human body. You build structure as protection. Not because you are fragile, but because you have learned what happens when you keep trusting your old impulses. Your old impulses did not come from evil; they came from adaptation. They kept you functional. But functional is not free. Functional has a price, and the invoice always arrives in the same currencies: health, energy, and peace.

A self-respecting discipline starts with one question you cannot talk your way around: what is my baseline, and who is responsible for it? If you keep waiting for motivation, you are waiting for a mood to do the job of a policy. Motivation is a visitor. Policy is a resident. When you are serious, you do not "feel like it." You decide what happens when you do not feel like it. That is the difference between a life that changes and a life that keeps repeating with better vocabulary.

Most people sabotage discipline because they make it dramatic. They start like they are going to become a different species overnight. They change everything at once, create a perfect routine, and then collapse the first time life becomes real. Then they interpret collapse as proof they are broken. They are not broken. They are untrained. The nervous system does not learn through speeches. It learns through repetition. It learns through small wins that become evidence. Evidence is what calms the body. Evidence is what makes your body trust you. And when your body trusts you, discipline stops feeling like a fight.

So, the real question is not "How do I become disciplined?" The real question is "What structure will I keep even on a bad day?" A bad day is not the day to invent your character. A bad day is the day your character is revealed. Becoming First in your body is designing a minimum standard you do not negotiate. Not because you are rigid, but because you have learned that when everything is negotiable, your worst habits become the negotiators.

Start with the basics that change the entire nervous system: sleep, food rhythm, movement, and stimulation. Sleep is not a luxury; it is the body's primary repair state. If you keep sacrificing sleep, you will keep paying in appetite, mood, impulse control, and anxiety. Then you will call it "stress" as if stress is something that just happens to you. No. Stress is also something you manufacture when you keep living in ways that teach your body it is not safe. Becoming First means you build a bedtime like a boundary, not like a suggestion. It means you stop letting screens, texts, late-night drama, or last-minute "just one more thing" decide how you will feel tomorrow. You do not need a perfect night. You need a protected one.

Food rhythm matters for the same reason. People want food to be a simple discipline story: calories, macros, willpower. But appetite is not only hunger; it is regulation. A dysregulated person will crave quick chemical changes: sugar, volume, salt, ultra-palatable hits, late-night grazing. That is not because they are weak. It is because their system wants relief. Becoming First means you stop feeding desperation. You feed stability. You eat before you are desperate, because desperation makes decisions for you. You do not wait until your body is screaming and then act surprised when you make choices that numb you. A stable rhythm is not dieting. It is nervous system management.

Movement, too, must be reframed. Movement is not a debt payment for eating. It is not a punishment for having a body. It is a discharge valve. It clears tension from the system, so your mind does not have to carry it all day. It creates a baseline where you are less reactive, less hungry for stimulation, less likely to search for relief in the wrong places. Becoming First means you move as care. Even when it is simple. Even when it is not heroic. Because your body does not need heroics. It needs consistency.

Then there is stimulation, which is the silent killer of modern discipline. Most people are not addicted to their phone because of content. They are addicted because the phone became a sedative. It became the fastest way to avoid internal discomfort. It keeps the nervous system activated, and then you wonder why you cannot rest, why you cannot focus, why you cannot sleep deeply, why you feel tired while you do nothing "hard." You are doing hard things all day: you are managing constant input. Becoming First means you stop living like your attention is public property. You protect quiet. Quiet is where processing happens. Quiet is where the body finally exits survival mode.

This is not about living like a monk. It is about living like a person who respects the costs. Because discipline is not moral superiority. It is cost accounting. It is you realizing that the "small" choices are not small when they repeat daily. One more late night. One more scroll into sedation. One more meal eaten standing up. One more day with no movement. One more afternoon carried by caffeine and adrenaline. One more night where you "treat yourself" with something that steals tomorrow. The body adds it up. The body keeps receipts. And eventually you call it burnout, aging, weight, anxiety, "I do not feel like myself," as if yourself is a mystery. No. Yourself is your pattern.

Becoming First in your body is the moment you stop waiting for a crisis to start respecting your baseline. It is the moment you stop bargaining with your health as if you can outsmart biology with confidence. It is the moment you stop using your body as a payment method for a life that does not fit. Because the strongest thing you can do is boring: a stable sleep window, consistent meals, daily movement, reduced stimulation, and a refusal to self-medicate the consequences of your own postponement.

And that is the deeper truth: discipline is not about forcing yourself. It is about no longer abandoning yourself. It is about making your body feel like home instead of a project you constantly manage, criticize, and punish. When you "go first" in your body, your mind gets quieter, your appetite gets saner, your emotions get less explosive, and your energy stops being a random lottery. Not because life becomes easy, but because you stopped treating your own baseline like it is optional.

When people say they want a new life, what they often mean is they want the same life with less consequences. Discipline is accepting that consequences are the curriculum. You either learn them early with small discomfort, or you learn them later with pain. Becoming First means you choose the smaller discomfort on purpose. You choose the discipline that protects you, not the chaos that drains you. You do not wait for anyone, not even for the version of you who finally "feels ready." You act like your future is already yours, and you start paying it respect today.

Becoming First in your Mind: Rewriting the Voice that Shaped Your Limits

If you want to understand why most people never truly change, do not look at their goals. Look at their inner voice. Look at the sentences they have been repeating in their head for years, and how those sentences quietly decide what they attempt, what they tolerate, what they postpone, what they settle for, and what they call "realistic." People think the mind is where dreams are born. It is also where dreams get strangled politely, with logic, with "timing," with "I just need to get through this week," with "it is not the right moment," with "I am not ready." And that is why Chapter 14 matters. Because "I go first" is not only about discipline and body. It is about refusing to keep living under an internal narrator that was trained in fear and then promoted to CEO.

Your mind is not always you. Your mind is also your history. It is your conditioning. It is the language you inherited. It is the tone you absorbed in rooms where you learned what love costs, what safety requires, what attention demands, what approval feels like, and what happens when you take up space. That is why someone can be brilliant and still self-sabotage. That is why someone can have evidence of success and still feel like a fraud. That is why someone can be loved and still feel disposable. Because the mind does not only run on facts. It runs on old agreements. And most people do not realize they are not failing because they lack discipline. They are failing because they keep obeying a voice that was designed to keep them small enough to survive.

For many people, the first voice they ever obeyed was not loving. It was demanding. It was critical. It was conditional. It rewarded them when they were useful, when they were quiet, when they were impressive, when they were agreeable. It punished them when they were inconvenient, when they were emotional, when they were honest, when they said no, when they wanted more. So they learned a rule: being yourself is risky. And then the mind took that rule and built a whole personality around it. A whole life around it. A life where you perform competence while you are terrified of being exposed. A life where you call anxiety "drive." A life where you call avoidance "being busy." A life where you call self-betrayal "keeping peace." And you can survive that way for years. That is the tragedy. You can survive it so long that you start calling it normal. You start calling it you.

Becoming First in your mind begins when you stop confusing that voice with truth. Not every thought deserves respect. Some thoughts deserve interrogation. Some thoughts are not guidance; they are inheritance. Some thoughts are not intuition; they are fear with better vocabulary. Some thoughts are not realism; they are a prison decorated with logic. And if you do not learn to separate your true self from your trained voice, you will keep living in a cage that sounds like you.

Here is the brutal part: your mind will always offer a reason to delay. Always. It will offer a reason to wait for confidence, to wait for clarity, to wait for permission, to wait until you are thinner, richer, calmer, more stable, more certain, more healed. It will say, "Once I fix this, then I will start." But that is not wisdom. That is the waiting game in its most sophisticated form. Because confidence is not the prerequisite. Confidence is the result. Clarity is not the prerequisite. Clarity is the result. Stability is not the prerequisite. Stability is the result. You do not get those things by thinking harder. You get them by moving first. That is why this chapter is titled the way it is. You do not wait for the mind to stop being afraid. You teach the mind through action that it does not get to run your life by panic.

Most people have a signature inner voice. You can almost predict it. It shows up when they are about to do something that would change their identity. It shows up when they are about to raise a boundary, end a pattern, ask for more, leave a relationship, start a project, claim visibility, speak with authority, stop tolerating disrespect, stop negotiating their time, stop being the one who absorbs. And the voice says something that sounds mature: "Do not be dramatic." "Do not overreact." "Be the bigger person." "Think about how they will feel." "Maybe you are asking too much." "Maybe it is your fault." "Maybe you should wait." "Maybe you should be grateful." That voice often does not scream. It whispers. Which is why it is dangerous. Because it can sabotage your life without ever sounding like sabotage. It can sound like maturity while it keeps you in the same loop forever.

Rewriting the voice is not about forcing positivity. That is childish. That is a temporary high. It is also exhausting. People try to fix a harsh inner voice by covering it with nice phrases. They talk about self-love while still negotiating their standards. They talk about worthiness while still chasing approval. They talk about mindset while still living in the same self-betrayal. The mind does not change with slogans. The mind changes with evidence. The voice changes when it no longer matches your behavior.

So the first step is not to become "positive." The first step is to become accurate. Accurate is different. Accurate does not flatter you and it does not degrade you. Accurate is clean. Accurate tells the truth without performance. And the truth is usually something like this: I have been obeying a voice that was built to protect me, and now it is limiting me. That is not a character flaw. That is not shame. That is simple diagnosis. And when you diagnose correctly, you stop treating your life like a moral failure and start treating it like a retraining process.

Your inner voice was shaped by repetition. That is why it feels automatic. That is why it feels "real." It was practiced. It was reinforced. It was rewarded. It was used as survival. Some people learned to criticize themselves before anyone else could, because if they attacked themselves first, they felt less vulnerable. Some people learned to minimize their needs because needs created conflict, and conflict felt dangerous. Some people learned to become hyper-competent because performance bought safety. Some people learned to become charming because charm avoided consequences. Some people learned to over-explain because over-explaining felt like a way to prevent rejection. Some people learned to accept less because asking for more created abandonment. These are not personality traits. These are strategies. And strategies can be replaced, but only if you stop treating them like identity.

This is where "I go first" gets psychological. Because going first in your mind means you stop letting your past negotiate your future. It means you stop treating old fear as a vote. Fear can speak. Fear can share information. Fear cannot hold the steering wheel. Fear is allowed in the car. Fear is not allowed to drive.

The mind will argue with this. It will say, "But what if I fail?" And the answer is not a motivational poster. The answer is: you have been failing quietly for years. Quietly failing to honor yourself. Quietly failing to set boundaries. Quietly failing to choose what you actually want. Quietly failing to stop repeating the same pattern. Quietly failing to build the life you keep imagining. That kind of failure is the worst kind, because it is invisible, so it feels like nothing is happening while your life is passing. You think you are waiting for the right moment. You are actually losing years. That is the invoice. That is the cost nobody wants to pay attention to: the cost of delay.

There is a particular voice I have seen in people who look strong on the outside. It says, "I can handle it." And they can. That is the problem. They can handle too much. They can handle disrespect. They can handle inconsistency. They can handle stress. They can handle chaos. They can handle being the one who carries. They can handle being the one who fixes. They can handle being the one who absorbs. And because they can handle it, they keep handling it. Until handling it becomes their identity and then they wonder why they feel empty, resentful, exhausted, and numb. That voice is not strength. It is conditioning. It is a trained tolerance for pain. And it is not noble. It is expensive.

So Part II is where we strip that voice down to its real function. Ask yourself: what does my inner voice protect me from? For many people it protects them from rejection. For others it protects them from responsibility. For others it protects them from visibility. For others it protects them from intimacy. For others it protects them from disappointment. For others it protects them from being accountable to their own potential. It keeps them in the safe zone where they can complain without changing. It keeps them in the zone where they can fantasize without committing. It keeps them in the zone where they can say "one day" and never face the humiliation of starting.

That is why rewriting the voice is not gentle work. It is honest work. It is the kind of honesty that scares people because it removes their excuses without removing their humanity. It says: you are not bad. You are not broken. But you are responsible. Responsible for the voice you keep feeding. Responsible for the stories you keep repeating. Responsible for the meaning you attach to discomfort. Responsible for the way you interpret a boundary as cruelty, a no as danger, a pause as failure, a lonely night as proof you are unlovable.

Most people do not realize how much meaning they attach. A delayed reply becomes "I am not important." A criticism becomes "I am not good enough." A conflict becomes "I will be abandoned." A mistake becomes "I always ruin everything." A quiet day becomes "my life is empty." A stable partner becomes "this is boring." A person who disappears becomes "this is intense, this is real." The mind is a meaning factory. And if you do not rewrite its core meanings, you will keep living as if your interpretations are reality.

Becoming First in your mind means you stop letting your brain narrate your life like a tragedy by default. Not by lying to yourself, but by changing the rules of interpretation. You change the meaning of discomfort. You change the meaning of boredom. You change the meaning of loneliness. You change the meaning of someone else's mood. You change the meaning of rejection. Because the meaning is what controls behavior. If discomfort means danger, you will run. If loneliness means worthlessness, you will chase. If boredom means emptiness, you will sedate. If rejection means death, you will shrink. But if discomfort means growth, you will stay. If loneliness means recalibration, you will hold your standard. If boredom means space, you will breathe. If rejection means redirection, you will move forward.

This is what people miss: mindset is not optimism. Mindset is definition. It is the definition of what is happening inside you when you feel something uncomfortable. And most people have definitions that were built in childhood and never updated. They are using old operating systems to run an adult life. Then they blame themselves when the system crashes.

So how do you rewrite the voice in practice, without therapy language, without pretending? You do three things: you expose it, you challenge it, and you replace it with evidence.

Exposing it means you catch the sentence. Not after the damage is done. Not after you spiraled, texted, ate, drank, scrolled, lashed out, or collapsed. You catch the sentence at the moment of activation. The sentence is usually fast and absolute. It uses words like always, never, nobody, everyone, ruined, impossible. It feels final. That is how you know it is not wisdom. Wisdom is nuanced. Trauma is absolute. Conditioning is absolute. Fear is absolute. If the voice is absolute, it is almost always old.

Challenging it means you stop treating it as a judge and start treating it as a witness. A witness can speak. A witness does not decide your verdict. You ask: is this sentence true, or is it familiar? Is it accurate, or is it protective? Is it guidance, or is it a reflex? Then you bring in one concept that changes everything: pattern. Not mood. Not a single moment. Pattern. Because the mind loves to build identity from one moment. It loves to label you from one slip. It loves to catastrophize. You correct it with pattern. You say: one hard day does not define me. One craving does not define me. One setback does not define me. One rejection does not define me. But a repeated choice does. So what choice am I repeating now?

Replacing it with evidence means you do not try to "think" your way into a new voice. You behave your way into it. The new voice cannot be imaginary. It must be earned. You earn it by doing the smallest thing that proves you are in charge. You earn it by choosing a standard in the moment your old voice demands relief. You earn it by not sending the message. By not reopening the door. By not negotiating the boundary. By going to bed when you are tired. By eating like stability matters. By doing the walk. By closing the screen. By holding the line. By tolerating the discomfort without turning it into a relapse. And every time you do that, the nervous system gets a new data point. Evidence. Proof. Not a speech. Proof.

Here is what changes when you collect enough proof: the voice stops being loud. Because the voice gets loud when you are uncertain. It gets loud when you do not trust yourself. It gets loud when your behavior has taught your mind that your standards are negotiable. When you become consistent, the voice has less authority. It can still speak, but it cannot dominate. Because it has been demoted by reality.

This is where the most important internal rewrite happens: you stop identifying with your feelings as commands. Feelings become information. The urge becomes information. The craving becomes information. The anxiety becomes information. The loneliness becomes information. The anger becomes information. You stop treating these signals as instructions. You stop living like every internal weather pattern requires immediate action. And that is what emotional maturity actually is. Not being "calm." Being able to feel without obeying.

Most people have never been taught that. They have been taught that discomfort is an emergency. So when they feel discomfort, they try to fix it instantly. They fix it with food, or sex, or noise, or conflict, or reassurance, or approval, or work. They do not realize they are not fixing the problem. They are training the problem. Every time you sedate discomfort immediately, you teach your nervous system: discomfort is dangerous. And then your nervous system produces more discomfort. Because it is trying to protect you from "danger." The loop tightens.

Becoming First in your mind is breaking that loop. It is you teaching your body a new rule: discomfort is tolerable. Loneliness is survivable. Boredom is not death. A no is not abandonment. Someone else being upset is not your responsibility. Silence is not rejection. Time passing is not failure. A slow season is not proof you are behind. It is just a season.

That last one is crucial: the voice that shaped your limits often lives in urgency. It makes you feel behind even when you are doing fine. It makes you feel like you must rush, fix, prove, perform. Urgency is not ambition. Urgency is fear. Ambition builds. Urgency panics. Ambition creates systems. Urgency creates shortcuts. Ambition respects time. Urgency tries to bully time. And when people live under urgency, they burn out and then they call themselves undisciplined. They are not undisciplined. They are living under a tyrant voice that never lets them arrive.

So you rewrite urgency into purpose. Purpose is calm. Purpose is stable. Purpose does not need to be dramatic. Purpose moves. Purpose goes first even when nobody claps. Purpose is quiet because it is not trying to prove worth; it is trying to build a life.

This is also where you rewrite the voice that shaped your limits in relationships. Because many people have an inner voice that says: do not risk disconnection. Do not say the truth too directly. Do not set a boundary too firmly. Do not make them uncomfortable. Do not ask for reciprocity. Do not demand consistency. Do not name the cost. Do not be "difficult." That voice created a certain kind of person: the person who is easy to take from. The person who over-functions. The person who keeps the peace by paying with themselves.

If that has been your pattern, your mind will interpret standards as cruelty. It will interpret self-respect as selfishness. It will interpret leaving as betrayal. It will interpret not replying as rude. It will interpret consequences as aggression. That is the old programming. And if you do not rewrite it, you will keep sabotaging your own healing by calling it "too much."

The rewrite is this: self-respect is not aggression. It is alignment. Boundaries are not punishment. They are clarity. Consequences are not cruelty. They are reality. A standard is not a threat. It is a promise you make to your nervous system: I will not keep putting you in environments you have to survive.

This is where the mind fights hardest, because the mind loves familiar roles. The mind loves identities. The mind loves being "the good one," "the strong one," "the forgiving one," "the patient one," "the one who understands." These identities can be noble. They can also be prisons. And for many people, the hardest part of going first is letting go of the identity that makes them feel valuable in dysfunctional situations. If you stop being the rescuer, who are you? If you stop being the one who absorbs, what happens to your sense of purpose? If you stop being the one who fixes, will anyone stay? That is the fear behind the voice. It is not a small fear. It is primal.

But the answer is simple and brutal: if someone only stays when you betray yourself, they are not staying for you. They are staying for the role. And a life built on role is not a life. It is a performance with a pulse.

So Part II is the psychological point of no return. This is where you decide what kind of voice leads your life. A voice that makes you smaller so others are comfortable? Or a voice that makes you honest so your body can finally relax? A voice that treats your needs as negotiable? Or a voice that treats your baseline as sacred? A voice that keeps saying "later"? Or a voice that says "now, imperfectly, but now"?

Your mind will still create arguments. It will say, "But what if I lose people?" And yes. You will. Sometimes. Or you will lose the version of them that existed only when you were easy to consume. And you will feel grief. Real grief. Because the mind confuses familiarity with love. It confuses attachment with safety. It confuses intensity with intimacy. It confuses being needed with being valued. When you remove those confusions, you feel the emptiness they were covering. And that emptiness is not proof you made a mistake. It is proof you stopped lying.

That is why going first in your mind is not a motivational moment. It is a lifestyle decision: you stop lying to yourself. You stop saying you are fine when you are not. You stop saying you will start tomorrow when tomorrow keeps moving. You stop saying you will change when they change. You stop saying you will rest when life calms down. You stop saying you will set boundaries when you feel less guilty. You stop saying you will be confident when you have more proof. You start acting like a person who is done postponing.

And when you do that, something shifts: your mind stops being the place where you lose the war before you start. It becomes the place where you lead. Lead does not mean you never doubt. Lead means doubt does not decide. Lead means fear does not vote. Lead means the old voice can speak, but it does not get to sign contracts on your behalf anymore.

This is the real rewrite: I do not need to feel ready to behave with self-respect. I do not need to feel confident to act with clarity. I do not need to be fully healed to stop betraying myself. I do not need permission to take my life seriously. I do not need to wait until my mood is perfect to keep my standard.

That is "I go first" in your mind. It is you refusing to let your internal narrator keep writing a life where you are always almost there. Always preparing. Always understanding. Always explaining. Always improving. And never arriving.

You arrive when you decide. You arrive when you do the thing while the voice complains. You arrive when you stop treating discomfort like an emergency and start treating it like a toll you pay to exit an old identity. You arrive when your inner voice begins to match your standards instead of your fear.

And then, quietly, without drama, you become someone else. Not a different person. A truer one. One who does not wait for the mind to be calm. One who makes the mind calm by keeping their word. One who stops using tomorrow as a hiding place. One who stops confusing thought with action. One who stops negotiating their own life into a corner.

Because the mind that shaped your limits was never your enemy. It was your protector. But you are not here to be protected from life. You are here to live it.

And if you have been waiting for the moment you finally feel strong enough to go first, here is the truth: you will feel strong after. Not before.

The Price of Self-Respect

The hardest part about raising your standard is not losing the wrong person. It is losing the version of yourself that made the wrong person possible. The version that answered too fast, softened too early, explained too much, forgave on credit, and called it "heart." The version that treated inconsistency like a personality trait instead of a warning. The version that kept negotiating obvious things because naming the truth felt like it would cost you access. It does cost you access. That is the point. The access was never free. You were paying with your baseline.

Self-respect is not a feeling. It is a behavior that has a price. If it costs nothing, it is not self-respect. It is convenience disguised as maturity. Real self-respect costs you the ability to stay in rooms where you are tolerated instead of valued. It costs you the ability to keep a situation alive through your own flexibility. It costs you your role as the emotional accountant, the one who balances the books, the one who keeps the peace by paying for it. And the first time you stop paying, everyone who benefited from you paying will call you different. Cold. Dramatic. Difficult. Proud. They will say you changed as if change is an insult. What they mean is you stopped being easy to manage.

Most people do not fear boundaries. They fear what boundaries reveal: that the connection only works when you accept a lower standard than you would ever recommend to someone you love. They fear the silence that arrives when you stop fixing everything. They fear the emptiness that comes when the chaos is gone and there is no longer a "situation" to obsess over. They fear that without the struggle, there will be nothing to hold. Because they were not holding love. They were holding tension. They were holding anticipation. They were holding intermittent warmth like a lottery ticket. And when you stop buying lottery tickets, the first thing you feel is withdrawal. The second thing you feel is grief. The third thing you feel is dignity returning like blood flow to a limb that has been numb for years.

A standard is where you stop making your peace dependent on someone else's mood. It is where you stop renting your nervous system to people who pay in inconsistency. It is where you stop allowing a text to reset your entire day. It is where you stop calling it "a misunderstanding" when you have understood it ten times already. And this is why standards feel brutal at first: they remove your favorite coping mechanism, which is the fantasy that you can explain your way into being treated well. Some people are addicted to being understood because being understood feels like control. They think if the other person finally gets it, the behavior will change. They keep delivering context, softness, patience, logic, empathy, their whole psychology thesis, as if respect is something you can purchase with better sentences. You cannot. If a person has shown you repeatedly that they can listen and still choose themselves at your expense, they did not need more explanation. They needed consequences. And you needed the courage to give them.

Most people keep the wrong dynamic alive through one thing: immediacy. Immediate forgiveness. Immediate access. Immediate replies. Immediate reassurance. Immediate "it's okay" while their body is screaming that it is not okay. They do this because tension feels unbearable. They feel the cold in the room and they rush to fix it. They feel the withdrawal of warmth and they chase it back. They feel someone's discomfort and they sacrifice themselves to restore comfort. They call this love. It is not love. It is nervous-system management. It is the reflex to make the room safe by making yourself smaller. And over time, you become so skilled at it that you forget there is another option: you can let the room be uncomfortable. You can let someone feel what they created. You can let silence exist without treating it like an emergency. You can tolerate the gap without filling it with self-betrayal.

The price of self-respect is that you stop performing closeness. You stop proving you are "easy." You stop proving you are "the bigger person" in situations where "bigger" actually means "more willing to absorb disrespect." You stop over-functioning to compensate for someone else's under-functioning. You stop being the one who makes the relationship work by being the one who breaks first. And yes, the moment you stop being that person, the relationship will either rise to meet you or collapse. That collapse is not failure. That collapse is information. It is the truth that the "connection" required you to abandon yourself to survive. That is not connection. That is a contract where you pay and they receive.

A lot of people confuse attachment with devotion. Devotion is chosen freely. Attachment is often chosen by fear. Fear of being alone. Fear of being unchosen. Fear of not being wanted. Fear of regret. Fear of the void. Fear of what you will have to feel if you stop using the relationship as a sedative. And this is where standards become real, because standards force you to sit with that fear without solving it through access. They force you to face the question you avoid in every loop: if nobody is choosing you right now, can you still choose yourself? If the phone is silent, can you still remain stable? If the other person is disappointed, can you still hold your boundary without apologizing for existing? If someone withdraws warmth, can you still breathe without chasing?

This is what people do not admit: sometimes the other person is not the primary drug. The drug is the repair. The drug is the comeback. The drug is the moment they return and you feel your body flood with relief. The drug is the "we are okay" conversation after you have been on edge. The drug is the emotional rollercoaster, because it makes you feel alive, and calm feels unfamiliar. Standards remove the drug of repair by refusing to participate in the cycle. You stop allowing the reset. You stop allowing the warm words to erase behavior. You stop allowing time to be treated as an apology. You stop allowing affection to function like bribery. You stop allowing apologies without change. You stop allowing the story to replace the pattern.

Patterns matter more than promises. That sentence is a dividing line. Some people will hate it because it ruins the fantasy that love is about intentions. Intentions are cheap. Patterns are expensive. Patterns cost effort, consistency, maturity, and the humility to change. That is why patterns are truth. If a person repeatedly disappears and reappears, repeatedly crosses a line and then offers sweetness, repeatedly speaks to you in a way they would never tolerate from you, repeatedly expects you to understand while refusing to understand you, then the pattern is the relationship. Everything else is decoration. And the longer you stay, the more your body learns that your needs are negotiable. Your nervous system learns that your boundaries are suggestions. Your self-worth learns that you will tolerate a lot for a little. That is the kind of learning that follows you into every area of life, not just love. It follows you into business. Friends. Family. Money. Health. You become a person who keeps paying for peace.

The cleanest standard is this: you do not participate in dynamics that make you smaller. Not because you are superior. Because you are done collapsing. You are done becoming a lesser version of yourself to keep the room warm. You are done being an emotional hostage negotiator. You are done offering yourself as ransom and calling it maturity. That does not mean you become harsh. It means you become final. You stop debating obvious things. You stop reopening doors that already proved their cost. You stop returning to conversations that exist only to keep you tethered. You stop giving someone "one more chance" when "one more chance" is actually a lifestyle.

This is where the fear hits: if you hold the line, you might lose them. Yes. And if you do not hold the line, you will lose yourself. That loss is slower, quieter, and more destructive, because it masquerades as devotion. You slowly become reactive. You slowly become anxious. You slowly become the person who is always scanning, always anticipating, always managing tone, always reading between lines, always adjusting your mood based on someone else's mood. You tell yourself you are "sensitive." You are not sensitive. You are trained. You are trained to monitor because you have learned that safety is not stable. That training is expensive. It costs sleep. It costs appetite. It costs your ability to feel calm without guilt. It costs your ability to enjoy a quiet day. It costs your ability to trust your own instincts because you keep overriding them to keep access.

Standards are how you reverse that training. Not with speeches. With behavior that does not bend. Behavior that makes your body exhale. Behavior that removes the constant negotiation. And it starts in the smallest place: response time. People who respect themselves do not respond like they are being graded. They do not respond like love is a timed exam. They do not respond like silence is punishment. They respond when it is clean for them. They respond from steadiness, not from panic. They do not surrender their day to prove they are available. Availability is not loyalty. Availability without boundaries is how you teach people they can enter your life whenever they feel like it and leave without consequence.

Then it becomes even cleaner: you stop granting access to people who have not earned emotional safety. Access is privilege. Access is not a right. Access is not owed. If someone repeatedly destabilizes you, they do not deserve more access. They deserve distance. If someone repeatedly disrespects your time, your body, your peace, your limits, they do not deserve more explanation. They deserve a closed door. And closing the door does not require anger. It requires clarity. The clarity that you cannot heal in the same environment that keeps injuring you. The clarity that your nervous system is not public property. The clarity that love cannot require you to be at war with yourself.

Some people will try to weaponize your standard by calling it ego. They will say you are "too proud." They will frame your boundary as an attack because it removes their convenience. But pride is not the issue. The issue is that your old version was a discount store. Everyone could walk in. Everyone could take what they wanted. No receipt. No consequences. No accountability. You raise the standard and suddenly there is a price tag. Not money. Behavior. Respect. Repair. Consistency. And people who were used to consuming you for free will call you expensive like it is an insult. It is not an insult. It is the correction.

This is the part nobody romanticizes: loneliness. Real standards create loneliness first. Not because standards are wrong, but because standards remove the noise. They remove the wrong connections. They remove the endless processing. They remove the late-night loops. They remove the dopamine. They remove the familiar instability. And in that quiet, you meet yourself. You meet the parts of you that were using relationships as sedation. You meet the grief you postponed. You meet the anger you swallowed. You meet the exhaustion you kept overriding. You meet the truth: you were not only tolerating them. You were also avoiding you. Standards bring you back to you.

If you cannot tolerate that quiet, you will return to the old dynamic and call it "missing them." That is not always missing them. Sometimes it is missing the distraction. Sometimes it is missing the role. Sometimes it is missing the feeling of being in a story. People stay in pain because pain gives them a plot. When the plot ends, the silence feels like death. But the silence is not death. The silence is your life returning to you. It is your nervous system finally getting the chance to settle. It is your body finally not waiting for the next shift. It is your mind finally not having to interpret mixed signals like it is doing forensic analysis. It is peace. Real peace. The kind that does not require you to betray yourself.

The ultimate standard is not how you handle the other person. It is how you handle the moment your body begs you to break your own rule. The moment you feel the pull and your mind starts negotiating: maybe I was too strict, maybe I should be softer, maybe it is not that serious, maybe I should be "mature." That voice is not maturity. That voice is the old contract trying to survive. It will dress itself in the language of compassion because compassion is the loophole your old self used to reopen doors that harmed you. But compassion that requires your collapse is not compassion. It is fear trying to stay respectable.

Real compassion includes you. It includes your sleep. It includes your health. It includes your baseline. It includes your right to be treated with consistency. It includes your right to not be spoken to like that. It includes your right to not be punished with silence. It includes your right to not be kept in suspense. It includes your right to not have to audition for basic respect. If a relationship requires you to abandon those rights to keep it alive, the relationship is not love. It is a transaction where you pay with your body.

The standard that costs you something is not the one you announce. It is the one you live when nobody claps. It is the one you keep on the nights you are tired and nostalgic and vulnerable. It is the one you keep when you are lonely and your nervous system is trying to buy relief. It is the one you keep when the person returns with warmth and you can feel your body wanting to melt, not because the behavior changed, but because the tension ended. That is where you either return to your old self or you become someone new.

And here is the truth nobody wants at first: you do not "feel ready" to hold a standard. You hold it and then your body learns it is safe. You do not wait for confidence. You act with integrity and then confidence arrives as a byproduct. Evidence creates self-trust. Self-trust creates stability. Stability changes your appetite, your sleep, your focus, your entire posture in life. This is why your relationships are not a separate category. They are a training ground. They either train your nervous system to trust you or train it to expect you to betray yourself again.

A person who keeps their standard becomes boring to chaos. That is not an insult. That is graduation. Chaos cannot feed off you anymore because you stop reacting on schedule. You stop answering the bait. You stop doing the dance. You stop explaining to someone who benefits from misunderstanding you. You stop over-giving to prove you are good. You stop chasing warmth like it is oxygen. You stop needing to be chosen to feel real. That is the shift. That is the moment your life begins to change without drama. Quietly. Cleanly. Permanently.

This is what "being first" looks like in real human terms: you become the person you can trust. You become the person who does not break their own rule to avoid discomfort. You become the person who can sit in the absence without running back to familiar pain. You become the person who does not confuse loneliness with emergency. You become the person whose peace is not rented. It is owned. And once you own your peace, you stop building your life around people who require you to lease it back to them.

You will still love. You will still miss. You will still grieve. But you will not make your heart a landfill where other people dump their inconsistency and call it "complicated." You will not keep paying for closeness with anxiety. You will not keep shrinking to keep access. You will not keep calling yourself strong while your body is breaking under the job of managing someone else's unpredictability.

The price of self-respect is that some doors close. The reward is that you stop bleeding out privately. You stop living in anticipation. You stop treating love like a test. You stop performing calm while bracing inside. You stop abandoning yourself to keep the atmosphere polite. Your body feels it first. Your sleep deepens. Your appetite stabilizes. Your breath stops living in your chest. Your jaw unclenches. Your shoulders drop. Not because life is perfect, but because your life is no longer built on the daily lie that you can tolerate what it is costing you.

That is the standard that costs you something. It costs you access to the old room. It costs you the old role. It costs you the old story. But it gives you back the one thing you cannot replace with any other win: a nervous system that trusts you, and a life that no longer requires you to betray yourself to be loved.

THE OATH: TODAY

The Thirty-Year Trade

For almost thirty years, I lived inside transactions. Not always with money. Sometimes with attention. Sometimes with access. Sometimes with a smile that was not free, with a promise that was not clean, with a handshake that came with invisible fine print. I sat across from people the world would call untouchable—kings in their own countries, presidents in their own rooms, stars who could shift a room's oxygen just by entering it, billionaires who spoke softly because they never needed to raise their voice. And I learned something that ruined the fantasy forever: status does not make a person whole. It just gives their wounds better lighting.

At every level of power, I saw the same hunger dressed in different fabrics. The same fear dressed in different suits. The same need to be seen, to be safe, to be in control, to be adored without being truly known. The names changed, the watches got more expensive, the tables got longer, the security got tighter, but the human pattern stayed brutally consistent. Everybody was negotiating. Everybody was protecting something. Everybody was trading something. And the most dangerous trade I watched—over and over—was the trade people make with themselves.

I watched men and women win entire industries and still beg silently for approval from a single person. I watched people who could buy anything still live as emotional employees, waiting for a mood to decide whether they were "good enough" today. I watched people with global influence become small, compliant, polite, apologetic—because one relationship, one gatekeeper, one audience, one parent, one lover still owned their nervous system. They could move money, move policy, move headlines. They could not move their own boundary.

At first, I thought I was studying them. Then I realized I was studying myself. Because my life also became a negotiation. I learned how to read rooms fast. I learned how to anticipate tone. I learned how to make people comfortable. I learned how to over-deliver so they would not question my worth. I learned how to swallow a truth and call it "strategy." I learned how to keep things smooth and call it "professionalism." I learned how to carry pressure and call it "strength." I became excellent at managing the external world while quietly postponing the internal one.

That is the part nobody sees. The part that does not show up in photos, deals, credits, accomplishments, introductions. The private cost. The accumulation. The way you keep moving, keep producing, keep performing, until your own body becomes the collateral. And you can do that for years. That is why it is so seductive. You can "make it" while you are bleeding out internally in slow motion.

The truth is, I did not just meet powerful people. I met power itself—how it smells, how it seduces, how it rewards, how it punishes, how it trains you to compromise without calling it compromise. Power rarely says, "betray yourself." It says something cleaner. It says, "Just this once." It says, "Be smart." It says, "Do not be dramatic." It says, "Timing." It says, "Not now." It says, "Later." It says, "You can handle it."

That last sentence is the one that almost destroys good people. Because they can. They can handle the disrespect. They can handle the mixed signals. They can handle the waiting. They can handle the emotional underpayment. They can handle the workload, the pressure, the chaos, the late nights, the compromises, the self-neglect. They can handle it so well that it becomes their identity. And then, one day, they cannot. Their body stops cooperating. Their sleep stops repairing. Their appetite stops listening. Their nervous system stops believing the lies. They call it burnout. They call it stress. They call it aging. They call it "I do not feel like myself." But it is not a mystery. It is the invoice for a life lived in negotiation.

I hit a point where the transaction fatigue became physical. Not dramatic. Not cinematic. Just a deep, quiet exhaustion with the same loop: trying to earn peace by paying with myself. Trying to stabilize the room by shrinking. Trying to be "understood" by over-explaining. Trying to be chosen by being easy. Trying to keep access by tolerating the cost. Trying to prove my value by never asking for what I needed. Trying to win without ever arriving.

And because I have lived around every level of status, I can tell you this with no romance left: the world does not reward the person who postpones themselves. It consumes them politely. It praises their resilience while it extracts their life. It calls them "strong" while they are quietly becoming numb. One day, I realized I had become too skilled at surviving—surviving a schedule, surviving pressure, surviving other people's moods, surviving expectations, surviving my own patterns, surviving my own appetite for intensity, surviving the addiction to urgency, surviving the need to be "on," surviving my own habit of waiting.

And something inside me said: enough. Not in a motivational way. In a tired, sober, final way. The kind of "enough" you say when you are done pretending you have time to waste. The kind of "enough" you say when you have seen what the trade costs over decades, not days. The kind of "enough" you say when you realize you have negotiated your own life into a corner and called it maturity.

I am not romantic about my growth. I am not interested in being admired for what I tolerated. I do not want a trophy for endurance. I want a life that is mine. So this is the truth that took me thirty years, a thousand rooms, and every kind of human interaction to learn: your life changes the day you stop making deals with your self-respect. Not the day you understand it. Not the day you talk about it. Not the day you post it. The day you stop trading your baseline for relief. The day you stop renting your peace to people who pay in inconsistency. The day you stop calling delay "timing." The day you stop calling self-betrayal "compassion." The day you stop calling your exhaustion "drive."

And that day is not someday. It is today. Because "today" is the only day that is not a fantasy. Today is where your patterns live. Today is where your excuses operate. Today is where your nervous system casts its vote. Today is where you either keep the old contract alive, or you end it. This is not a chapter about goals. It is not a chapter about being inspired. It is not a chapter about becoming a new personality. It is a chapter about an oath.

An oath is what happens when you are done negotiating. An oath is what happens when you stop waiting for the world to cooperate and you decide you will cooperate with your own life. An oath is not pretty. It is not soft. It is not a mood. It is a line you do not cross anymore, even when you are tired, lonely, tempted, nostalgic, or afraid. And I am telling you the truth, without performance: I am tired. I have done enough transactions. I have done enough waiting. I have paid enough. I have given enough "one more chances" to people, to seasons, to patterns, to versions of myself that kept promising they would change tomorrow.

Tomorrow is a liar, and you have proof. Today is the only honest thing left. So I am writing the oath the only way it works: not as poetry, not as a slogan, not as a mood you borrow for a page and return at midnight, but as a contract you can feel in your body—one you can sign without applause and still honor when the phone is silent, when the craving rises, when the old door opens, when the old version of you tries to negotiate the price down. Today, you do not negotiate. Today, you go first.

An oath is not a sentence you admire. It is a sentence you obey. It begins the moment you stop needing the emotional permission of "feeling ready," because you finally understand what readiness really is: not confidence, not clarity, not the absence of fear—exhaustion with your own postponement. It is the quiet disgust you feel when you hear yourself say "tomorrow" and you know you have been saying it for years. It is the moment your body stops cooperating with your excuses and your soul stops cooperating with your charm. That is why the oath has to read like a contract, not like a vibe. The negotiating part of you will try to turn this into an "inspirational moment," and then it will return to the old relief the moment the night arrives. It will try to make "today" symbolic instead of literal, to keep the door open "just in case," to keep the old version of you alive by calling it maturity, patience, compassion, realism. Today is where that ends.

And the reason I am writing it like a contract is because your old life has been a contract too—you just never admitted it. You signed it with habits. You signed it with response time. You signed it with sleep sacrificed for stimulation. You signed it with boundaries negotiated into apologies. You signed it with standards turned into "maybe." You signed it with self-talk turned into a courtroom where you are always guilty. You signed it with the way you kept paying for comfort using your future as collateral. So, this is the moment you sign something else—not to impress anyone, not to punish yourself, not to become a robot, but because you are done living a life where your best intentions get outvoted by your worst patterns at midnight.

The oath is long because the mind is clever. It hides in technicalities. It survives through ambiguity. It loves soft language that leaves you an escape hatch. So the oath must be clean, specific, and non-negotiable where it matters—human enough that you can keep returning to it without shame, firm enough that your old self cannot misread it as a suggestion. This is the oath, written for the part of you that is tired of being brilliant and still repeating.

Today, I stop waiting. I stop waiting to feel confident before I act with self-respect. I stop waiting for someone else's behavior to give me permission to live like my life matters. I stop waiting for the perfect week to begin. I stop waiting for the world to calm down so I can finally treat myself like a person, because the world will never calm down on command and my well-being is not allowed to be held hostage by circumstances. Today, I choose action over analysis when analysis is just fear wearing intelligence.

Today, I stop making deals with my baseline. I stop treating my body like an employee I can exploit. I stop borrowing energy from tomorrow with late nights, overstimulation, and false "rewards" that steal my sleep, and then steal my mood, and then steal my appetite, and then steal my focus, and then steal my dignity. I stop pretending the body will forgive unlimited inconsistency. I stop acting surprised when the invoice arrives, because I finally respect cause and effect. Today, I treat my sleep like a boundary, not a privilege; I treat my food like stability, not anesthesia; I treat movement like care, not punishment; I treat quiet like medicine, not emptiness.

Today, I stop obeying impulses as if they are commands. I acknowledge cravings, urges, and emotional storms as information—not as instructions. I recognize that the part of me that wants immediate relief is not evil, but it is not in charge. It can speak. It can protest. It does not get to sign contracts. Today, I practice delayed relief on purpose, because I refuse to keep choosing comfort that costs me my future.

Today, I stop negotiating with my own word. I stop making promises to myself that I break privately and then calling myself strong in public. I stop living a double life where my standards exist only in my imagination. Today, I become a person my body can trust. I become consistent enough that my nervous system can stop scanning for the next betrayal coming from me.

Today, I rewrite the voice that shaped my limits. I stop confusing familiar thoughts with true thoughts. I stop letting old fear narrate my future. I stop letting urgency impersonate ambition. I stop letting guilt impersonate morality. I stop letting nostalgia impersonate love. I stop letting "what if" become a cage. Today, I choose accuracy over self-attack and over self-flattery. I tell the truth cleanly: if I keep doing what I have been doing, I will keep getting what I have been getting, and I am done pretending surprise.

Today, I stop using language as a hiding place. I stop explaining my way out of accountability. I stop intellectualizing pain, so I do not have to change what causes it. I stop calling avoidance "being busy." I stop calling fear "timing." I stop calling self-betrayal "peace." I stop calling endurance "love." Today, I speak to myself like an adult: calm, exact, and non-negotiable where it matters.

Today, I stop renting my peace. I stop giving other people the power to reset my nervous system with a text, a tone, a disappearance, a return, a crumb of warmth, or a manufactured crisis. I stop treating someone's mood as my weather. I stop living like my stability is public property. Today, I protect my mind the way I would protect a child, because I finally understand what is at stake: my life.

Today, I choose reciprocity as the minimum, not a luxury. I stop confusing attention with care. I stop confusing chemistry with consistency. I stop confusing intensity with intimacy. I stop confusing being needed with being valued. I stop giving access to people who have not earned emotional safety. I stop calling it love when my body prepares for impact. Today, I make one decision that changes everything: patterns matter more than promises, and I will not build my life on promises anymore.

Today, I stop reopening doors that keep proving their cost. I stop participating in loops that train my nervous system to expect me to abandon myself again. I stop being the person who repairs tension by collapsing. I stop being the one who keeps the room warm by burning my own life for heat. Today, I allow consequences to exist without drama. I allow distance to be a form of respect. I allow silence to be information instead of an emergency. I allow people to experience what they created without me rushing in to soften the truth for them.

Today, I accept the price of self-respect without bargaining. If holding my standard costs me the wrong connection, I pay it. If it costs me the old identity, I pay it. If it costs me the dopamine of chaos, I pay it. If it costs me being misunderstood by people who benefited from misunderstanding me, I pay it. I pay it because I have paid a higher price for years: sleep, appetite, peace, focus, and the slow erosion of my dignity. Today, I choose the honest price over the familiar price.

Today, I stop waiting to be chosen correctly. I choose myself correctly. Not in a narcissistic way. In a survival way. In a sanity way. In a life way. I stop confusing self-respect with selfishness. I stop treating my needs like an inconvenience. I stop treating rest like laziness. I stop treating boundaries like cruelty. Today, I treat my well-being as sacred because it is the foundation of everything else I claim to care about.

Today, I do not need applause. I do not need a witness. I do not need a perfect streak. I do not need the fantasy of a flawless new identity. I need one thing: a clean return. I need to return to my standard every time I drift. I need to return without self-hatred, without drama, without the old identity story of "I always ruin everything." I return because returning is what builds trust. Returning is what builds a new life. Returning is what makes "today" real.

And today, I go first. Not tomorrow. Not when I feel ready. Not when they apologize. Not when the week becomes easier. Not when the world stops demanding. Not when the fear disappears. Today—while fear is present, while discomfort is present, while cravings are present, while history is present, while the old voice is still talking. Today, I still go first.

An oath only matters when it meets resistance. Not the kind you would dramatize, but the kind that arrives quietly and expects you to fold: the ordinary night, the familiar itch for relief, the reflex to reopen a door because it is unlocked, the urge to negotiate your standard down to something convenient. This is where your old life tries to survive—not through chaos, but through "reason." It will offer you a softer version of truth, a more flexible version of boundaries, a more polite version of self-betrayal, packaged as maturity. The mind does that. It has done that. It will keep trying. And now you do something it does not expect: you do not argue with it, you do not romanticize it, you do not hate yourself for it—you simply stop signing its paperwork.

Final does not mean loud. Final means clean. It means your baseline stops being a mood and becomes a rule. It means you stop paying in small installments for a life you keep postponing: one more late night, one more excuse, one more compromise, one more "I will start when…," one more "I deserve this" that is really anesthesia. It means you stop letting exceptions become an identity, because that is how the old contract stays alive—through technicalities, through loopholes, through "just this once" repeated until it becomes a lifestyle. The world will always offer you a deal. People will always offer you a cheaper version of yourself. Your own nervous system will sometimes beg you to return to what is familiar. But familiar is not safe. Familiar is simply practiced.

Your body understands one language: evidence. Not intention. Not explanation. Not motivation. Evidence is what teaches your nervous system that you are not going to abandon it again. Evidence is what turns "today" from a sentence into a reality your biology can relax inside. Sleep becomes a boundary, not a luxury you "earn" after you burn yourself out. Food becomes stability, not a reward you use to silence discomfort. Movement becomes care, not punishment. Quiet becomes medicine, not emptiness. These are not lifestyle tips. They are the infrastructure of self-respect. This is what it looks like when you stop living like your future is optional.

Your mind will keep offering commentary; it is built to do that. The shift is that commentary stops being command. Fear can exist without drafting your decisions. Doubt can speak without being given the steering wheel. Shame can knock without being invited to live in the house. When discomfort tries to turn into an emergency, you do not buy relief with self-betrayal. You do not negotiate your standard because you are lonely. You do not hand your power back because someone returns with a little warmth and a familiar story. You let the moment be uncomfortable, and you stay loyal anyway. That is where strength actually lives—not in how much you can tolerate, but in how consistently you stop tolerating what drains your life.

This is where relationships finally become honest. Not because people suddenly behave better, but because you stop training them to get access through inconsistency. You stop confusing attention with care. You stop confusing chemistry with consistency. You stop confusing relief with respect. You stop treating someone's mood as your weather. You stop repairing tension by collapsing. You stop performing closeness to avoid consequences. You let consequences exist without theatrics, because drama was never your power—clarity was. And clarity changes everything. People either rise to meet you, or they reveal that they were only comfortable with the version of you who paid first and called it maturity.

There is a cost, and it is real, and you feel it at first. The cost is not only losing certain connections; it is losing an identity that once protected you. The version of you that survived by being agreeable, available, endlessly understanding, endlessly resilient, endlessly willing to absorb. That version may have looked "strong," but it lived exhausted. When you stop over-functioning, there can be an unfamiliar quiet, and the mind will try to label it loneliness, so you run back to noise. Do not confuse silence with emptiness. Silence is space. Space is where your life returns to you. Space is where your breath deepens, your jaw unclenches, your shoulders drop, your appetite becomes sane, your sleep begins repairing again. That is not small. That is your life force coming home.

And then something else returns—something most people forget exists because they have lived too long inside negotiation. Clean joy. Not the spike of relief when chaos pauses, not the high of being chosen for ten minutes, not the intoxication of intensity. Clean joy is quieter, deeper, and it stays. It shows up when you wake up without feeling like your body is a debt. It shows up when you do not need a text to regulate your nervous system. It shows up when you stop punishing tomorrow to comfort today. It shows up when you realize that being alone is not abandonment when you are finally on your own side. That is what happens when your baseline becomes non-negotiable: you stop leaking energy into loops that were never going to pay you back.

So, this is how it ends—without performance, without bargaining, without a new personality, without waiting for the perfect moment. It ends with one standard becoming law inside you. Not next week. Not after you "feel ready." Not after the apology. Not after the timing improves. Today, with fear present. Today, with discomfort present. Today, with history present. Today, with the old voice still talking. The difference is that the old voice is no longer the authority. The oath is.

Close the book and let it land where it is supposed to land: in your behavior. Let "today" mean what it says. Let it be the day you stop negotiating your life into a corner and calling it maturity. Let it be the day you stop paying for peace with self-betrayal. Let it be the day you stop outsourcing your worth to moods, outcomes, attention, and permission. Let it be the day you become loyal to your future in a way you can feel in your body. Say it once. Mean it. Live it. Today, I go first—because today, I Become First.

Francesco Vitali
Become First

ABOUT THE AUTHOR

Francesco Vitali is a founder, publisher, and strategist who writes with one rule: no performance, no comfort words, no permission slips. His work centers on accountability—because it is the only place power can return to its rightful owner.

Based in Los Angeles, he has built across media, publishing, and technology, creating human-centered ventures and leading projects where pressure is not theoretical. Become First is not a motivational concept. It is a decision, written for readers who are tired of insight without change.

For updates and new releases, visit: VitaliAdvice.com.

IF YOU ARE READY TO BECOME FIRST — STAY IN TOUCH

If this book spoke to you, do not let it be a one-time moment.
Stay connected — and keep the work alive.

Join my newsletter
Short, direct notes that keep you sharp, grounded, and moving forward.
Sign up here: **VitaliAdvice.com/Newsletter**

Message For Success
If you want a daily rhythm — a daily reset — this is the companion.
Find it on Amazon and Audible:
https://www.amazon.com/Message-Success-daily-keeping-track-ebook/dp/B0CFFZQ67G/

Connecting on Social
Come join the community — daily clarity, real talk, and reminders to keep becoming.
Find me across your favorite platforms: **@VitaliAdvice**

"Stop competing. Start becoming."

— **Francesco Vitali**